Meaning and Mystery

D1190435

Meaning and Mystery

What It Means To Believe
In God

David M. Holley

A John Wiley & Sons, Ltd., Publication

This edition first published 2010
© 2010 David M. Holley

Blackwell Publishing was acquired by John Wiley & Sons in February 2007. Blackwell's publishing program has been merged with Wiley's global Scientific, Technical, and Medical business to form Wiley-Blackwell.

Registered Office
John Wiley & Sons Ltd, The Atrium, Southern Gate, Chichester, West Sussex, PO19 8SQ, United Kingdom

Editorial Offices
350 Main Street, Malden, MA 02148-5020, USA
9600 Garsington Road, Oxford, OX4 2DQ, UK
The Atrium, Southern Gate, Chichester, West Sussex, PO19 8SQ, UK

For details of our global editorial offices, for customer services, and for information about how to apply for permission to reuse the copyright material in this book please see our website at www.wiley.com/wiley-blackwell.

The right of David M. Holley to be identified as the author of this work has been asserted in accordance with the Copyright, Designs and Patents Act 1988.

All rights reserved. No part of this publication may be reproduced, stored in a retrieval system, or transmitted, in any form or by any means, electronic, mechanical, photocopying, recording or otherwise, except as permitted by the UK Copyright, Designs and Patents Act 1988, without the prior permission of the publisher.

Wiley also publishes its books in a variety of electronic formats. Some content that appears in print may not be available in electronic books.

Designations used by companies to distinguish their products are often claimed as trademarks. All brand names and product names used in this book are trade names, service marks, trademarks or registered trademarks of their respective owners. The publisher is not associated with any product or vendor mentioned in this book. This publication is designed to provide accurate and authoritative information in regard to the subject matter covered. It is sold on the understanding that the publisher is not engaged in rendering professional services. If professional advice or other expert assistance is required, the services of a competent professional should be sought.

Library of Congress Cataloging-in-Publication Data

Holley, David M., 1948–
  Meaning and mystery: what it means to believe in God / David M. Holley.
    p. cm.
  Includes bibliographical references and index.
  ISBN 978-1-4051-9345-0 (hardcover: alk. paper) – ISBN 978-1-4051-9344-3 (pbk.: alk. paper)
  1. God (Christianity) 2. Storytelling–Religious aspects–Christianity. 3. Christian life.
4. Faith. I. Title.
  BT103.H66 2010
  211–dc22

                                            2009018443

A catalogue record for this book is available from the British Library.

Set in 10.5/13pt Minion by SPi Publisher Services, Pondicherry, India
Printed and bound in Malaysia by Vivar Printing Sdn Bhd

01   2010

To Joyce

Who Awakened My Heart

Contents

Preface

The beginnings of this book go back to an occasion when I listened to a very bright high-school senior telling a group of people that he was trying to decide about whether to continue believing in God. This student had been brought up by Christian parents who had taught him their faith, but he had come to a point in life where he thought he needed to decide things for himself. His reflections took the form of considering various facts about the universe in an attempt to discover whether God was needed as an explanation of things. He set out to evaluate what could be said for and against this kind of explanation as objectively as he could. In the end he found the evidence insufficient for resolving the question of God's existence one way or the other, leaving him puzzled about whether to continue believing or not.

The kind of thinking used was familiar to me. I could recognize it as resembling standard philosophical reflection on the existence of God that proceeds by considering classic arguments that have been developed by historical and contemporary philosophers. I had on numerous occasions directed students in college classes in considering these kinds of arguments. But as I listened to this young man, my intuitive reaction was a sense that the kind of thinking he was doing was the wrong way to try to decide about belief in God. Here was a belief that had played an important role in his life. Keeping or abandoning it would make a significant difference in how he understood his place in the world and what he judged important. Yet he was proceeding as if he could decide about the belief by a type of thinking that eliminated the need for any personal involvement. Surely something was wrong in the assumption that the appropriate way to decide about a potentially life-shaping conviction, such as belief in God, was through the kind of detached theorizing that was being displayed.

I did what many philosophers do when they have an intuitive reaction, but no clear sense of its precise meaning or ramifications. I started to write, eventually publishing an article in a philosophical journal in which I argued against the adequacy of a relatively disengaged form of reflection about belief in God that treats the matter as a theoretical question and for a more involved type of reflection appropriate to the practical nature of the issue.[1] This book could be thought of as a continuation of my thinking on the subject. However, I develop my position here by means of the central concept of a life-orienting story. Belief or disbelief in God, I claim, arises in a practical context in which we acquire a narrative that enables us to find orientation in life. Some of us find orientation through a narrative that denies the reality of God and others find it through a narrative that affirms God.

The most relevant kind of reflection on God's existence focuses not on an isolated proposition, but on a story that that can structure an understanding of our experiential world. We all have such a story, though it may not be something we could clearly articulate. Nevertheless, it forms the backdrop for understanding our identity and discerning what it makes sense to do. Serious reflection about belief in God means considering the possibility of an alternative to the life-orienting story we are using, but to move from a story that makes sense of our experiential world to a different one involves a major shift in the way we think. It is less like deciding you were mistaken about whether you kissed your spouse goodbye this morning and more like deciding you were mistaken in thinking that you had a spouse.

Becoming convinced of such a fundamental mistake means losing confidence in the interpretive structures by which you have ordered your life. Maintaining this kind of confidence or losing it is not a matter to be settled by a dispassionate consideration of obvious facts. When the upheaval is this fundamental, the question is what facts are to be trusted. Becoming convinced by a theistic narrative or by an atheistic narrative involves coming to trust an apprehension of what things mean that we cannot certify through objectively considering agreed-upon evidence. Our confidence that a particular narrative is true develops as we are drawn into an understanding that we find plausible and discover to be reliable as a guide to shaping our lives. Giving up such an understanding makes sense only as we are drawn into an alternative narrative that can take its place.

One of the things that struck me about the student described earlier was how he thought about the question of God's existence as if it were a purely theoretical issue, but neglected to consider what it would mean to live in a reality without God. It was not belief in God as it might actually function to guide someone's life that he was considering, but belief as a hypothesis to account for puzzling facts. But by framing the question in a way that allowed him to put the issue of God at arm's length, he was effectively blinding himself to the kinds of considerations that actually convince people of the activity of God in the world. He was assuming, for example, that claims to revelatory experiences would be acceptable only if validated from a third-person standpoint in which we reflect in disengaged fashion about alternative hypotheses that might explain these experiential claims, rather than the perspective of someone who approaches a revelatory story in the light of a pressing need to find an orientation in life that is convincing.

I have written this book with people like this student in mind. That is, I am addressing it to people who, whether they believe in God or don't believe, feel the need to reflect on the issue. While I assume an audience with the discipline and curiosity to explore unfamiliar territory where the path is sometimes demanding, I have tried to write in a way that people without much background in philosophy will find understandable and interesting. My central message for these readers is that their reflection on God needs to be done in a way that allows them to approach the question, not just as theoreticians, but as individuals who are attempting to find an understanding sufficient for shaping a way of life. They need to decide about God in the context of asking the fundamental practical question, "How shall I live?"

Some professional philosophers will be put off by the way this book is written. They will assume that because I sometimes adopt a fairly breezy style that minimizes technical terminology and does not engage with all the relevant discussions of these matters in the philosophical literature, I am not doing serious philosophical work. I think they are mistaken. The philosophers I most admire exhibit an ability to deal with substantive philosophical issues in ways that engage nonspecialists, and I have attempted to imitate their example. In doing so I refrain from addressing some of the concerns professional philosophers might have, and I intentionally avoid writing in a way that would be appropriate in a philosophical journal, but opaque to a wider audience. However, because I am trying to say something philosophically important, I occasionally pull my general readers into deeper waters than they will find comfortable and address some matters that are likely to strike them as odd, obscure, or unimportant. The result may be something that satisfies neither audience, but I have attempted to strike a balance that I hope will appeal to intelligent nonspecialists while also providing enough for my substantive positions to be taken seriously by philosophers.

I am challenging the way most philosophers think serious reflection on belief in God should be done. Philosophers tend to assume that it is sufficient to consider the idea as a theory about reality (a metaphysical hypothesis). I claim that when we are thinking about the kind of belief that is religiously significant, we need to consider it as part of a larger complex that serves a practical function. What makes the existence of God believable is coming to trust a way of ordering our lives in which interaction with God is a crucial feature. What makes the existence of God deniable is coming to trust a way of ordering our lives that has no significant place for God.

When we approach the question of God as part of a potential answer to the fundamental practical issue of how to live, considerations that tend to drop out of metaphysical discussions take on a central importance. For one thing it is important to consider whether a particular way of linking reality with a way of life not only fits the facts we acknowledge, but illuminates our judgments of value and motivates us to live a life we can think of as worthy. Being convinced by a story about God or by a story of a godless reality is not just a matter of giving assent to a truth, but becoming engaged in a way of life.

Note

1   David Holley, "Disengaged Reason and Belief in God," *Faith and Philosophy*, 19, 3 (2002), 317–30.

Acknowledgments

I am grateful to the University of Southern Mississippi for a sabbatical leave during the fall 2008 term. This time enabled me to complete the manuscript much sooner. Several friends have read and commented on portions of the book. Bob Kruschwitz provided helpful suggestions for many of the chapters. I have also benefited by responses to particular chapters from Dennis Sansom, Erik Anderson, Sam Bruton, and Doug Henry. Houston Craighead provided a thoughtful response to material from the first chapter that I presented at a meeting of the Society for Philosophy of Religion in February of 2009. I also wish to thank two anonymous external reviewers chosen by Wiley-Blackwell for extensive comments on the introduction and first seven chapters at the time of initial submission and another anonymous reviewer and series editor who provided comments on the complete manuscript. I am grateful to all who helped to make this book better. I have made numerous changes in response to comments at various stages, but I have sometimes resisted suggested alterations, so none of the readers should be blamed for any deficiencies that remain. Finally, my wife Joyce gave me unfailing support and encouragement throughout the project. It is to her that the book is dedicated.

Permissions for Chapter Epigraphs

John Haught (chapter 1). Accepted as fair dealing by Cambridge University Press. From *Is Nature Enough? Meaning and Truth in the Age of Science*, 2006, p. 46.

Christian Smith (chapter 1). By permission of Oxford University Press. From *Moral Believing Animals: Human Personhood and Culture*, 2003, p. 78.

Louis Dupré (chapter 2). Reprinted by permission of the publisher; all rights reserved. From *Religious Mystery and Rational Reflection*, Wm. B. Eerdmans Publishing, 1998, p. 26.

Michael Buckley (chapter 2). By permission of the publisher. From Michael Buckley: *Denying and Disclosing God: The Ambiguous Progress of Modern Atheism*, Yale University Press, 2004, p. 138.

C. Stephen Evans (chapter 3). Reprinted by permission of the publisher; all rights reserved. From *Faith Beyond Reason: A Kierkegaardian Account*, Wm. B. Eerdmans Publishing, 1998, p. 94.

Michael McGhee (chapter 3). Accepted as fair dealing by Wiley-Blackwell Publishers. From *The Meaning of Theism*, ed. John Cottingham, Blackwell Publishing, 2007, p. 85.

Paul Helm (chapter 4). By permission of Oxford University Press. From *Faith With Reason*, 2000, p. 96.

John Cottingham (chapter 4). Accepted as fair dealing by Cambridge University Press. From *The Spiritual Dimension: Religion, Philosophy and Human Value*, 2005, p. 139.

Alasdair MacIntyre (chapter 5). By permission of University of Notre Dame Press. From *After Virtue*, 3rd edition, copyright © 1981, 1984, 2007 by Alasdair MacIntyre, p. 217.

Todd Tremlin (chapter 6). By permission of Oxford University Press. From *Minds and Gods: The Cognitive Foundations of Religion*, 2006, p. 101.

Julian Baggini (chapter 8). By permission of Oxford University Press. From *Atheism: A Very Short Introduction*, 2003, p. 37.

John Cottingham (chapter 9). By the kind permission of Taylor and Francis Books UK. From *On the Meaning of Life*, Routledge, 2003, pp. 38–9.

Susan Neiman (chapter 9). By permission of Princeton University Press. From *Evil In Modern Thought: An Alternative History of Philosophy*, 2002, p. 323.

David Wiggins (chapter 10). Accepted as fair dealing by Wiley-Blackwell Publishers. From *Needs, Values, Truth: Essays in the Philosophy of Value*, Basil Blackwell, 1987, p. 89.

Charles Taylor (chapter 10). Reprinted by permission of the publisher from *A Secular Age* by Charles Taylor, p. 680, Cambridge MA: The Belknap Press of Harvard University Press, copyright © 2007 by Charles Taylor.

Introduction:
Does Anyone Actually Believe in God?

It can be frustrating to talk to an intelligent person whose thinking about important issues differs from your own. You feel as if there ought to be something you could say that would help that person to see the light. Or perhaps, if you are somewhat more humble, you may think that there is something the other person might say that could enlighten you. But when someone's beliefs are alien to your own, it can be difficult to develop an empathetic understanding of how anyone could find such beliefs convincing.

One recent author, reflecting on arguments for God's existence says, "I began to wonder whether the arguments were ever really seriously endorsed; and this led me to wonder whether anyone actually believed their conclusion. That is, I began to wonder whether anyone really did believe in God."[1] Judging that there is no reason at all to accept claims about God, he decides that people who say they believe in God are simply self-deceived. They don't really believe what they claim to believe.

Well, that's one way to respond to someone who says something that seems to you obviously wrong, but it's a pretty extreme way. An alternative would be to try to determine whether there are any assumptions implicit in your own perspective that lead you to view what you reject as not only false, but unbelievable. A key theme of this book is that ways of thinking about belief in God that seem natural in our culture distort the way we reason about it. Both believers and nonbelievers are tempted to think about the idea of God as if it were an empirical hypothesis, posited to explain general features of the world or particular experiences that defy natural explanation.[2] One result of this way of thinking is that when we try to talk about whether there is good reason to believe in God, we end up talking about things that bear little relation to the kind of belief intelligent religious people hold or to the considerations that actually convince them of the truth of their belief.

Asking for Reasons

The problem is not that we ask for reasons. Asking for reasons is part of what we do when we encounter beliefs that seem puzzling or doubtful. If your best friend has suddenly given up eating meat and become uncomfortable around others who still eat it, it seems appropriate to ask why she thinks she should not eat meat. Suppose that the answer turns out to be a personal experience with the operation of a factory farm that has produced a reaction of intense disgust. Even if you are not convinced to change your own habits, you might find the changed beliefs and practices of your friend to be understandable. You know something about how she changed her mind, and you can at least imagine thinking in the way she does. Sometimes what a reason does is to make a particular view understandable in the sense that we have some grasp on how someone might accept it.

Of course, we can describe beliefs that would not be so understandable. If your friend claims to believe that babies are delivered by storks, you would likely suspect that she is putting you on. If she proceeds to give you a reason, such as the experience of having seen a baby delivered by this method or having read about it in some source she takes as authoritative, you would be unlikely to regard these reasons as serious answers. If you were convinced that she was serious, you would likely wonder whether she has lost touch with reality. Or perhaps you would decide that she must be speaking metaphorically and did not mean what she said to be taken literally.

So what about the case of giving reasons for believing in God? If you don't believe yourself, but discover that someone you know well has this belief and ask for reasons, what kinds of reasons might you expect? If you have been indoctrinated into standard philosophical models, perhaps you would expect a rehearsal of some well-known arguments for the existence of God. But suppose someone actually appeals to such arguments as the basis of his belief. Would that render the belief intelligible to you? Perhaps you could understand how someone might acquire a theory about the cause of the universe through this kind of reasoning, but would such a theory amount to belief in God? What would be unintelligible is how someone might acquire the kind of belief that could have life-transforming significance or be held as a fundamental conviction. In other words such reasons would not account for the acquisition of a distinctively religious belief.

To think about the kinds of reasons that might make belief in God intelligible, we need to have some understanding of the context in which this belief functions. In the first place, belief in God does not arise as acceptance of an isolated proposition. The idea of God is ordinarily understood in relation to a larger story in terms of which people form some understanding of what human life is about and how it should be lived. Accepting the larger story means acquiring a way to interpret the meaning of everyday experiences. A believer views her experiences in the light of the story and evaluates choices in terms that the story makes intelligible. In other words acquiring a belief in God is inseparable from acquiring a way of life.

So when someone asks a believer, "Why do you believe in God?" it may not be easy to know how to answer. The answer is unlikely to be a simple piece of evidence that convinces the believer that her experience should be interpreted in the way she does or that her way of life is fitting. Accepting the existence of God in a religiously significant way won't be like adding a hypothesis that there is a hitherto undiscovered moon of some planet. In that case you might point with relative ease to the specific evidence you found convincing. But while there may be specific experiences that a believer takes as indicators of divine activity, the idea of God permeates the believer's experience at a fundamental level. To point to the evidence, she would need to point to the kind of intelligible order that using a theistic story makes possible. Reasons for accepting the belief will be bound up with whatever considerations have made the story in which the idea of God functions compelling.

Narrative Framing

To understand the particular judgments that people make, we often need to know the patterns of thought that lie in the background of their assessments. The female CEO of a major corporation gives an apparently uncharitable assessment of a young female executive who is attempting to balance her duties to the company with the demands of family life. The judgment turns out to be related to the CEO's personal story. Closely connected with her own sense of identity is a narrative of how she worked her way up the company ranks through single-minded dedication that surpassed that of her male counterparts. There were necessary sacrifices, including sacrifices to family life. She thinks of herself as a trailblazer for other women, and from this perspective she views the young executive who is apparently less single-minded as someone who is squandering the opportunity that she and others like her have provided.

The background stories people have often furnish them with paradigms that lead them to weigh evidence in different ways. Political disputes about issues such as poverty or the use of military power often turn on the ways that people consider information from alternative narrative perspectives that frame its significance. One sees the situation of the poor in terms of a social oppression story, and another sees it in terms of a personal responsibility story. We tend to recognize as significant those things that fit into the frames we are using and marginalize things that don't seem to fit. Sometimes our failure to recognize the importance of something is irresponsible, but recognizing the irresponsibility typically involves enriching the narratives we are using, rather than approaching the facts without some narrative that enables us to sort out what is significant.

Our stories shape our perceptions at different levels. At the highest level of generality, we have stories about the nature of human life and the world in which we live that I call life-orienting stories (discussed in Chapter 1). They put our lives in a context that enables us to interpret the significance of our choices and develop a coherent mode of life. Religious stories of this sort tend to describe the significance of our lives in relation to dimensions of reality that transcend ordinary empirical observation and verification. They speak of such things as gods or God or karma or Nirvana, invoking these transcendent realities as keys to making sense of our lives.

It is tempting for someone who does not accept any religious account to view an appeal to transcendent realities as a kind of empirical hypothesis that is formed on the basis of flimsy evidence. But to do so is to miss the way that any talk about what is ultimately real makes claims that go beyond the empirically verifiable. One sociologist in a discussion of the centrality of narratives for understanding human behavior, points out that neither narratives that invoke transcendence nor those that deny transcendence limit their claims to what can be tested empirically. He notes, "… the belief that the only and total reality that actually exists is that which humans can empirically observe is itself a statement of faith, whether or not its adherents recognize and admit it as such."[3] What makes such a claim about reality believable is not that it explains empirical evidence, but that it shapes a particular understanding of the world in which the categories and methods used in natural science are viewed as providing the tools for the most fundamental and complete explanation of everything. It is in using this vision as a guide to thought and action that a person comes to believe what it presupposes about reality.

In a similar way people who believe in God are convinced, not by a process of reasoning from publicly available evidence to the conclusion that God exists, but by a narrative vision in which the idea of God plays a fundamental role. When they are able to use this narrative to orient themselves in life by discerning the kinds of significance it highlights, the conception of reality it presupposes becomes believable.

Alternative Narratives

It is possible to reflect on the life-orienting narratives that persuade us, but any such reflection should be governed by the realization that we need some story of this kind to order our lives. We can reject one story only if we can explicitly or implicitly substitute some alternative, and only a limited number of alternatives will seem like viable options to us. So our judgment about life-orienting narratives is fundamentally a comparative judgment. Is one of the viable alternatives superior to the others?

The superiority in question involves accounting for accepted facts, but such considerations are unlikely to narrow the options to a single one. There will be theistic stories and atheistic stories, developed in ways that can accommodate the facts that can be generally agreed upon. Matters on which we don't have general agreement are often more important in assessing these stories. How should religious experiences be weighed? Can we rule out claims to miraculous events? Do our emotional capacities and our discernment of value have a role to play in gaining insight into the nature of things? Because we fail to agree on these kinds of issues, we may also fail to agree about what the relevant facts are and how they should be weighed.

Even if we could agree about factual evidence, the superiority of one narrative over another is not just a matter of determining which one fits established facts better. Life-orienting narratives, whether theistic or atheistic, provide ways of ordering the value-laden world we experience as agents who must determine how to act. The accounts of reality they contain are woven into a vision of the human good and of a moral order that is authoritative for us. Their capacity to evoke our love for the good and motivate us to live in accordance with that moral order is crucial. We reflect on these stories, not just as detached theorists, but as individuals with moral and aesthetic sensibilities that may or may not be engaged by a particular story.

The point here is not that one is attracted by a particular vision of human fulfillment and decides that it must, therefore, be true. It is rather that life-orienting stories have to make sense from a practical perspective, not just from a theoretical perspective. If we cannot be drawn into the vision of human good supported by a particular story, reasons for believing the account of reality it portrays are unlikely to be convincing. Conversely, when a story portrays a vision of human good that resonates with our moral impulses, we are likely to be receptive to potential confirmations of the truth of the story. The evidence for a godless reality seems more convincing when we find a moral vision of human life without God to satisfy our aspirations for independence and autonomy. Potential signs of divine benevolence seem more convincing when we approach them with an attraction for a kind of spiritual development that depends on the truth of a theistic narrative.

Revelation and Reason

The author quoted at the beginning of this introduction, who found no reason at all to believe in God, was very likely thinking that the idea of God is an empirical hypothesis that turns out not to be needed to explain anything. When we look at the relevant data, we discover that we can get along perfectly well without this idea. There is another way of thinking about the idea of God, however, that is prominent in theistic stories. People are said to learn about who God is and what God does through revelatory experiences. Consider, for example, how someone might come to believe that there is a loving God. Such a belief does not arise from reflecting on the good and bad of life and deciding that God is needed to explain an excess of good over bad. Rather the conviction that God cares about human life arises from becoming convinced that in particular events God's nature has been revealed.

The typical philosophical assumption is that there is a proper order to follow. You have to decide whether God exists before moving on to the question of whether there is a revelation of God's nature.[4] But the convictions of religious people ordinarily proceed in the opposite direction. They are exposed to a story that includes accounts of what God has done or communicated and become convinced about God. This sort of response may depend on predispositions that do not rule out the possibility of God as greatly implausible, but having such predispositions to entertain the idea of God is fairly common, and they need not depend on a process of reasoning that independently establishes the probability of God's existence.

Suppose you receive a letter from someone who calls himself or herself a "secret admirer." You might regard the letter as a hoax, dismissing the possibility. Perhaps you have independent reasons for thinking that no one could admire you in this way. But it is also possible that reading the letter convinces you that there really is a secret admirer who has chosen this way to communicate with you. Perhaps there are details in the letter that convince you the author is a genuine admirer. It is the contents of the letter, not some prior proof of a secret admirer, that functions to produce belief. Similarly, in theistic religious communities particular accounts of divine action and divine communication purport to tell people about God's nature and intentions. Coming to believe these accounts is not a matter of having a proof of God and then having a proof that this is a divine revelation. It is more a matter of finding the story convincing enough to "try it on" as a way of understanding your life.

Of course, an initial impulse to believe a revelatory story is not enough. When a story purports to make sense of your life, it needs to be usable as a guide to interpreting your experience and regulating your pattern of living. A story that seemed initially promising might later be recognized as defective. But finding a story usable is not a matter of finding the kind of reasons that could convince anyone. There is testing that can be done, but not the kind of testing that proves once and for all that a particular story is correct. Furthermore, the perspective from which we can test any life-orienting story is in relation to other possible stories that might seem viable. We are not in a position to abandon a story that might seem problematic unless we have on the horizon a way of interpreting the meaning of our experience and shaping our lives that seems more convincing.

Mystery

It can seem odd to someone who thinks that the meaning of human experience is to be understood in terms of what we can observe and verify that anyone would think that the key to making sense of things lies in a dimension of reality beyond ordinary empirical observation. Furthermore, when sophisticated theists talk about God, it becomes clear that when they invoke various analogies and images, they are trying to speak about something that stretches the limits of human language. It seems strange to think that one explains something by positing something beyond understanding.

However, that way of putting it distorts what belief in God is about. Talk about God is not so much an explanation of what seems puzzling, but a way of expressing an apparent apprehension of a deeper meaning. All of us are familiar with the experience of going beyond a surface meaning to an awareness of significance it discloses. A certain look or gesture tells you that someone is flirting. An act of giving in to temptation reveals that you are not the person you imagined yourself to be. An awareness of suffering triggers the realization that you must respond. Our ability to read deeper meanings is surely fallible, but it is also part of what allows us to find our way around in the world.

People who believe in God think that experience discloses depths that are not immediately apparent when we look at surface meanings. But discerning the depths comes through awareness of a revelatory story that tells us of the purposes and plans of God. When we view our own lives in relation to this larger drama, everyday activities take on a different significance. The believer's experiential world includes things like awareness of divine guidance, divine judgment, and divine empowerment. The revelatory story becomes a kind of key that unlocks awareness of these deeper meanings.

The kind of understanding claimed is not what we might want as theorists concerned with making everything comprehensible. It is instead an understanding conducive to shaping a life that fulfills a particular vision of the human good. The believer who seeks to align herself with divine purposes needs some idea of what those purposes are and how to think about what God has done or is doing, but the kind of knowledge needed for practice might leave a great deal unexplained. A religious vision, properly understood, does not clear everything up, but allows one to articulate particular meanings and live in accordance with them, while recognizing that the articulation is from a very limited point of view.

Life-orienting stories that deny transcendence invite us to think about things we don't understand as puzzles that might be cleared up with more investigation. Life-orienting stories that invoke something transcendent invite us to attend to mysteries that defy human comprehension.[5] The denial of mysteries is connected with a confidence in the powers of human reason that is useful in many contexts. But the danger of this approach is the temptation to ignore or minimize what does not fit into the available explanatory patterns. If we think we know that there is nothing mysterious about the world we live in, nothing that might serve as a pointer to a deeper meaning, we are unlikely to be open to stories that attempt to convey such a meaning.

The idea that no reasonable person could really believe in God might seem plausible if we rule out the possibility of revelatory disclosures. What seems apparent, however, is that not everyone rules them out. For some people the possibility that particular events and particular experiences might function as signs of a deeper meaning than empirical testing could verify seems worthy of consideration. Some people find it natural to approach questions of who we are and what our lives are about as mysteries calling for an openness or receptiveness to the possibility of revelatory insights.

Does anyone actually believe in God? If we imagine that the only respectable kind of belief would be one that treats God as an empirical hypothesis and we think that this hypothesis fails to be supported by some minimal level of verifiable evidence, then it may seem charitable to say no. But if we recognize the role of life-orienting stories in our belief formation and acknowledge that a person might be convinced by some story of what God has done or communicated, we can easily imagine someone forming the kind of belief that shapes his or her experiential world.

Furthermore, thinking about the matter in this way helps us to see that disbelief in God is not just a rejection of an empirical hypothesis, but rejection of a certain kind of story as a guide to life. To make sense of rejecting god stories, we need to know what kind of story takes their place, for we can't get along without some story about what is ultimately real and how it connects with the human good. The question is not whether we can prove the assumptions about ultimate reality in our stories, but what kind of story we find adequate as a guide to how to live, for the closest we come to truth in these matters is in discovering an experiential reality we find compelling and a way of life that engages us.[6]

Notes

1   Georges Rey, "Does Anyone Really Believe in God?," in *The Experience of Philosophy*, 6th edn., eds. Daniel Kolak and Raymond Martin (Oxford: Oxford University Press, 2006), 336.
2   Recent bestselling opponents of theistic religion explicitly say that they are arguing against the existence of God as a scientific hypothesis. For example, see Richard Dawkins, *The God Delusion* (New York: Houghton Mifflin, 2006),

50. See also Victor Stenger, *God, the Failed Hypothesis: How Science Shows That God Does Not Exist* (Amherst, NY: Prometheus Books, 2007). In Chapter 2 I discuss the philosophical tendency to treat belief in God as a metaphysical hypothesis or as based on a metaphysical hypothesis.

3   Christian Smith, *Moral, Believing Animals: Human Personhood and Culture* (Oxford: Oxford University Press, 2003), 100.

4   Sandra Menssen and Thomas D. Sullivan present evidence that this is a standard philosophical assumption and then argue against it in *The Agnostic Inquirer: Revelation from a Philosophical Standpoint* (Grand Rapids, MI: William B. Eerdmans Publishing Company, 2007). I agree in rejecting this assumption, but offer different reasons for thinking it defective.

5   The distinction between "problem" and "mystery" is based on the discussion of Gabriel Marcel. He thinks of problems as potentially solvable, whereas mysteries escape objective understanding. See *Creative Fidelity*, trans. Robert Rosthal (New York: Fordham University Press, 2002).

6   Compare this to Kierkegaard's claim that "*An objective uncertainty, held fast through appropriation with the most passionate inwardness, is the truth*, the highest truth there is for an *existing* person." Johannes Climacus, *Concluding Unscientific Postscript to Philosophical Fragments*, ed. and trans. Howard V. Hong and Edna H. Hong (Princeton: Princeton University Press, 1992), vol. 1, 203.

1

Life-Orienting Stories

"For human subjects the world is not experienced, at least in a rich or interesting way, apart from stories." (John Haught[1])

"It is by finding ourselves placed within a particular drama that we come to know our role, our part, our lines in life – how we are to act, why, and what meaning that has in a larger scheme of reality." (Christian Smith[2])

Imagine that you wake up some morning in an unfamiliar house. You have no memory of arriving at the house and no idea of why you are there. A woman comes to the door of your room and tells you that the house is a clinic, and she is your doctor. She informs you that you have apparently experienced some kind of trauma, resulting in memory loss of events since early childhood. You were brought to the house the previous evening in a state of confusion. The head of the clinic examined you and assigned you to her. She says that she will be looking in on you regularly and gives you some medications and instructions, stressing the importance of following the instructions carefully. Despite your confusion, her manner gives you confidence that you are being well cared for. Accepting what she has said, you set about to follow your doctor's orders. On subsequent days you meet other residents of the clinic who speak highly of the place and with great respect for the clinic head. Some give personal testimonials of their own progress. Everyone gives you encouragement to be confident that the prescribed regimen will restore you to health.

A few weeks later, however, while you are walking on the grounds, a man whom you take to be an employee of the clinic pulls you aside and delivers a quiet, but insistent, warning that something ominous is going on. He presents you with evidence that an imposter has replaced the true head of the clinic and put people with questionable backgrounds on the medical staff. He claims that your memory loss is very likely drug-induced and hints that people on the clinic staff are pursuing some nefarious purposes, perhaps working for your enemies. For the moment you are apparently being kept out of the way, but when they no longer need you, your life may be in danger. You should cease taking the prescribed medication and take an alternative medicine, which he slips into your hand, claiming it will bring you in a few weeks to a state of clarity. He stresses the importance of getting away from this place as soon as possible and offers to help you escape to a place of safety, where you will find a community to provide support.

While you are puzzling over this new development, you return to your room and fall into a dream-like state. In this state a figure, claiming to be yourself, appears and tells you that you are a professor of clinical psychology. According to this account, you have been engaged in a series of experiments, connected with producing deep hypnosis. In early experiments you have discovered ways of experiencing very vivid scenarios. The people you meet in these scenarios and the situations experienced are convincing enough that you have no trouble entering into and participating in them, but there is some danger that you may get permanently sucked into these hypnotic scenarios and be unable to return. So the vision messenger is a fail-safe device for helping you get out. You are to practice a series of meditative techniques that will remind you of your true situation and eventually allow you to withdraw from the quasi-reality produced by deep hypnosis.

Needless to say, this parade of conflicting messages leaves you thoroughly disoriented. You are not sure what to believe. Furthermore, you are faced with the immediate, possibly urgent, practical question of what to do next. Accepting the wrong account could lead to misguided action, and it might even prove disastrous, but waiting until you are sure which account is correct could also produce unfortunate consequences. You need some background story that will enable you to comprehend the nature of the situation you face and evaluate your options, but it is not immediately apparent what story to accept.

Now expand the house. You find yourself an inhabitant of planet earth. You have come to this place without any memory of how you arrived or why you are here. As you grow up, your parents teach you particular ways of thinking and behaving that enable you to navigate your world and regulate your activities. Included in their teaching is the claim that you are a creation of God and that God has put you here for a good purpose. They tell you emphatically that obeying God's commands and finding your place in God's plan are vitally important. Others in the community to which you belong reinforce these teachings. As you grow older, however, you come to realize that not everyone has received the same lessons. Some people have been taught things about God and the human situation that differ subtly, or even markedly, from what you have been taught. Furthermore, you encounter a few people who reject the whole idea of being placed here by God. You have come to exist in this universe, they claim, as a byproduct of a physical process that has no purposes or plans. You need to accept this fact, they urge, and leave behind comforting fairy tales of a loving Creator in the sky.

At first you dismiss these alternative stories and cling to your own. But as you mature, you find yourself somewhat confused and disoriented by the conflicting accounts. It seems to make an important difference what account you accept. Different ways of understanding your situation lead to different conclusions about what is valuable and what kind of life to live. But reflecting on the diverse beliefs that people hold makes you wonder whether there is any way of reaching the truth. Other people, you realize, seem just as attached to their own background stories as you have been to yours, and when you are challenged to prove that the teachings you have been relying on are correct, you find yourself at a loss. You are faced with the very practical problem of acting on the best understanding you can attain, and settling on such an understanding is not something you can put off indefinitely, for what kind of life will you live while you are waiting for the truth to become apparent?

Life-Orienting Beliefs

It is not merely simple curiosity or the urge for intellectual mastery that propels you to look for a frame of reference that will enable you to comprehend the meaning of your situation. It is rather the need to orient yourself so that you can order your life. It would be nice to have a kind of roadmap and tour guide to help you make sense of what you are doing and give you some understanding of what to expect. Or if you cannot obtain such detailed instructions, it would at least be helpful to have some sort of general explanatory account of the human condition. Without some plausible way of construing the nature of your situation, you are likely to be lost as you try to find your way through life.

Most people have had the experience of getting lost. When we get lost, we need some way to find our bearings: a familiar landmark, a path that we think leads to the river, directions from a local, a map that shows our location. By such devices we attempt to alleviate our confusion with regard to where we are and attain the means to get to where we want to go. When we realize that we are lost, the belief that a certain direction is north could function as an *orienting belief*, a belief that enables us to get our bearings and formulate a course of action. To be disoriented in such a situation is to be left without sufficient understanding to develop a coherent plan for reaching more familiar territory. Of course, a particular orienting belief might turn out to be incorrect, but when we need to act, there may be few viable options but to rely on some understanding of our situation, even if it is adopted only provisionally.

Losing our sense of where we are spatially is only one kind of disorientation. A person might wake up from a coma, having lost a sense of what day, or even what year it is, unable to orient herself with regard to time. Someone might develop a disease such as Alzheimer's and become confused about the identity of close friends and relatives, losing a kind of social orientation. An individual in an alien cultural situation might become disoriented because of the absence of a shared understanding of the meaning of common practices or gestures.

Some of the beliefs we rely on for orientation transcend the needs of particular situations. We utilize them to find our way around in life. These *life-orienting beliefs* include some understanding of the human situation and of the ethical norms we should live by. An important source for such beliefs is found in teachings deriving from various religious traditions. These traditions propose answers to such questions as, "Who am I?" "How does human life fit in some larger scheme of things?" "What is important in life?" "How should I treat other people?" "How can I deal with suffering?" Such answers become understandable within the context of the particular tradition's *life-orienting story*, which links an account of what is ultimately real with a particular way of living.[3]

There are other sources for life-orienting stories besides religious traditions. In subsequent chapters I will be discussing some nonreligious orienting narratives that function as alternative ways of integrating a fundamental picture of reality with an account of what is worth doing and worth aspiring to. But for most of humanity, religious traditions have been the primary source of the orienting dramas in terms of which people understand their lives. The orienting stories of developed religious traditions typically contain a diagnosis of a problem that keeps human beings from achieving harmony with the nature of things. Religions offer prescriptions for dealing with the problem that involve following a designated path conducive to achieving a superior mode of life. Explaining the problem and the ideal typically involves some account of a reality beyond the reach of ordinary sense experience. Traditions develop particular ways of conceiving this reality and describing how to orient one's life in relation to it.

It is possible for a life-orienting story to be relatively bare in terms of specific guidance; however, the stories of developed religious traditions tend to provide a good deal of instruction about how to live. In both explicit and implicit ways, these traditions define for adherents the standards that ought to govern their choices, the priorities that should claim their attention, and the attitudes and character traits that they need to develop. Furthermore, they stimulate a range of motivations to live out the way of life that the story presents as an object of aspiration.

A life-orienting story is like a lens through which one looks to find a particular way of living intelligible and attractive. Events looked at through the lens of different orienting stories can have very different meanings. (Think of the difference involved in understanding what is happening through the lens of the therapeutic story or the paranoid story or the hypnotic adventure story at the beginning of the chapter.) While some may say that different stories are just different ways of looking at the same facts, the story a person accepts helps to determine what will be taken as a fact. Furthermore, an action that seems reasonable and obvious from the point of view of someone utilizing one story might seem bizarre and unintelligible from the point of view of someone with an alternative story.

If we think of the orienting story as like a lens, the lens is not to be imagined as a pair of glasses that can easily be taken off and put on, but more like a semi-permanent implant. Someone who habitually uses the categories of a particular religious tradition to order experience may find it easy or natural to construe the meanings of events in terms conducive to that tradition's story, while finding it difficult even to imagine how things might seem from the viewpoint of an alternative story. Even when we are able to imagine a very different understanding of life, we may not be able to entertain it as a real possibility for us.

While it is possible to move from one life-orienting story to a different one, these stories would not achieve their function if we were frequently able to switch. We need ways to conceive our identity and order our life that are relatively stable. We can within limits modify our understanding of the orienting story we are using, but losing the story altogether is like a major trauma. Hence, as we use a life-orienting story, it typically remains unquestioned unless it becomes unwieldy as we attempt to live out the kind of life it supports or is destabilized by encounters with competitive stories that weaken our confidence in it. Even then, the story that has shaped our understanding may not be easily abandoned, since the prospect of changing from one fundamental orienting story to another calls for a major shift both in how we think and in how we live.

Belief in God

Some people's story about life makes use of the idea of God. In fact some people have difficulty telling their own story without referring to God. Their theological vocabulary is crucial to explaining their identity and the deeper meaning of their everyday activities. For these people belief in God is a life-orienting belief that is connected with a structured way of understanding who they are, what they are doing, and what is worth doing. To lose their belief in God would not be a minor modification in their thinking. It would be more like an upheaval in the way they perceive ordinary events and construe the meaning of their activities.

Obviously not everyone who claims to believe in God has the kind of belief that means this much. It is possible to hold a belief in a supernatural reality that has little relevance for our thought or behavior. David Hume compared belief in God to the belief that an elderly relative, whom you have never met, has left you an estate.[4] If you think that you have such a benefactor, Hume claimed, this remote sort of being could not be the object of genuine emotional responses. Nor is the existence or nonexistence of such a being particularly relevant to the question of how to live your life. For many people the idea of God is a hypothetical creator, who set the universe with its law-like structures in motion, but has no real involvement in it. They could decide that there is no such deity, and not much of practical importance would have to change.

By way of contrast, consider the belief of Socrates. One of the charges against Socrates at his trial in ancient Athens was not believing in the gods, or perhaps not believing in the right gods. Part of Socrates' defense involved telling the story of how he began the kind of behavior that made people want to get rid of him. He describes how he came to view his activities as expressions of a mission that had been assigned to him by God, one that he carried on at considerable personal cost. Given this understanding, if the authorities of the city should offer to drop the charges against him in exchange for a promise not to continue his mission to examine people for their pretense of wisdom and virtue and to challenge them for exhibiting concerns for money and reputation that crowded out more important values, he would have to decline. His orders come from a higher authority, and he must continue his god-given calling.[5]

Toward the end of Socrates' defense, he replies directly to the charge of not believing in the gods with the assertion that he does believe – and in a deeper sense than any of his accusers believe.[6] The kind of belief Socrates affirms has resulted in an extraordinarily demanding quest to fulfill his divinely given mission, wherever it may lead. He has adopted a way of understanding his situation that occupies his time and shapes his identity. In contrast to orthodox believers who assent to the standard doctrines of the city, but treat those doctrines like a theory with only peripheral connections to their central concerns, Socrates lives out his belief. It is a vital part of a story that provides an orientation, structuring his understanding of who he is and what he needs to be doing.

Religious Belief and Its Counterfeits

Sometimes people confuse the kind of belief that functions to orient an individual in life with the kind of belief that can be held at arm's length. This confusion is common with regard to belief in God. Instead of discussing belief in God in the religiously significant sense, we substitute unwittingly the question of whether to accept God as a metaphysical hypothesis. But the question of whether a being called God is needed to explain the physical universe is not the same as the question of whether to accept an orienting story in which the concept of God plays a fundamental role. One question is basically theoretical in nature; we can consider it as thinkers who are dealing with a kind of intellectual puzzle. The other question is practical; we approach it as active agents who need an orienting story to order our lives.

It is sometimes thought that while there may be more to belief in God than acceptance of a theoretical hypothesis, we can examine this belief by thinking of the metaphysical hypothesis as a kind of pared down core. But if the idea of God arises fundamentally in the context of seeking a life orientation, the most compelling sources of belief may be considerations whose significance is apparent from a practical point of view, but drop out when we focus on the theoretical question of what is needed to explain natural phenomena. One who has accepted the idea of God, as part of a life-orienting story, need not have an opinion about the value of the idea for metaphysical theorizing. Conversely, someone who finds the idea useful for constructing a metaphysical account may have little use for the idea as part of an orientation for a way of life.

People who come to believe in God in a religiously significant way ordinarily do so as the result of being exposed to teachings from religious communities that convey to them a fundamental orienting story that elaborates a particular understanding of what is real, what is important, and what is meaningful. Sometimes such a story is accepted on the basis of confidence in those who relate it. But for the story to take root, people need to find a kind of resonance between the religious account and their own experience. Making a religious story your own involves more than intellectual assent to its truth; it means coming to understand the events of your life in the light of the orienting story and aspiring to live the kind of life that understanding renders fitting. When the life-orienting story is a theistic one, the person who has his or her life-world shaped by the story believes in God.

Acquiring this kind of belief is not a matter of adopting the hypothesis of God to explain the natural world and then considering some god-story. Response to a story that provides practical orientation is the primary source of belief in God, and any theorizing about the idea of God or reflecting on whether accepting the existence of God would be justified by reasoning from observations of the natural world is secondary. A believer whose experience has been shaped by a theistic life-orienting story may find reflection about order in the world or the contingent nature of physical things to lead to satisfying ways of thinking about the god encountered through the story, but that is very different from viewing these lines of thought to be the basis for belief in God. If we speak of a basis at all, it will be in the lived experience of a normative order that is structured by a theistic life-orienting story.

To speak of how people acquire belief in God and find it confirmed in their experience is not to deny the possibility of rational reflection on that belief. However, I will be arguing throughout this book that the most central form of reflection about a religiously significant belief in God is reflection about how to live. Genuine belief in God is something that we display through involvement in a particular orienting drama, and to consider that belief is to consider whether we can enter into or sustain such an involvement. This sort of reflection is different from evaluating a purely theoretical hypothesis. For one thing we approach a potential life-orienting story from the perspective of someone who already lives on the basis of some understanding of our life situation. The issue is not whether to accept a particular story or go without one, but whether to stick with the story we are using or to try to restructure our lives in terms of a different story. Furthermore, we confront this kind of issue as interested parties who are vitally concerned with understanding our lives in a way that makes sense. This intimate connection between believing and our way of life tends to be obscured when we disconnect the idea of God from the practical context in which belief in God arises.

Alternative Stories

If we lived in a world where only one ultimate orienting story had any plausibility, the question of whether to accept it would not arise. But in our world whatever stories we have been taught or come to accept, we are aware of alternative stories. While we may rule out many of these religious and nonreligious options on various grounds, more than one viable competitor are likely to remain. Our position is analogous to that of the person at the beginning of this chapter who is presented with multiple ways of understanding the puzzling situation, but with no obvious procedure for determining which to accept.

In such a situation many people follow the strategy of holding to the story they have been taught, abandoning it only if it is found to be unworkable in practice. But unlike other eras in which you could simply take your own story for granted because everyone around you was taking it for granted, the modern era presents us with a pluralistic world in which it is difficult to avoid coming into contact with people who have significantly different understandings. While these encounters may or may not result in doubt, they make it more difficult to regard one's own views with the same sense of certainty. Reflective people, even if they do hold fast to a familiar story or retain their story with some modifications, find it hard to avoid considering why they should accept this story rather than another.

We can ask this question at different levels. One level is whether to accept a particular story, such as the Christian story or a particular version of the Christian story. But it is also possible to raise the question at a more general level. For example, "Why accept a religious story, as opposed to a naturalistic one?" While it is next to impossible to give an uncontroversial definition of religion and religious ways of life, I would suggest generally that religious orienting stories tend to appeal to a reality that is beyond what is typically accessible through ordinary sensory experience, and naturalistic accounts reflect the view that our descriptions of reality should stay close to the empirically observable.[7]

The naturalistic intuition is that there is something excessive and unreliable about appeals that posit something out of the reach of ordinary sensory observation. Is there a corresponding religious intuition? Perhaps it is the idea that getting a deep understanding requires us to go beyond what we find on the surface. Plato's story of the cave compares the world given in ordinary sense experience to a realm of shadows in relation to a deeper reality. Hindu thought characterizes ordinary experience as having the illusory status of *maya*. We live in a dreamlike sort of realm that hides something more fundamental. In each case the suggestion is that we can be led astray if we take a kind of surface presentation as ultimately real. We need to look beyond the appearances to a more basic level of reality.

From a naturalistic perspective this way of thinking sounds like an open door to endless flights of fancy. If we license claims to realities inaccessible to empirical testability, we lose the prospect of being able objectively to distinguish between truth and speculation. However, someone who has felt the attraction of a religious vision of reality may be equally convinced that adopting naturalistic modes of thought is like putting on blinders that keep us from awareness of deeper meanings. Such a person might suspect that limiting reality to what we can verify empirically is likely to result in missing whatever does not conform to our testing procedures.

But why should anyone think that there is something mysterious or hidden or beyond the purview of ordinary sense experience? Perhaps it is not so much thinking it in the abstract as it is encountering stories referring to the transcendent that seem to provide a kind of intelligibility to the human situation. Many kinds of experience can suggest a transcendent dimension. When a story of the transcendent is available, it can provide a satisfying way of making sense of these experiences. Additionally, religious stories satisfy a persistent human urge to make sense of our lives in terms of our value aspirations. When a story tells us how ultimate justice will be done or how human fulfillment is possible, it is speaking to matters that concern us. If it takes something transcendent to fit our value aspirations with reality, our concerns give us motivation to entertain such a possibility.

The kinds of experiences that might suggest transcendence are numerous. They include such things as visionary experiences, meditative experiences of a unity behind diversity, moments of fearful awe at something majestic, a sudden insight that has a transforming effect, the sense of being guided in a time of crisis, an overwhelming awareness of beauty. It is not that these experiences cannot be explained in some way compatible with naturalistic intuitions. It is rather that they can strongly suggest that there is more going on than what appears on the surface. When an orienting story with transcendent categories is available, it can seem compelling as a way to understand such experiences. Sociologist Peter Berger tells of a psychoanalyst friend who had orthodox Freudian views of religion. Berger asked him if he ever had doubts about his account of religion. After some hesitation he replied that he had doubts whenever he listened to the choral portion of Beethoven's Ninth Symphony.[8]

In addition to the prospect of ordering these intimations of a transcendent dimension, some religious stories appeal to a persistent human longing to find our lives intelligible in a way that satisfies our value aspirations. We can think that human suffering has neither rationale nor remedy. But a well-known religious story tells us that it is a product of distorted craving that can be overcome by a path leading to the egoless state of Nirvana. We can regard the events of our lives as lacking in meaning or significance, but in a certain kind of religious story they are portrayed as part of a process by which a benevolent creator seeks to transform us from egocentric beings, trapped in our own follies, to persons who are fully free to love. In each case the background story appeals to a deep longing for finding orientation in terms of an order we can regard as worthy. In other words what is sought is a kind of union between our understanding of the facts and our valuing nature.

Of course, such a longing is not a reason for thinking the story that satisfies it is true. Reality may be out of tune with human longings for this kind of intelligibility. But what is the appropriate attitude toward this sort of longing? We could distrust it, thinking that anything other than our ability to assess evidence is irrelevant to the question of truth. However, in a famous discussion William James suggests that the concern to eliminate the influence of what he calls our passionate nature from our quest for truth seems to derive itself from the passion for a kind of certainty that is free from the risk of error.[9] That passion, he argues, as it manifests itself in the demand that we should suspend judgment on any matter that is not confirmed by evidential considerations, endorses a procedure that is neither accurate as an account of how any of us think, nor of how we should think. We justifiably rely on aspects of our nature other than our ability to consider evidence in our pursuit of truth.

One of the examples James cites has to do with belief in moral truths. All of us are taught that there are ways we ought to behave and ways we should not behave. We learn, for example, that telling lies is generally forbidden and that showing compassion is generally a good thing. At some point we may reflect on our moral beliefs with a skeptical eye, wondering whether our ideas of goodness or obligation are only "odd biological phenomena" or whether there is real moral truth that we need to recognize as authoritative. It is well known that a person can be a moral skeptic, reducing apparent truth claims about the moral realm to something that lacks a compelling authority over us, and it is difficult to see how someone who assumes a distrustful attitude toward the capacity for recognizing moral truths can be shown undeniable evidence to the contrary. If there are moral realities, it may take a kind of trusting attitude to bring us in touch with them. As James puts it, "If your heart does not *want* a world of moral reality, your head will assuredly never make you believe in one."[10]

The point is not that receptiveness to moral reality creates that reality, but that a kind of receptiveness is needed for recognizing it. Similarly, James posits that our recognition of religious truth could depend on a receptive attitude toward it. Religious stories present to us visions of life in which human values are brought into a kind of harmony with our understanding of the nature of things. The question of whether or not there is a transcendent order that makes such a harmony possible is something we are unlikely to be able to decide on the basis of publicly accessible evidence. Yet whether we believe in such a reality and orient our lives in accordance with that belief could make a major difference in how we live.

So if someone is presented with a religious life-orienting story that satisfies the urge to make sense of the world in value terms and finds that she has a strong inclination to believe the story, should she veto that inclination on the grounds that the evidence doesn't settle the matter? While such a choice is an apt response to the fear of error, that fear cannot be assuaged without risking the loss of truth and the loss of the kind of life that may be in the truth. If there is something about the nature of reality with the potential to fulfill the longings for the kind of intelligible order that religious stories describe, giving veto power to the fear of being wrong or the fear that it may be "too good to be true" could keep us from a way of life that might constitute our deepest fulfillment.

If we consider whether there is a dimension of reality beyond the empirical order as a theoretical question, we may think that the appropriate response is, "Who knows?" But the claims about transempirical realities come to us in the context of stories that purport to provide orientation for a way of life. In that context we cannot simply shrug off the question. We will either live as if we believed in some kind of transcendent order, or we will live as if we do not. So when we encounter a religious story that offers orientation in terms of an appeal to the transcendent, the central question is not whether we have a foolproof way to establish the existence of such transempirical realities. It is whether we have found a way of living that does a better job of orienting us so as to render our experiential reality intelligible and motivate us to live in accordance with the values we find compelling.

Orienting Stories and Truth

Of course, not every orienting story is one that we can or should entertain. Starting from background beliefs that we assume to be well established, we will find some stories too implausible or unlikely to be considered. Even people who accept a religious orienting story may find many other religious stories to be outlandish. Someone whose thinking is shaped by a naturalistic point of view may find no religious life-orienting stories worthy of serious consideration. On the other hand, someone whose imagination has been captured by a religious vision may have difficulty finding any plausibility in a naturalistic account.

Trying to evaluate someone else's orienting story is difficult for a variety of reasons. One is that it is difficult to achieve a genuine understanding of a point of view that is alien to your own. It takes effort to try to imagine how someone could think so differently, and often we are content to reject alien ideas on the basis of a superficial understanding that relies on relatively uncharitable interpretations. Another reason is that we are apt to take for granted a great many things that would be regarded as questionable or false by someone with a different orienting story. We absorb from our communal context a variety of ideas that become de facto starting points of our thinking. If we come to question some of these ideas, there will always be others that it does not occur to us to question. Even if we become aware that a particular starting point is contestable, we may be unable to take an alternative seriously.

Despite these difficulties we sometimes do make an effort to listen to others' stories and examine our own. Sometimes we even abandon an orienting story that has been fundamental to our own understanding and adopt an alternative one. But the process of trying to get at the truth is not nearly as neat as in areas where there are more or less agreed upon ways to distinguish between truth and falsehood. Noting the difficulty of getting decisive verification or falsification, some philosophers have concluded that when we get to the point of talking about ultimate orienting stories, we are no longer talking about truth.[11] But such a conclusion is often connected with an overly idealized notion of what truth-seeking involves or a privileging of truths that are easy to come by over those that we struggle to acquire.

When people reject particular orienting stories, they often do so on grounds that sound very much like evaluations of truth claims. A story is judged implausible because it flies in the face of obvious facts. For example, suppose it posits an account of creation of the world that conflicts with overwhelming scientific evidence. Often such criticisms turn out not to be the last word. A defender of the story might suggest that the version that contradicts science contains elements that are not essential to the religious view. All of this sounds very much as if the question of truth is being taken seriously. Reformulating an account that does not square with agreed-upon facts is often a reasonable way of proceeding.

It is easy to underestimate the capacity of religious traditions to reflect on and adjust their stories. While some religious communities have exhibited relatively little interest in revising their accounts to deal with the range of human experience or to cohere with new understandings, developed religious traditions are often remarkably resilient in reinterpreting their stories to adapt to changing circumstances or knowledge. A theistic tradition, expounded in terms of an overly simplistic idea that obedience to God means prosperity and disobedience means punishment, faces obvious pressure to rethink the idea in the light of the observation that the wicked prosper and the righteous suffer. A long-lasting tradition may come to view some of its earlier beliefs and practices as primitive and superstitious. It may, for example, reject portrayals of God that are clearly present in its own sacred texts as anthropomorphisms that need to be understood in less literal ways. Religions that show themselves incapable of this kind of reflection risk ceasing to exist, and those that do survive often acquire intellectual resources for responding to potential objections.

Some might see this tendency to revise an orienting story to accommodate recalcitrant facts as a determined effort to hang onto the story without being willing to consider whether it is true. Undoubtedly it is often just that, but on the other hand, recognizing the need to reformulate beliefs in the light of problematic data can be an expression of a concern for truth. If you are convinced of the correctness of a view, it is often an intellectual virtue not to discard it too quickly, but to explore the possibility that objections arise from simplistic understandings of what the view means. The need for some degree of tenacity is particularly understandable when we are dealing with orienting beliefs that structure our practical life. Holding on to a basic orienting story is often inseparable from holding on to a stable identity.

Furthermore, in practical terms rejecting a life-orienting story makes sense only when we are aware of a superior alternative. A person might be very aware of difficulties in a particular story, but find no alternative to be as believable. Additionally, we sometimes find ourselves in a position, like that portrayed at the beginning of the chapter, of needing to commit ourselves to some story and act on the basis of the understanding it provides. In the process we may find the perspective we have adopted increasingly compelling or we may discover that it has become increasingly cumbersome and implausible. Only rarely, however, is either experience like encountering evidence that makes it clear, once and for all, that the story is correct (or incorrect). Our pursuit of the kind of truth that matters most to us is not typically so simple.

With regard to many of the beliefs that matter most to us, we proceed by forming interpretations that seem plausible and adjusting our interpretations in the light of experience and reflection. In the realm of interpersonal experience we are constantly forming interpretations of the meanings of others' actions or intentions that furnish a basis for our own response. I may, for example, believe that someone I work with is rigid and uncooperative and regulate my own behavior accordingly. Sometimes we revise our interpretations and come to an understanding we regard as superior. What I took to be rigidity is actually a function of having certain core convictions – on many matters there is ample flexibility. This sort of reinterpretation in pursuit of deeper understanding is a feature of our practical beliefs that may be missed if we think of seeking truth only in terms of gaining indisputable verifications or falsifications. In the interpersonal realm the truth that we act on is rarely so indisputable that an alternative interpretation could not be defended. Yet we are obliged to act on the basis of judgments we find plausible.

As we seek fuller insight, we are understandably reluctant to abandon beliefs that have served to orient us. Consider the case of a wife who has adopted the orienting belief that her husband loves her. It might be a belief around which much of her life is organized. Presumably she has some evidence in his behavior to confirm the belief. But insofar as the belief provides a kind of orientation that structures her understanding of events, she will not continually treat the belief as an object of examination. But suppose questions arise from some things the husband does or fails to do. There are situations in which the evidence against his love may be overwhelming enough that the belief, and the orientation that goes with it, ought to be abandoned. But it is also possible in some circumstances to imagine the wife revising her paradigm of love as too limited, perhaps even learning to recognize in her husband a deeper and unexpected kind of love. Similarly, someone who has gained some confidence in the orienting story of a particular religious tradition may expect that within the tradition are deeper understandings than the particular ones she has mastered. Past experiences of working through puzzlement might strengthen this kind of confidence.

We are not in a position to construct our life-orienting stories from the ground up. When we try to consider fundamental components of our story, we inevitably do so from a standpoint constituted by assumptions that might be questioned. Someone using a theistic story may consider whether God exists, just as someone using a naturalistic story may consider whether physical categories are genuinely ultimate. But in either case the question will be considered from the point of view of what seems plausible, and our judgments of plausibility are shaped both by assumptions we find difficult to question as well as assumptions that we are not even aware of using. The aspiration to certify our starting points from a point of view that is beyond question can never quite be satisfied.

Nevertheless, we come to trust the stories that orient us. As we habitually adopt the patterns of thought a particular story calls for, we either develop confidence in those patterns or we lose confidence, sometimes even to the extent that our capacity to use the story is compromised. But the question of when it is reasonable to hold onto a story and when we ought to abandon it for an alternative is not one for which a clear-cut and indisputable decision procedure is available. Dealing with doubts about a story that has structured our way of life is often intensely personal, and the perspective from which we think about such matters is not one we can expect everyone to share.

Philosopher Nicholas Wolterstorff wrote a journal of his thoughts following the tragic death of his son in a mountain-climbing accident. In the journal he reveals a struggle in trying to come to terms with the death and to reconcile it with his belief in a loving God. In the midst of his questioning, some of his friends suggested that he scrap the idea of God, which seemed to be contributing to his turmoil. Wolterstorff's reply to the suggestion was that he was unable to stop believing. The belief, he reported, springs up irresistibly.[12]

We cannot simply turn on or turn off the confidence we develop in life-orienting stories. For these stories to perform their orienting function, the patterns of interpretation they call for need to penetrate deeply, forming cognitive and emotional habits. There are, of course, people who profess to live by a story that is only loosely connected with the life they are actually living. Tolstoy tells of an incident in his teenaged years when he dropped his religious practice because of the realization that he no longer believed what he had assumed he believed. The collapse of his faith was more like the realization that there was only a pretense of faith that was unconnected with the rest of his life.[13] But for someone who has relied on a story to shape his or her life, puzzling life experiences are often insufficient to override a confidence that arises from finding in a story the key to understanding what is significant and what is valuable.

Fallibilism

You may be convinced that your life-orienting story is true. You may have overwhelming confidence in it. You have, so to speak, bet your life on it. But could you be wrong? If orienting stories are neither true nor false and anybody's story is as good as anyone else's, we don't need to worry about the possibility of being mistaken. But if we regard these stories as matters of truth and start to make judgments about which stories are closer to the truth and which should be rejected as false, we have to face up to the risk of getting it wrong. With regard to life-orienting stories, whether religious or nonreligious, human beings are limited and prone to error.

Even if you believe that you have attached yourself to a religious tradition that is an infallible source of truth, this tradition will have to be explained and understood by fallible interpreters. With regard to any major religion, we find not just one account of what the religion means, but many. So if some version of Buddhism or Judaism is true, which one is it? Even if we can reach agreement about some of the basics of any authoritative tradition, there are still disputes about how these understandings should be put into practice. Some Muslims understand their sacred texts to authorize suicide bombs against civilians, and some Muslims judge the activity to be a repudiation of their religion. Some Jews find biblical authorization for Israelite territorial claims extending from Egypt to Syria, and other Jews reject such claims. Even the clearest teachings have to be applied by fallible human beings.

The recognition "I could be wrong" about some of the basics around which I have organized my life need not keep anyone from seeking truth and gaining confidence in the truth we believe we have found. It doesn't need to keep us from making judgments about views we think are in error. But especially when we are talking about fundamental orienting stories, the realization of our fallibility might suggest the appropriateness of caution about condescending attitudes toward others who may also be seeking truth. I may be absolutely convinced that the Christian story provides the key to understanding the human condition and committed to helping others see things this way. But that does not justify me in regarding those I cannot convince as unworthy of my respect.

On the other hand, some people think that the way to show respect for others who have very different fundamental beliefs is to treat all such beliefs as equally legitimate. None are more true or false than any others. However, this position results in a kind of pseudo tolerance that does not take seriously the people you are purporting to respect. You can make all religious beliefs true only by reinterpreting them in a way that renders them unrecognizable to the people who hold them. The willingness to engage in civil discourse that disagrees with another's view, but treats it seriously, can be a greater sign of respect than refusing to acknowledge that a disputable truth claim has been made.

While there is a risk of being wrong about a life-orienting story, it is a risk we cannot avoid. As the parable at the beginning of the chapter suggests, we need to act on the basis of some life-orienting story. We can afford to remain uncommitted about many questions, but we do not have the option of being uncommitted about how to live, and ways of life that maintain neutrality regarding contestable claims about reality are hard to come by. Our attempts to withhold judgment on an issue whenever we lack theoretical certainty are sabotaged by the need to act. The understanding displayed in our mode of life will effectively override our stances of pretended neutrality. For example, if we decide to withhold judgment about God, we will most likely shape our lives in accordance with a picture of reality that does not include God. In practical terms we will live as if God does not exist or as if God's existence makes no difference.

We may or may not be aware of the pictures of reality that shape our behavior and govern our sense of what we are doing. When you are looking through a lens, you tend not to notice the lens itself. When we become aware of the lens, and aware of the fact that not everyone is using the same lens, we may be tempted to throw up our hands at the futility of knowing for sure. Or we may get on with the business of living by the story that convinces us, realizing that there is no better alternative than making our own the story we find compelling.

Notes

1 John Haught, *Is Nature Enough? Meaning and Truth in the Age of Science* (Cambridge: Cambridge University Press, 2006), 46. The use of this quotation as an epigraph has been accepted as fair dealing by Cambridge University Press.

2 Christian Smith, *Moral Believing Animals: Human Personhood and Culture* (Oxford: Oxford University Press, 2003), 78. The use of this quotation as an epigraph is by permission of Oxford University Press.

3 What I am calling a life-orienting story resembles what some authors call a worldview. My account is influenced primarily by sociological discussions of the importance of narrative for human understanding of what is real or significant. See, for example, Christian Smith, 63–94. A worldview is an abstract representation of what functions practically more as a background narrative. Philosophical discussions of narrative include Paul Ricoeur, *Time and Narrative*, vol. 1–3, trans. Kathleen McLaughlin and David Pellauer (Chicago: University of Chicago Press 1984, 1985, 1988) and Alasdair McIntyre, *After Virtue* (Notre Dame: University of Notre Dame Press, 1981), 204–25. There is a vast literature on the topic of narrative, including authors who are skeptical of the value of some uses of this category.

4 David Hume, *New Letters of David Hume*, eds. R. Kilbansky and E. C. Mossner (Oxford: Oxford University Press, 1954), 13.

5 Plato, *Apology* (29d) in *The Trial and Death of Socrates: Four Dialogues*, ed. Shane Weller (New York: Dover Publications, Inc., 1992), 30.

6 Plato, *Apology* (35d), 36.

7 William James characterizes the religious life as consisting of "the belief that there is an unseen order and that our supreme good lies in harmoniously adjusting ourselves thereto." *The Varieties of Religious Experience* (New York: The Macmillan Company, 1961), 59.

8 Peter Berger, *Questions of Faith: A Skeptical Affirmation of Christianity* (Oxford: Blackwell Publishing, 2004), 2.

9   William James, "The Will to Believe," in *The Writings of William James: A Comprehensive Edition*, ed. John J. McDermott (Chicago: The University of Chicago Press, 1977), 717–35.

10 James, "The Will to Believe," 730.

11 D. Z. Phillips is a prominent example of philosophers who have used ideas suggested in Wittgenstein to develop nonrealist accounts of religious beliefs. On his view talk about God expresses a particular attitude or perspective on human life, but does not refer to a transcendent reality. For an interesting critical discussion of philosophers who have applied Wittgenstein's thought to religious language, see Felicity McCutheon, *Religion Within the Limits of Language Alone – Wittgenstein on Philosophy and Religion* (Aldershot: Ashgate Publishing, 2001). Another helpful discussion of issues related to a realist interpretation of theism may be found in Peter Byrne, *God and Realism* (Aldershott: Ashgate Publishing, 2003).

12 Nicholas Wolterstorff, *Lament For a Son* (Grand Rapids, MI: Eerdmans Publishing Company, 1987), 76–7.

13 Leo Tolstoy, *A Confession and Other Religious Writings*, trans. Jane Kentish (New York: Penguin Books, 1987), 19–21.

2

God of the Philosophers

"To conclude to a transcendent ground, or to postulate such a ground in order to make the real intelligible, is not yet to attain the idea of God as religious faiths have traditionally conceived it." (Louis Dupré[1])

"One will not long believe in a personal God with whom there is no personal communication, and the most compelling evidence of a personal God must itself be personal." (Michael Buckley[2])

In science fiction stories people sometimes ask questions of a computer that the computer declines to answer. Typically the reason for not getting the desired response is that the question has been badly formed. For instance, it may contain ambiguities or vague terms that make it unclear exactly what is being asked. Or the question might be asked in a way that leaves out crucial variables. For example, someone asks how long a given task will take, without mentioning the number of people or type of machinery available to work on it. Evidently computers of the future are smart enough to refrain from attempting an answer until they are given a good enough question.

Even when a question appears to be formulated in a clear and precise manner, deciding what kind of answer is called for may involve considerable contextual understanding. If someone asks you what you are doing for lunch, the question might be about your availability for a lunch meeting or an inquiry into whether you are still pursuing your odd diet or it might be about whether your social life is picking up. Giving an appropriate answer can require some discernment into what the point of the question is. If we misconstrue the purposes of the inquiry, we may offer the wrong kind of answer.

It might be thought that a question such as "Does God exist?" would be immune from this sort of misunderstanding. Surely there is a straightforward answer to this question, regardless of our purpose in asking it. Sometimes, however, apparently straightforward answers can be unresponsive to what we primarily want to know. Suppose, for example, that the question of God's existence arises out of a concern to discover how to live my life. I want to know about God's existence because I think it will make some difference for what I should be concerned about and what activities should engage me. I want to know whether it makes sense to join some community of believers and devote myself to practices, such as praying and studying sacred texts.

Imagine that someone responds to my question by offering convincing reasons for thinking that the universe had a First Cause or an Intelligent Designer. While I might recognize this response as relevant to my question, I might also be disappointed in it. Even if the answer I have been given is correct, it is not what I was trying to discover. The kind of god I was inquiring about is one who would make a difference in how I live, and yet I might very well accept the idea of a First Cause or an Intelligent Designer without thinking that such a fact had much to do with me at all. Even if I think that I have learned something important, I might judge myself to be not very close to answering the question that motivated my inquiry.

The question of whether God exists is often interpreted as an expression of a kind of theoretical concern, arising out of our desire to understand things. When viewed in this fashion, it is tempting to equate it with an inquiry into whether some being beyond the universe is needed to explain the existence of the universe. Once we frame the question in this way, we may find promising lines of inquiry. We might think, for instance, that the starting point should be some scientific account of the nature of the universe and focus on whether there is some kind of explanation that science cannot give. But even if we can get a satisfactory answer to this kind of question, it seems doubtful that this procedure would get to the heart of what people are looking for when they ask about God's existence.

What most of us want to find out when we ask about God's existence relates to the God we have heard about in religious traditions. We wonder whether the object of worship in religions such as Judaism or Christianity is a reality. Discovering that we needed an entity called God to serve as an explanation of the universe might be worthwhile information, but it does not really answer the questions we are primarily concerned to answer. Can you pray to this theoretical entity? Is there some way to make contact with it? Does it care how you live? Issues that are of central importance in an inquiry about the object of worship in particular religions would be left untouched by an answer to the question of whether a being called God is needed as an explanation of the physical universe.

Perhaps someone might think that the answers to all these other questions are properly addressed only after we have resolved the explanation question. If it turns out that you do not need to posit such a being to explain the universe, we might imagine that this would somehow undermine a religious belief in God. But why should we think so? Did adherents of theistic religions decide that God exists because they thought that God was needed as an explanation of the universe, or is their confidence that God exists based on different considerations? If belief in God does not develop out of an attempt to form a theoretical understanding of the ultimate cause of things, we run the risk of distorting the belief when we construe it in these terms. If we are primarily concerned with God's existence as a religious question, we need to be careful not to confuse that inquiry with some other type of question.

Religious Questions and Metaphysical Questions

In describing how he came to develop his philosophical defense of Christian belief, Richard Swinburne writes,

> [O]nce I had seen what makes scientific theories meaningful and justified, I saw that any metaphysical theory, such as the Christian theological system, is just a superscientific theory. ... A metaphysical theory is a highest-level-of-all theory. It seeks to explain why there is a universe at all, why it has the most general laws of nature that it does (especially such laws as lead to the evolution of animals and humans), as well as any particular phenomena that lower-level laws are unable to explain. Such a theory ... is justified if it is a simple theory and leads you to expect the observable phenomena when you would not otherwise expect them.[3]

What Swinburne proposes is not idiosyncratic. His assumption that the idea of God should be evaluated in the context of seeking a metaphysical theory is the assumption that philosophers make when they attempt to discover whether general facts about the universe can justify an inference to the conclusion that God exists. Swinburne interprets standard arguments for God's existence as inductive arguments and uses the tools of confirmation theory to make a cumulative case argument. But he assumes that the way to justify belief that God exists is to show it as part of a general human concern to develop a theoretical explanation of things that starts with publicly available factual evidence.

In discussing cosmological arguments for God's existence, Swinburne says that while natural science cannot explain the existence of the universe, "God can provide an explanation. The hypothesis of theism is that the universe exists because there is a God who keeps it in being and that laws of nature operate because there is a God who brings it about that they do."[4] Whatever might be said for or against this claim, it should not escape our notice that the idea of God is treated as a hypothesis that is justified by providing a certain kind of explanation. Once we accept that assumption, the rules and procedures for discussing whether God exists become in effect the rules and procedures of metaphysical argument.

But is there any alternative? Isn't the idea of God a metaphysical idea that ought to be evaluated on metaphysical grounds? To answer this question, we need to distinguish between two senses of "metaphysical." In one sense of the word any claim about reality is a metaphysical claim. So, for example, if I speak of my next door neighbor graciously agreeing to mow my lawn while I was away, I am making metaphysical claims about the entity I call my neighbor, my lawn, and implicitly myself. However, when I start taking claims about reality to call for the particular kinds of explication or justification that metaphysicians develop, I am doing more than saying they are claims about reality. I am treating them as part of a certain kind of theoretical enterprise that operates in accordance with recognized standards of evaluation.

When we ask metaphysical questions in this more specialized sense, we are trying to construct an account of reality that meets requirements of precision and argumentative rigor that are understood components of philosophic practice. We can treat the idea of God in this way. We can put on our objective evidence-evaluation hats and consider whether the idea provides a better explanation of commonly accepted data than alternative hypotheses. When we do so, it may be tempting to think that our metaphysical investigation is a way of trying to answer the question of whether the being religious traditions refer to as God actually exists. But there are some significant reasons for being cautious about too close an identification between the metaphysical issue and the religious issue. Here are a few:

1.   **Acceptance or rejection of God as a metaphysical hypothesis is primarily an intellectual matter.** The focus is on gaining some kind of conceptual understanding that can be rationally explicated and defended. Religious belief in God, however, is not a product of a detached examination of the world. It arises most fundamentally out of participating in the practices of a religious community. In such a community adopting a belief in God is wrapped up with accepting particular attitudes and values that are connected with a shared way of life. It is at least not obvious that the question of whether to adopt such a belief and the way of life that goes with it is to be answered by the kind of dispassionate reasoning we think appropriate for pursuing theoretical understanding.

2.   **The kind of belief that could result from a metaphysical inquiry into God's existence does not give rise to the sort of commitment characteristic of religious belief.** When we treat the existence of God as a metaphysical question, it seems appropriate to imagine someone assenting to a hypothesis or a conclusion based on the evidence currently available, but holding the belief with a kind of tentativeness that is open to new evidence that might overturn it. However, anyone who accepted a belief in God in only a tentative manner would not be holding a religious belief. To be genuinely religious, belief in God must have the centrality characteristic of a fundamental conviction, making it inappropriate to think of the belief as a hypothesis in the ordinary sense of that term.

3.   **Thinking of God as a metaphysical concept means treating the idea as an inference from known data to something unknown.** By contrast someone with a religious belief in God will think of God as an experiential reality. It seems odd to pray to or worship a being that you have posited to exist as a result of some chain of reasoning. But the kind of belief that could be called religious will be exhibited through activities that engage the believer in a way that produces some sense of contact with God.

4.   **The content of a metaphysical belief that God exists is different from the content of a religious belief.** Anyone familiar with metaphysical thinking about God will recognize that the categories used are much more austere and abstract than the rich range of conceptual tools characteristic of religious traditions. A metaphysician might think about whether there is an uncaused cause or a necessary being, while a believer will think primarily in terms of images such as father or light or redeemer. Even terms that

might be given an abstract rendering, such as "creator," have for the believer an evocative power connected with appropriate responses, such as gratitude and praise.

The point is not that metaphysical thinking about the existence of God is inappropriate. A religious believer, who is inclined to do such thinking, might hold that the idea of God can be defended as a promising metaphysical hypothesis. On the other hand, a religious believer might be indifferent to metaphysical speculation, thinking perhaps (as many nonbelievers do) that human ability to reach reliable conclusions about ultimate matters through such reasoning is very limited. The point is that the question of whether the idea of God is needed for metaphysical purposes is distinguishable from the question of whether to believe in God.

Unfortunately, both believers and nonbelievers have found it all too easy to conflate the two questions. Even when the issues are understood as separate, it is often assumed that belief in God needs to be based on some kind of metaphysical reasoning. But, as I will try to make clear, it is far from obvious that religious belief either needs or could have such a basis. I am not questioning the appropriateness of reflecting on religious belief, only the assumption that substituting the metaphysical question of God's existence for the religious question is the best way to do that reflection. Throughout this book, I will suggest that closer attention to the features of religious belief in God will give us a better sense of what sort of reflection is most relevant to the issue of whether to have such a belief.

God of the Philosophers

The seventeenth-century mathematician Blaise Pascal had an overwhelming religious experience, which he memorialized in a note that he carried with him (sewed in the lining of his coat) until the end of his life. Through the note, he apparently attempted to remind himself of what he took to be a decisive, revelatory experience. In a now-famous phrase he claims that he had not encountered the god of the philosophers and scholars, but the "God of Abraham, Isaac, and Jacob."[5] What did Pascal mean in contrasting the philosophers' god with the biblical God? In part he may have been distinguishing the kind of reality that he believed he had contacted experientially with the kind of being who might emerge as a conclusion of a process of reasoning. In one case there is an inferred deity that fits into some system of thought. In the other case something enters into a person's life with a compelling immediacy. In his attempt to remind himself of what he had encountered, Pascal repeatedly uses the word "fire," suggesting something wild and uncontrollable. From his perspective the god of the philosophers is a domesticated deity who occupies a determinate place as an object of thought, but the God Pascal speaks of is an awe-inspiring presence who cannot be locked in our conceptual cages.

The deity who appears in the writings of the seventeenth-century philosopher Descartes is a good candidate for the god of the philosophers. Descartes wanted to put human knowledge on a firm basis, and he set out to do so by using a process of systematic doubt. By setting aside beliefs he could not be absolutely sure of, Descartes hoped to arrive at the kind of truth that could not rationally be doubted and then build on this foundation a secure body of knowledge. When he subjected his beliefs to his method of doubt, Descartes put himself into a skeptical hole that he climbs out of only by invoking God as a guarantee of the reliability of his sense experience and his thought processes.[6] Presumably Descartes, as a faithful Catholic, had a religious belief in God, but as a philosopher, he brings in God as a theoretical entity, performing a needed function in his philosophical system.

When the idea of God becomes a theoretical entity that can be useful to us, we have shifted the context from personal encounter to a context in which we can contemplate the idea with a degree of detachment. We are no longer dealing with the God who overwhelms and disturbs us, but a god who enters into our thinking on terms we set. Whatever does not contribute to our intellectual goals is likely to escape our attention.[7]

The kind of god needed for philosophical purposes will be one that contributes to the goal of intelligibility. Achieving this end is in some tension with the religious affirmation of an experiential reality that overwhelms our powers of comprehension. While a philosophical account of God may acknowledge that there is something beyond our understanding, the aim of making the whole intelligible makes it tempting to marginalize whatever our concepts cannot convey. Great theologians, such as Augustine or Aquinas, are able to use philosophic categories, while still affirming that they are dealing with a mystery they can barely hint at. But the philosophic urge exerts a pressure against genuine openness to a mystery that is beyond our grasp.

Another source of tension is between using metaphysical models of God and maintaining the interpersonal context in which theistic religions place encounters with God. It is tempting for a philosopher to think that some abstract set of categories supersedes the personal language of theistic practice. Reflective theists recognize the need to qualify anthropomorphic understandings of the divine, but it can be a short step from eliminating objectionable analogies between the divine and the human to eliminating the model of personal agency altogether. When metaphysical thinking about God is placed in an interpersonal context, it can supplement the portrayals arising from theistic practice. But when the interpersonal context is removed, the idea of God retains only the remotest connection to religious conceptions.

When we contrast God as an object of theoretical understanding with God as an object of experiential encounter, one obvious difference is with regard to who is in control. Pascal describes the kind of encounter in which the object of experience is not merely a means to completing his agenda, but something that actively takes charge. By contrast someone who is theorizing about God may feel relatively secure about manipulating a set of philosophical concepts, in accordance with the rules of logic, like pieces of a puzzle that are being put together to form a satisfying intellectual product. There is little danger that the puzzle pieces will rise up to assert control.

When God is thought of as an agent, beyond our comprehension, who dwarfs us in knowledge, power, and goodness, our yearning for control suffers a blow. Contemplating such a God is not something we can do with an attitude of aloofness from a safe distance. The God of Abraham won't sit still while we figure out how to do things on our own terms, but enters with disturbing demands that challenge our agendas. To take seriously the idea of a Divine Other who judges and commands us is to enter a different realm from the abode of the god who passively fits into our projects.

The twentieth-century philosopher Martin Heidegger protests against the kind of god that emerges from philosophical thinking as an intellectual construct, noting that we can neither pray to nor sacrifice to such a deity. A god who is derived from classical metaphysical thought, he suggests, does not provoke a person to "fall to his knees in awe nor can he play music or dance before this god."[8] But why speak, as he does and as Pascal does, of two different deities? Why not regard metaphysical inquiry as a different mode of access to the same deity? At least part of the answer might be that the categories of understanding that dominate metaphysical thinking represent an object that we can consider at arm's length. When we think about a prime mover or an intelligent designer, we imagine a being whose existence can be considered with the kind of dispassionate objectivity we try to maintain in areas such as science. But there is reason to wonder whether God is the kind of entity who can be considered in this way. Perhaps we can understand Pascal to be suggesting that when we try to maintain the aloofness of an objective investigator, the object of thought is a truncated version of deity that is no longer recognizable as God. What we arrive at by means of such investigations is so remote from what religious people call God that it is misleading to claim that we are dealing with the same object.

Consider an analogy. Suppose someone does an analysis of the genetic code that makes up the body of a person you care about. You are given a description of the person by means of a computer printout, listing details of the code. Without denying the legitimacy of the account, you might claim that this sort of description misses what you regard as most important about the person. While there is a sense in which the analysis is just talking about the person in a different way, what is described is so different from what you know through encounter with this person that it seems like a stretch to say that the object of analysis is the same as what you call the person. Thinking about the person as an entity that can be objectively described, using categories other than those derived from personal encounter may tell you something, but knowing the person requires you to think in different ways.

Similarly, someone who believes in God might find the descriptions resulting from a metaphysical account of God to be so remote from the patterns of thought characteristic of communal religious practices that identifying the object of worship with the object of metaphysical thinking seems problematic. Just as the kind of knowledge needed for dealing with other people at a personal level differs from the kind of knowledge we seek in objective theorizing, the kind of knowledge claimed by the religious believer differs greatly from the kind sought in metaphysical analysis. One way to understand the difference is to recognize that in theoretical knowing we have artificially narrowed our purposes by conceiving ourselves as something like spectators on the object of knowledge. In most of life we are not spectators, but participants who are concerned to achieve various goals and respond appropriately to the kinds of reality we encounter. What we need to know is practical in the sense that the focus is on regulating our concerns and our actions. Religious belief can be treated as a theoretical matter, but it is more like the interpersonal understanding that we use to guide our practical living. As such, it calls for a participative frame of mind that contrasts with the approach of the spectator who is considering things from afar.

For purposes of some kinds of investigation, we follow a policy of putting our emotional reactions and values on hold. But there are some truths that we genuinely understand only when we have grasped their significance for our lives, and this kind of awareness arises out of something other than dispassionate detachment. Imagine someone who accepts the claim that an avalanche is imminent and will crush the house in which he and his family are living, yet makes no effort to evacuate the house. Or imagine a woman who hears that the spouse she adores has betrayed her, but has no emotional reaction. In such cases we might wonder whether the person has really understood. There are some kinds of understanding that occur only when we do our thinking as embodied agents who care about and respond to things, not as intellects, who can manipulate facts with sublime indifference.

The Kind of Belief that Matters

There are some beliefs that people can hold without much personal investment. I might believe that a particular celebrity will make an appearance in my city, but not care whether she does or not. I might believe that there is intelligent life in some other galaxy. But unless I feel the need to devote much time or effort to searching for signs of that life, the belief can sit comfortably on the edge of my belief system, along with other beliefs that have little impact on how I live. On the other hand, there are beliefs that matter to me a great deal. The question of whether my spouse really loves me is unlikely to be something toward which I can adopt a nonchalant attitude. The belief that I am competent in my profession might be vital to my sense of self-worth. I will have a major stake in the truth or falsity of such beliefs.

No sharp dividing line exists between beliefs on which a great deal is riding and beliefs that have minimal practical significance. Some obscure bit of knowledge about snake poison, which I have tucked away, might in some situation make the difference between life and death. Nevertheless, some beliefs are of more central relevance for the way we conduct our lives. Among these are beliefs that are closely connected with our core values or sense of identity.

One of the sources of confusion in trying to discuss belief in God is that it can be thought of in a way that puts it in the class of beliefs with little practical importance. If we equate the question of whether God exists with the issue of what is needed for explaining the existence of the universe, such a belief seems a little like an individual's idle speculation about the existence of intelligent life in other galaxies. We can imagine someone who affirms a belief that there is some intelligence behind the universe and refers to her affirmation as belief in God, even though the belief makes little practical difference for her life. If she came to think that her belief was mistaken, giving it up need not be especially troubling. Contrast this sort of belief with a genuinely religious belief in God. To believe in a way that is recognizably religious is to stake your life on something that is closely connected with your sense of who you are and what it is important to care about.

One way to obscure the practical significance of the question of God's existence is to think about the idea of God in isolation from the range of ideas that are used in any religious tradition to connect it with the believer's life. Hence, for example, a Christian belief in God functions in relation to concepts such as sin, creation, redemption, commandment, and grace. Grasping what the belief means also calls for an awareness of connections between these concepts and activities such as prayer, praise, confession, seeking God's will, and repentance. We don't really comprehend what it means to believe unless we can imaginatively comprehend what it would mean to use a set of religious categories to structure our thoughts and attitudes and engage in the practices associated with internalizing this understanding.

If we look at religions in a very general way, we can see them as responses to central human concerns about ordering our lives. Major world religions typically present a comprehensive diagnosis of the human condition that locates a fundamental problem with our approach to life. Depending on the religion, the problem might be in some confusion about the human situation or some basic perversity that results in a distorted set of attachments and pursuits. Particular religions offer ways to overcome the problem and attain genuine fulfillment. However, achieving such fulfillment is not typically a matter of satisfying our present cravings. It is instead a matter of grasping the futility of our egocentric perspective and adopting a wider point of view that will open the door to liberation or salvation.

In theistic religions the idea of God is central both to understanding the human predicament and moving toward a superior mode of life. A vision of the goodness of divine purposes and activities functions to reveal to us our own deficiencies and our need for redirection. The means by which change can occur involves accepting these purposes as our own. As we adopt the practices prescribed by the religious tradition, we begin a spiritual path that is supposed to reorient us and empower us toward a pattern of concerns and actions that will lead to a higher quality of life.

When we recognize that a religiously significant response to the idea of God occurs within the context of encountering a life-orienting story that offers a way of salvation, we should be able to understand why treating the idea primarily as a metaphysical hypothesis for explaining the universe distorts our thinking about whether to believe in God. We can consider whether the idea works as a metaphysical hypothesis by standing back and impartially examining evidence. But when the question of God's existence is bound up with the question of how we should live, considerations other than our need for theoretical understanding become relevant. For one thing it is relevant whether we can appreciate and be attracted by the way of life connected with acceptance of God. Indeed, finding a resonance between a theistic way of life and our deepest aspirations is a significant step toward belief in God.

Hence, paradigmatic religious experiences, such as conviction of sin or receiving grace can be vehicles to appreciating the package of beliefs in which belief in God is included. Being able to experience emotions like awe or reverence in the right situations or coming to think of life as a deep mystery can be ingredients in a religious response to life. Rather than being a matter for intellect alone, being drawn to a way of life in which belief in a divine source is a key component depends on whether the emotional and value reactions needed for responding to a being of supreme power and love can be evoked.

Knowing about the god of the philosophers is an intellectual task. It calls for assessing evidence and making inferences. To the extent that we have a personal stake in the outcome of such an inquiry, our interest needs to be put on hold so that the evidence can be considered from an unbiased point of view. The kind of evidence to be considered needs to be put in a form where we can assess it objectively. If there are essentially private religious experiences, they will enter the picture as claims to have had an experience that is described or interpreted in particular ways. If there are human inclinations that might pull us in a particular direction, we need to rein them in so that we won't jump to premature conclusions.

By contrast knowing about the God of Abraham, Isaac, and Jacob is a task calling for personal engagement, involving capacities other than our ability to draw logical conclusions. When we are presented with a life-orienting story that gives a particular diagnosis of human needs, our ability for self-assessment and our openness to unpleasant self-knowledge are vital factors in responding positively or negatively. When the story portrays a normative order that is rooted in God, our capacity for being attracted by or repelled by the values embodied in that order is crucial for any assessment. When imaginatively entering a story evokes inclinations to believe, our willingness or unwillingness to trust these inclinations is pivotal.

Philosophical Foundations

There is a persistent idea that we ought to be able to decide about the existence of God apart from the wider context in which we might consider life-orienting stories. We can acknowledge that *if* God exists, it would make a radical difference, but consider *whether* God exists with a degree of objective detachment. By impartially examining the evidence, we can make a judgment about whether the available evidence supports the existence of a being with characteristics similar to those religious traditions ascribe to God.

However, it is unclear what this kind of investigation is supposed to tell us. If we decide that there is strong objective evidence for some kind of deity, perhaps we would think it worthwhile to investigate the claims of a particular religious tradition. But are we still to maintain the attitude of objective detachment? Would we approach these claims with a kind of academic suspicion? In that case it would not be surprising if the beliefs and practices of participants in the tradition seemed alien or even unintelligible. But what if we made an effort to understand the religious community at a deep level, participating in their practices and imaginatively entering into their life-orienting story? At this point whether we come to share their belief system or not, we are no longer playing the role of detached investigators. Instead we are opening ourselves to a way of life. Whether that way of life becomes our own is not just a question of evidence that could be objectively assessed. It is also a question of whether we find in ourselves something that responds powerfully to the religious life-orienting story, making it seem compelling.

On the other hand, what if we assess the evidence for some kind of deity from our position of objective detachment and find it inconclusive? Should we then conclude that investigating the claims of particular traditions is, therefore, unnecessary? It is conceivable that if we had done such an investigation with a receptive attitude, we might have come to accept the life-orienting story of some tradition. Would we have been wrong to do so without prior confirmation independent of the tradition of the existence of a deity?

When people come to accept a religious account of the human situation, they might be mistaken. But it is confused to think that the kind of full-fledged belief in God that results from responding to the stories and practices of a religious community is defective without some independent validation from an objective assessment of evidence for a generic deity. Many of our most important beliefs are acquired not as individual propositions, but in contexts where we respond to an integrated complex of beliefs that come to make sense as a whole.[9] Belief in God comes about as a response to a specific narrative about God, and it is only within such a context that the question of belief can be raised in a religiously significant way. Whatever doubts there may be about the whole complex of beliefs won't be resolved by breaking it into parts to decide about God in a context that insulates us from the possibility of religious engagement.

Michael Buckley has argued that the rise of Western atheism is paradoxically the result of attempts to provide philosophical defenses of belief in God that prescind from the specifically religious sources of that belief. Theologians and philosophers sought to found a generic belief in deity on simple observations and conclusions of reasoning that might be done without personal involvement and then treated actual religious belief as based on this philosophical foundation. As it came to be thought that religious belief needed this sort of philosophical construction, questions about the particular defenses resulted in a cloud of suspicion around the religious beliefs they were supposed to justify.

Buckley claims that the substitution of a god known through inference for the object of religious awareness is at the root of the problem. He writes,

> While religion presupposes personal engagement as the permeating and fundamental relationship with god, philosophical inference introduces a third term or warrant other than this involvement, namely the evidence through which one is informed about god and from which god is deduced. In one way or another, religion involves god as a living presence; philosophic inference demonstrates that there is a god as "a friend behind the phenomena."[10]

The problem is not with metaphysical reasoning about God as such; it is with the tendency to think of this reasoning as necessary for validating the experiential involvement with a life-orienting story that furnishes the real basis for belief in God.

What Metaphysical Reasoning Can Do

Even though it is a mistake to think of religious belief as founded on philosophical arguments for God's existence, there is a role that philosophical reasoning can play in relation to belief in God. A positive response to a religious story will depend upon a prior disposition not to regard fundamental assumptions of the story as utterly implausible. So, for example, we do not accept stories that tell us about fairies or leprechauns as accounts of reality because we are confident that there are no such creatures. Similarly, someone presented with a story about God might think that no such stories should be taken seriously because thinking that God exists is on a level with thinking that fairies exist.

One role for metaphysical thought about God is to clarify the difference between belief in God and belief in the various agents that populate fairy tales. Philosophical reflection on the idea of a creator makes it apparent that an intelligence that could produce and sustain the universe would have to be a different and more fundamental kind of reality than the physical things and agents we perceive through our senses. While particular beliefs about God might be dismissed as superstitious, the idea of a creator can be connected with reflection on the nature and existence of the universe. The universe doesn't appear to explain its own existence, and the idea of a necessarily existing ultimate that explains why there is a universe seems at least worthy of consideration.

Furthermore, metaphysical arguments for a creator present the idea in ways that can display it as an option for belief. One way to view arguments for God's existence is to see them as identifying a possible option for understanding things and attempting to show its superiority to alternative possibilities. So, for example, one form of teleological argument appeals to the way fundamental features of the universe near the "Big Bang" give the appearance of being fine-tuned for the eventual production of living and intelligent beings. The apparent fine-tuning suggests that the basic laws and constants have a purposive explanation: Some agent transcending the universe arranged things so the universe could produce living and intelligent beings. Given the evidence, there are only a few viable alternatives. One is to posit what has been called the "many universe hypothesis," which purports to explain the appearance of purposiveness by some random process that produces a very large number of universes, some small percentage of which have life-producing potential. Someone advancing the fine-tuning

teleological argument will attempt to show that the purposive explanation
is superior to alternative explanations, that the best understanding of things
is to view our universe as produced by a creator who sought to produce
living and intelligent beings.

Suppose that attempt is inconclusive. Suppose there is room for rational
disagreement about what the best explanation is. The argument might still
accomplish something significant. Even if this kind of teleological argument fails to establish that explanation in terms of a purposive agent is the
only viable explanation or the best explanation, the identification of a few
viable alternatives may be enough to establish that a purposive explanation of the universe is a possibility that needs to be taken seriously. Showing
even this much removes at least some potential obstacles to taking seriously a story that purports to reveal something about the activities and
nature of a creator. The possibility that there might be a creator could
provide a reason to investigate accounts that purport to offer revelatory
knowledge.[11]

Of course, some people find metaphysical arguments for a creator to
establish much more than a bare possibility. However, even if they are
correct in their assessments, we should not confuse the very limited belief
that might arise from a metaphysical argument for a creator with a belief
produced by encounter with a life-orienting story. Someone who has
responded to a theistic life-orienting story might be able to consider a
philosophical argument for God's existence and say what Aquinas says at
the end of each of his Five Ways: "… this everyone understands to be
God."[12] If this identification means merely that the object of encounter in
religious communal experience might be correlated with the ultimate
arrived at in metaphysical discourse, it need not be problematic. But when
it is concluded that, without such reasoning, claims about God would
lack rational foundation or that religious discourse reduces to metaphysical discourse, a potentially helpful correlation has become a source of
confusion.

Belief and Experience

It is easy for people in our culture to assume that the idea of God is primarily a type of explanation of what we might otherwise find puzzling, and
for anyone who makes this assumption, it can seem as if the proper way to

consider whether God exists is to try to decide whether God is a good explanation or not. Do we need God to explain why the universe exists or why things in the universe are ordered as they are? Does God help to explain our sense of moral obligation or our experience of beauty? When we frame the issue in this way, the question to be resolved is whether there is enough evidence to convince us that we need to postulate God to account for facts that we all recognize.

For people who find this way to approach the issue natural and obvious, the suggestion that there is another way to proceed may seem puzzling. How else could one come to know whether God exists than by reasoning from well-established facts to a transcendent cause that explains them? A first step toward recognizing the possibility of an alternative is to notice that hardly anyone who actually believes in God bases the belief on this kind of reasoning. While most believers would affirm that God helps to explain some general facts about the world, more central to becoming convinced about God is learning to use the idea of God in their understanding of everyday life. People with a religiously significant belief are likely to engage in activities such as speaking to God in prayer or have experiences they describe as receiving God's forgiveness or God's guidance. It's not that God is an inference from these activities or experiences; rather the activities and the experiences are understood in such a way that belief in God is an implicit component.

Consider an analogous case. Imagine thinking about the philosophical question of whether to believe that other people have minds. It might seem as if the proper way to answer this question is to consider the idea of a mind as an explanation for something. So, for example, we might think that the hypothesis that other people have minds explains purposive behavior and speech originating from bodies that resemble our own. But thinking in this way requires us to imaginatively put ourselves into a world in which we don't assume the existence of minds other than our own until we have evaluated the evidence. Needless to say, none of us live in that kind of world. We can entertain the idea of what it would be like not to think there are other minds, but whatever argument we can make from that world to our own wouldn't be the basis for our belief in other minds. The real basis has to do with the way the idea of other minds is implicit in our thinking about our activities and our experience. We find this idea indispensable for describing the world we actually inhabit.

Similarly someone who genuinely believes in God will find the idea indispensable for describing the experiential world in which she lives. Thinking of God as a hypothesis to be inferred from specifiable data means starting from an understanding of the world that does not presuppose God, but belief in God is not a matter of moving from such a world to a reality in which God is included. It is matter of finding yourself within the kind of world where God is implicit already. One who finds herself inhabiting such a world can still raise doubts about it. In that sense belief in God is different from the belief that other people have minds, which no one seriously doubts. However, doubts about the existence of God should not be construed as doubts about whether the idea works as an explanation for certain general facts that can be agreed to by people who believe as well as people who don't. They are better construed as doubts about the adequacy of a person's understanding of his or her experiential world. When belief in God is the matter to be decided, the central question is whether you can and should allow yourself to retain or be drawn into the patterns of thought that make the believer's world what it is.

The considerations that draw people into understanding their experiential world in terms of God do not arise primarily from the perspective we take as investigators, standing back from the world and constructing explanations. Rather it is as agents who need to make sense of and order our lives that we accept or reject the idea of God. The idea of God typically comes to people as part of a larger package that conveys some understanding of the place of human life in a wider frame of reference, the ways we can live lives of value in relation to that wider frame, and what fulfillment we can hope for. A response of belief or unbelief is to the total package. The persuasiveness of its diagnosis of the human condition and its portrayal of a superior mode of life plays a vital role in making the idea of God seem plausible or implausible.

When people encounter the idea of God in the accounts that come from theistic religions, they are offered an interpretive key, not only for understanding the events of their lives, but for ordering their concerns, their judgments of value, and their longings. For a believer the idea of God plays a significant role in answering questions such as, "What is worthy of my love and devotion?" "Do the things that capture my attention contribute to a worthwhile life?" "How can I deal with failure, suffering, and death?" The answers we give to such questions help to spell out the contours of a way of life. Finding the idea of God compelling is tied up with finding a particular way of life compelling.

The point here is not that we have certain problems and come to the conclusion that belief in God would help us to deal with them. It is rather that we misconstrue the question of God's existence when we think of God as a possible answer to a theoretical question that arises from our concern to understand puzzling facts. We get closer to the heart of the matter when we understand belief in God as arising in a practical context where the central concern is to find guidance about how to live. When we view an account of the human condition in which the idea of God is an important component in the light of that concern, we are in a better position to notice the considerations that might lead to belief.

It is important to recognize that whether we believe in God or don't believe, we need some understanding of our situation that enables us to orient ourselves in life. People who are not persuaded by any religious narrative will explicitly or implicitly rely on a nonreligious story to structure their understanding of the events of life. It might, for example, be a story about how human life is an unintended byproduct of a vast physical system. It might suggest a path to liberation through ridding ourselves of any superstitious notion of something beyond the physical order or of any kind of causality other than physical causality. Accepting these truths might be thought to be a vital part of devoting ourselves to genuine values and developing real autonomy. Such an alternative to a theistic guide to life is built around the denial of a transcendent order beyond the physical, and the denial of such an order is usually believed in a way that parallels the way belief in God is acquired – as part of a narrative that provides a persuasive account of how to live.

Belief or disbelief in God is less like a hypothesis adopted to explain some observation or set of observations and more like an assumption that, as part of a larger narrative, gives guidance about interpreting and responding to the events of life. People accept a particular assumption because the interpretive account in which it is embedded provides a way of understanding their experiences and their choices that they find convincing. Of course, assumptions can be questioned. For someone whose daily life involves activities such as seeking God's help or looking for God's purposes, or enjoying God's blessings, it is certainly possible to reflectively consider whether this mode of life is guided by a faulty understanding of reality. But for a believer to give serious consideration to that question is to consider alternative ways to interpret the meaning of everyday experience and to explore the question of whether he or she could be drawn in to an alternative that leaves out God.

To seriously consider the idea of God means "trying on" an understanding of how to live that is permeated by the idea. To reject the idea of God is to find some account of how to live that excludes God more compelling. While we can speculate about theism or atheism as theoretical constructs, these beliefs become important for us only when they are viewed as components of an understanding of the human condition that structures a way of life. The answers that we want are about the god of a possible life-orienting story, not the god of the philosophers.

Notes

1   Louis Dupré, *Religious Mystery and Rational Reflection* (Grand Rapids, Michigan: Eerdmans, 1998), 26. The use of this quotation as an epigraph is by permission of Eeerdmans Publishing Company.
2   Michael Buckley, *Denying and Disclosing God: The Ambiguous Progress of Modern Atheism* (New Haven: Yale University Press, 2004), 138. The use of this quotation as an epigraph is by permission of Yale University Press.
3   Richard Swinburne, "The Vocation of a Natural Theologian," in *Philosophers Who Believe: The Spiritual Journeys of 11 Leading Thinkers*, ed. Kelly James Clark (Downers Grove, IL: InterVarsity Press, 1993), 186.
4   Swinburne, 191.
5   Blaise Pascal, *Pensées*, ed. and trans. Roger Ariew (Indianapolis: Hackett Publishing Company, 2005), 266 (S742, L913).
6   Rene Descartes, *Discourse on Method and Meditations*, trans. Laurence Lafleur (Indianapolis: The Bobbs-Merrill Company, Inc., 1960), 61–143.
7   My discussion in this section is indebted to ideas from Merold Westphal, *Transcendence and Self-Transcendence* (Bloomington, IN: Indiana University Press, 2004).
8   Martin Heidegger, *Identity and Difference*, trans. Joan Stambaugh (New York: Harper and Row, 1969), 72.
9   Michael McGhee, "Seeke True Religion. Oh, Where?" in *The Meaning of Theism*, ed. John Cottingham (Oxford: Blackwell Publishing, 2007), 85.
10 Michael Buckley, *At the Origins of Modern Atheism* (New Haven: Yale University Press, 1987), 348.
11 See Sandra Menssen and Thomas D. Sullivan, *The Agnostic Inquirer: Revelation from a Philosophical Standpoint* (Grand Rapids, MI: William B. Eerdmans Publishing Company, 2007). Menssen and Sullivan use philosophical arguments to establish the possibility of God as a prelude to considering the claims of a fuller revelatory account.
12 Thomas Aquinas, *Summa Theologiae* (London: Blackfriars, 1964), vol. 2, 13ff. (Ia, q. 2. a. 3).

3

Reasons for Believing in God

"Suppose that a set of religious beliefs were true, but that the intellectual practices designated as 'reasonable' in a society ... were such as to make it impossible to recognize those truths." (C. Stephen Evans[1])

"It is the narrative that is basic. That there is a God is ... implicit in assent to the narrative of his deeds." (Michael McGhee[2])

A scene that has been played out with minor variations in countless introductory philosophy classes begins with the professor asking whether there are any good reasons to believe that God exists. With a bit of encouragement, a few students will suggest some reasons. The professor dutifully records their suggestions on the board. After a list has been generated, some of the proposed reasons are quickly eliminated. They are not really reasons for thinking something true, but only expressions of desire. Or they beg the question by assuming something that anyone who doubts God's existence would not accept, such as the authority of some sacred scripture or claims that miraculous events have occurred. In the end the surviving reasons are recognized as rudimentary formulations of classical arguments that have been proposed by philosophers. The arguments purport to derive the conclusion that God exists (or a being with an important attribute of God exists) from claims that should seem obvious or at least highly plausible to anyone who thinks about them in the light of a generally available understanding of the nature of the world. The class proceeds on the assumption that the appropriate way to consider the question of God's existence is to evaluate these standard arguments.

On the surface the procedure followed might seem to be an obvious way to think about a matter on which people disagree. From some kind of neutral standpoint, consider reasons that might be given in support of (or against) the controversial belief. But the professor's way of framing the question and guiding the discussion is less innocent than it might seem. Behind it is a paradigm of what is needed for a belief like this to be acceptable. Two elements of this paradigm stand out. One is that the proposition that God exists needs to be examined by itself, not as part of a larger set of beliefs and practices. It is assumed that before we can consider any story about God, we first need to settle whether God exists. The second element to notice is that the justification procedure focuses on facts that everyone should acknowledge, which might lead to the conclusion that God exists. It assumes that the appropriate way to decide about God is to reason from what is obvious, putting aside starting points about which we might disagree.

The first two chapters of this book question the idea of trying to decide about the existence of God in isolation from the larger context in which belief in God arises. I have claimed that belief in God in a religiously significant sense arises in connection with accepting a life-orienting story in which the idea of God is central. While accepting such a story presupposes that God exists, the relevant reasons are reasons for accepting the story rather than reasons for believing the individual proposition that asserts God's existence. There is a philosophic urge to pull beliefs apart and attempt to discover something foundational. However, often the foundation is not to be found in individual propositions, but in a larger complex. As Wittgenstein puts it, "When we first begin to *believe* anything, what we believe is not a single proposition, it is a whole system of propositions. (Light dawns gradually over the whole.)"[3] When someone is convinced by a life-orienting narrative about God, that person acquires a belief that God exists, but we should not assume that such a process requires reasons for believing in God's existence that are independent of reasons for accepting the narrative.

The other questionable element in the picture of seeking reasons for belief in standard arguments for God's existence has to do with the kinds of reasons that will be considered. Reasons that appeal to indisputable facts, such as the existence of the universe or the law-like regularity of natural phenomena will be in order, but reasons that appeal to experiences or to events that can't be validated by publicly available evidence are likely to be regarded as deficient. Reasons that can be evaluated independently of any concerns or attitudes we might bring to the inquiry will be acceptable, but reasons whose appreciation might depend on our frame of mind or receptivity will be viewed with suspicion. The question is not just whether a believer has reasons but whether there are reasons that fit well in models of objective investigation that are assumed to be appropriate for this kind of inquiry. Whatever does not fit will be pushed to the margins of the discussion.

Also pushed to the margins will be features of God that are particularly important for religious belief. The focus of this discussion is likely to be the kind of god who could account for the existence of the universe, not on the kind of god who exhibits a particular care or concern for human life. If we imagine an inquiry into the existence of a benevolent deity with whom people can make contact, the obvious question is whether there are experiences that indicate the activities of such a deity. Theistic communities have their narratives of revelatory events, along with confirming experiences by members of the community. But considering such claims leads us away from the kind of reasoning characteristic of theistic arguments. Rather than moving from general facts about the world to a judgment of whether a theistic account is needed to explain these facts, the central issue becomes whether to accept particular events and experiences as indicators of the activity of God.

Being convinced by a revelatory narrative that there are signs of divine activity in the world is less like reasoning from indisputable facts to an undeniable conclusion and more like getting into a frame of mind where an apparent meaning emerges. There is a point in Jane Austen's *Emma* where the heroine comes to the realization that she loves someone. An emotional reaction to an event triggers her awareness of various behaviors and thoughts that suggest love. She had been aware of these as facts, but when she attends to them as possible signs of love, their meaning becomes clear. Once she has gained this apparent insight, she finds it irresistible.[4]

A story can sometimes be a vehicle that enables one to grasp a meaning that was previously hidden. Imagine that after your mother dies, a relative tells you a story about things your mother had done for you, which you never knew about. Many of these involved significant personal sacrifices that leave you amazed. While she was alive, you had thought of her as cold and manipulative, but the story leads you to rethink all this. As you consider what you thought you knew, you realize that many of your assessments may have been mistaken. You can see that actions you took one way may have meant something altogether different. The possibility that the story is true opens the door to a shift that could alter your understanding of who your mother was and what you meant to her. Of course, you may not be able to verify that what the relative has told you is true. Nevertheless, as you reconsider the past in the light of the story, you might become convinced of the truth of the story.

In a similar way theistic revelatory stories function as pointers to what is hidden. They can be thought of as invitations to attend to the world in a way that makes signs of God's activity recognizable. Look at your world in the light of a story about a benevolent deity whose good purposes for human life are revealed in paradigmatic encounters described in scriptural texts. See how the story about God can illuminate your awareness of the significance of things and serve as a guide for ordering your life. The story is not a proof of God, but when it seems credible enough, it can suggest ways of understanding the human context that people find worthy of consideration. One who considers his or her experiential world in the light of the story may become convinced that the benevolent God described by the story is real.

Obviously this sort of confidence is not a guarantee of truth. People have apparent insights of various kinds that turn out to be false, and the claim that past events and present experiences reveal signs of divine action can certainly be denied. But how should we evaluate a claim about revelatory events? No doubt we can dismiss many particular claims to revelation on a variety of grounds, but it is another thing altogether to dismiss the possibility that some theistic revelatory story might be true. If we are confident that there is no deity or no deity interested in communicating important truths about the human condition, we can be confident in rejecting all such stories. But should we be confident in thinking that any such story can be judged very unlikely? If we are, it seems likely that our confidence arises out of being convinced by a different type of narrative that precludes this possibility. But in that case, how should we decide which narrative is more credible?

Theoretical and Practical Points of View

Approaching the question of God by means of standard theistic arguments depends on the assumption that we can treat the issue as a theoretical one for which we appropriately assume the role of objective inquirers. We are to approach the question as if our sole concern is to determine what the facts require us to acknowledge. No thoughts about what accepting or rejecting God's existence might mean for how we need to live our lives should be allowed to influence us. No biases that might interfere with a dispassionate consideration of evidence should affect our judgment. The possibility that what we discern or how we construe what we discern about potential signs of God's existence might depend on our receptiveness or openness to the prospect is not to be considered. It is assumed that we can treat the process as one of evidence gathering and evaluation, where the relevant evidence should be recognizable by anyone with some minimal level of intellectual skills.

Such a procedure seems perfectly in order if we imagine belief in God's existence to be a speculative hypothesis that is being proposed to explain generally acknowledged facts. But while we can undoubtedly treat the idea in that way, it should not escape our notice that in theistic religious traditions belief in God is not a product of objective theorizing by dispassionate observers. God comes to seem plausible to people who approach the possibility in the light of a variety of practical concerns, including concerns about how they need to live. A story that situates them in relation to a powerful agent who creates the world and acts within it appeals to them, not primarily as theoreticians, but as agents who need some account of the context in which they operate in order to know what to do. For people who approach the matter from this practical point of view, it may be difficult to resist believing an account of that context that seems to render their personal experience intelligible and connect it with a vision of human fulfillment they find compelling.

Suppose, however, that a student in the imagined philosophy class says to the professor,

> I believe in God because a particular religious tradition (Jewish, Christian, Muslim, or whatever) has given me a description of the human situation that makes sense to me when I try to understand my experiences and determine how I need to live. When I think about my life in terms of the problem of sin and when I follow the procedures described in the tradition for seeking forgiveness, it feels as if I am put back on the right track. When I shape my conduct and my concerns in conformity with the teaching my tradition provides about good living, I am convinced that I am tapping into deep insights about what humans ought to be. When I think of other people, using images, such as "children of God" I discover that I treat them better. When I pray and seek to see my concerns in the light of God's point of view, I become less self-centered. Occasionally I get a glimpse of how I might serve some divine purpose for life, and occasionally I think I understand how God is using

situations I face to shape my character. There are plenty of things that happen that I can't make sense of, but if I didn't believe in God, I would lose some of the most trusted ways I have for discerning the significance of what I experience and ordering my life in accordance with that understanding.

What might the professor say in response? Perhaps she will explain that this answer won't do at all. It's too subjective. It appeals, not to anything publicly verifiable, but to an individual's sense of how things seem to him. It appeals to ideas as effective for achieving certain ends, but whether they are effective or not is irrelevant to their truth. In other words the professor will likely push the discussion away from any alleged reasons connected with using the interpretive tools a tradition provides for living a religious life toward evidence that is available from a more generically human point of view that puts such interpretive overlays under suspicion. Perhaps she will point out that the kinds of confirmations the believer finds are unlikely to be persuasive to anyone who is trying to think about whether God exists in a way that is unclouded by potential desires or wishes. Perhaps she will say that before we entertain the possibility that any comprehensive theistic account might be true, we need some independent verification of the assumption of God's existence.

However, the likelihood of this kind of wholesale dismissal of reasons deriving from the experience of using a theological vocabulary to order one's life shows why the seemingly neutral procedure is rigged against discovering any genuinely compelling reasons for believing in God. The process is set up to seek the kind of justification that infers God's existence from facts that do not presuppose God. But even if there are legitimate inferences of this kind, they would not provide the kinds of reasons that could produce anything like religious belief. Religious belief depends on finding signs of God within the experiential world, and finding such signs would be more like discovering a kind of intelligible order within experience than trying to infer such an order from a reality devoid of it.

When a believer is asked to remove theological descriptions from the experiential world, this might be understood as getting to the real facts, but from the point of view of someone whose experience is infused with theological meanings, it can seem more like speaking an impoverished language that removes the possibility of describing important aspects of experience. You could, as a thought experiment, remove all your moral categories from your descriptions of situations. But it would be misguided to imagine that this perspective provides a deeper understanding of what is going on. What you have done is more like blinding yourself to a certain kind of meaning that your moral categories allow you to articulate. Similarly, a theist might acknowledge that describing experience without theological meanings is possible, but regard the resulting perspective as deficient, failing to reveal what is centrally important. For someone who thinks in this way, the kinds of reasons that seem most relevant to belief in God are features of experience that incline him or her to speak in theological terms. Describing such reasons is largely a matter of highlighting aspects of experience that evoke this inclination, but feeling the pull of such reasons means assuming a perspective different from the objective theoretical point of view that is assumed appropriate for discussions of classical theistic arguments. It is from the point of view of agents who are concerned to shape a life that people find themselves attracted by a narrative about God.

Life-Orienting Stories

The prestige of scientific patterns of thought makes it relatively easy to draw us into a discussion of standard theistic arguments. We are aware of how scientists frame hypotheses to explain observational evidence and how the evidence can be regarded as supporting or not supporting a hypothesis, and it seems as if this method ought to be applicable to any genuinely factual issue. So we frame the idea of God as a kind of hypothesis to be considered, one that is offered as an explanation of puzzling facts like why the universe exists or how complex things like human intelligence came to be. But when we consider the question in these terms, we are drawn away from the kind of thinking that produces belief in God, as opposed to acceptance of a theoretical construct. John Cottingham comments about the usual philosophic way of reflecting on religious belief, "One has a strange feeling that the intellectual analysis, however acute, does not capture what is at stake when someone gives, or refuses, their allegiance to a religious worldview. The focus is somehow wrong."[5]

People ordinarily come to believe in God in the context of encountering a narrative that purports to tell them how human life is to be understood, what is ultimately real, and what way of life is best. In earlier chapters I have called this kind of narrative a life-orienting story. Life-orienting stories satisfy a practical need. They make sense of our world in a way that allows us to order our lives. To accept a particular life-orienting story means understanding your experience in the light of it and seeking to form your identity in accordance with the values that story presents as normative for a worthy life. Accepting a life-orienting story is not like accepting a theory to explain a set of facts that are already obvious. These stories will have a great deal to do with shaping our ideas about what the facts are and what they mean.

Life-orienting stories carry with them assumptions about what is ultimately real, but the claims they make about ultimate reality are not subject to the kind of verification we seek in science. When these stories tell of a transcendent reality with which human life needs to be harmonized or when they deny that there is any such reality, they go beyond what we could evaluate by objective empirical testing. There are experiences that can be taken as signs of transcendence and reasons that can be offered for thinking that there is no such thing. But the question of whether there is or is not a transcendent reality corresponding to the symbolic representations of religious traditions won't be settled on scientific grounds.

The point here is not that the assumptions about reality made in life-orienting stories are arbitrary. Saying that the ultimate reality is God, or a physical system governed by natural law, or a source reality beyond the personal in which the distinctions we are aware of in ordinary perception disappear is not just idle speculation. In each case there will be experiential sources that are taken as interpretive keys to making sense of the world. Theistic stories are rooted in claims about experiencing revelatory events in which God has acted. Naturalistic stories are elaborations of the human experience of finding in the world an order that we can predict and to some extent control. Monistic stories appeal to a certain kind of meditative experience that puts one in touch with a reality beyond subject–object distinctions.

If we think of the realities posited in these alternative stories as theories, we are unlikely to be able to establish the supremacy of one over the others in a way that does not beg the question. But it is not at the level of theory we have to decide. We have to decide on an understanding of things that will order our lives. With theoretical questions, we can usually hold back on decisively committing ourselves until all the evidence is in, but we don't have this same option with regard to issues that make a difference in how we live. Living on the basis of a story that posits the physical universe as the ultimate reality precludes living on the basis of a story that posits God as the ultimate reality, and the manner of life may be substantially different. The practical necessity is to find a story that we actually believe and can live by.

Obviously we want to shape our lives on the basis of a story that is true, but we approach the question of truth with starting points that are disputable. Some people view all religious stories as so implausible that they can be dismissed out of hand, while finding it obvious that some naturalistic life-orienting story is correct. Other people begin with a sense that there is a depth to reality that scientific categories cannot capture and look to religious stories as ways to articulate that sense. Such diverse predispositions are bound to affect our judgments of truth. But even if we can't certify the narratives we find ourselves believing to everyone's satisfaction, we test them indirectly by attempting to shape our lives in accordance with them. Sometimes life-orienting stories collapse as we try to hold together our understanding of the world and our convictions about what is important and worthy. But sometimes we become increasingly convinced that a particular story is the best option or even the only viable option for making sense of life. The patterns of thinking it provides become embedded in our surest sense of who we are and what we are doing, convincing us of their truth.

Stories About God

At one level the answer to why a person accepts a particular life-orienting story is fairly easy. Someone might describe how she was taught a particular story at an early age and got used to understanding her life in terms provided by the story. Or someone might describe having a story that she came to doubt and being introduced to a new story that seemed to make better sense of things. Such accounts give us something close to how people acquire beliefs that God does or does not exist. But they may not fully satisfy us when we ask for reasons, for part of what we want to know is why someone would find credible a story that posits a transcendent reality such as God.

The answer to such a question is likely to be fairly complex. But we might start with the observation that people find it relatively easy to think in terms of a powerful purposive agent who creates the world and acts in it, and when they encounter a religious story about such an agent, they are often ready to entertain it as a possibility. Cognitive psychologists have done considerable empirical work on our belief-forming capacities in recent years, and many of them have concluded that formation of the idea of God is a natural product of the way our brains work. We have a tendency to think in terms of agents when we encounter apparently purposive phenomena, and purposive phenomena that are not caused by natural agents suggest to us supernatural agents.

Of course, such a tendency can lead to a wide variety of beliefs that seem extravagant or superstitious to people in our cultural context. It might lead, for example, to the postulation of spirits where we have learned to think in terms impersonal forces. So given background assumptions that restrain the operation of this tendency, it will not work quite the same way for us as it might for someone in an ancient context. But even with an understanding of the world that is formed in relation to fundamental assumptions associated with natural science, the tendency to think in terms of purposive agency can make a monotheistic view seem plausible. One cognitive psychologist proposes that the tendency to form a belief in God is natural for humans in a way that parallels the formation of belief in other human minds.[6] Given the ease with which we form this belief, he devotes a whole chapter of his book on how belief in God arises to explaining how atheism is even possible.[7]

To notice that there is a kind of ease with which human beings think in terms of a transcendent agent is not to give an argument for (or against) the truth of the belief. An atheist is likely to regard this process of belief formation to be unreliable, while a theist might view it as a means by which God creates conditions conducive to recognizing the truth. But recognizing the pervasiveness of the tendency to form beliefs in supernatural agency can explain why theistic stories function for many people as reasonable starting points to be adopted unless there are decisive objections or better alternatives.

To claim that people find the idea of God plausible is different from claiming that they accept the idea as the best hypothesis to explain particular data. We don't form the hypothesis that other people have minds as the best explanation of behavior that seems purposive. Rather we perceive a world in which agents act in purposive ways. Similarly people are strongly predisposed to construe their experience in theological terms. They find it easy to perceive the natural world as a creation or view a particular path as divinely ordained or see themselves under divine judgment. Just as certain phenomena trigger our tendency to construe the world in terms of human agents, there are phenomena that draw people easily into understanding their experience in terms of divine agents.[8]

Kant is known for powerful criticisms of classical arguments for God's existence. When he comes to what he calls the "physico-theological proof"

Kant pauses to say that the "proof always deserves to be mentioned with respect. It is the oldest, the clearest, and the most accordant with the common reason of mankind."[9] He represents the argument as inferring God from purposive order in the natural world. While Kant thinks this argument can't work as a proof of God, he speaks expansively about how contemplating the purposive order perceived in nature produces a "belief in a supreme Author [of nature] that ... acquires the force of an irresistible conviction."[10] What Kant recognizes is the ease and the persuasive power of thinking about the world and events in the world in terms of a supreme agent. People don't need to be argued to the conclusion of God when they find it so easy to understand features of their context in terms of God.

The kind of belief one might acquire in this way is fairly vague unless it is given more specificity by a religious account of the nature of supernatural agency. When religious traditions provide such stories, people who are predisposed to think in theological categories are often receptive to them, especially when they are passed on as authoritative teaching. Needing some kind of life-orienting story, people are likely to accept accounts that are provided by trusted sources. As long as a story can function fairly well to guide their lives, and as long as they come across no competing stories that could do a better job, they are likely to believe the story they have. In our society, however, in contrast to more monolithic societies, people become aware of a range of competing stories. Whatever life-orienting story we use, we are likely to encounter people who accept a different one, and in such a context it is inevitable for reflective people to question their stories.

Reflecting on a Theistic Story

Some questioning involves an examination of the need to revise a story to achieve more consistency within the story or greater coherence with other beliefs. But some questioning is more radical. By raising questions about very fundamental assumptions of a theistic story, such as God's existence, one is considering the possibility of a life-orienting story that eliminates God. However, raising such a possibility is like spinning wheels on an icy pavement unless there is an available alternative that an individual views as a viable option. Since God's existence is accepted as part of a life-orienting story and we can't get along without some story, rejecting it means accepting a different life-orienting story. The judgment that God does not exist gets little traction until one can contemplate what it would mean to live in a world devoid of God and be drawn toward taking this possibility seriously.

Alternatives to a life-orienting story that posit some transcendent reality such as God are certainly available. We could propose, for example, a story that tells us that the physical universe, understood in terms of scientific accounts that describe its operations, should be taken as ultimate. Human beings arise as byproducts of this physical system, operating in accordance with certain natural regularities. We are not the result of any intention or purpose, but of a process utilizing natural selection that has adapted us to our environment. We need to reject any thoughts of beings or realms beyond the physical order. We also need to reject ideas that events such as surprising rescues or unexpected recoveries from illness reveal any transcendent purposes. The physical order will sometimes produce results that we like and sometimes results that we don't, but there are no higher-level purposes beyond human purposes, only an impersonal causal law. Living intelligently involves understanding and adjusting to how these natural regularities work.

To make this alternative into a life-orienting story, we would have to add some additional features. For example, we would need to add some kind of account of how this sort of universe is connected with our experience of moral order, exhibited in ideas such as right and wrong, good and bad, noble and ignoble, etc. What kind of moral order should we recognize? How does it become authoritative? How specifically should our ideas of moral order direct our lives? What would constitute the good for us individually and collectively? With such additions would it be a superior story to one that posits a reality like God? That depends. How sure are we that there are no experiences in which individuals make contact with a power or a kind of reality beyond the physical realm? How confident are we that human beings are a product of an unintended process? Can we really know in advance that all extraordinary events are fully explained without reference to anything beyond the natural order? Can a story that removes purposive order accommodate norms with sufficient authority to govern our lives? This story, like god stories, proposes a kind of comprehensive vision of the way things are, and the adequacy of any such account depends on how well it works as an interpretation of the world we experience and a guide to living in it.

Which story we judge more adequate seems to depend in part on how we think the world works. People who believe in God tend to disagree with philosophical naturalists about some of the facts of the matter, and their disagreements, while important practically, are not the kind that we should expect to be resolved by scientific testing. A naturalist may be quite sure that something like intercessory prayer can make no difference, other than possibly in the mind of the person who prays. A theist might be just as confident that prayers can make a difference, even if not quite understanding how. A person who rejects supernatural agency will reject any providential events, while a believer might regard certain events as clear indications of a higher purpose or meaning.

The point here is that a reflective judgment about whether to understand one's life in terms of some story about God is a comparative judgment. It is not a matter of trying to start from indisputable data and infer the existence of God, but of finding a theistic story better or worse at providing a plausible understanding of the significance of our experience than an alternative story without God. Arguments are involved in our assessments of life-orienting stories, but the kinds of arguments that are most relevant are those that undermine our confidence in a particular vision by leading us to contemplate discordant elements or those that evoke confidence by highlighting features of our experience that fit well with a particular vision.

Attitudes and the Discernment of Meaning

What we accept as true in addition to the way we fit our understanding together into an overall vision involves a kind of weighing in which certain experiences are taken as vital clues about the nature of existence. But what we take to be the clues and how we understand their significance is affected by how we approach the issue. In a well-known story Bertrand Russell was asked what he would say if he discovered in an afterlife that God does exist. Russell replied to the effect that he would inform God that he had not provided enough evidence. Russell's remark suggests that he took it as obvious that the default position is not to believe in God until acquiring evidence of a certain kind, presumably the kind that allows for no viable alternative to the conclusion that God exists. The appropriate attitude on his view is a kind of skeptical waiting for evidence. There are times when such an attitude is commendable, but there are also times when it seems misguided. Sometimes the pursuit of truth takes the form of trying to discern the meaning of something, a task that may call for getting into a frame of mind conducive to recognizing potential meanings.

In a well-known article Martha Nussbaum calls our attention to cases in which knowing comes about as a result of attending in a way that a concern to give a detached evaluation of evidence would sabotage. Her central example is taken from a story in which a woman comes to the realization that she loves a man. Discovering her love is not a matter of considering evidence from some objective point of view. It is only as she thinks in a more involved way, letting down her defenses, yielding to particular imaginative urges and trusting certain inclinations that she recognizes her own love. Her ability to read the signs depends on going beyond a surface meaning to find a deeper meaning in particular actions and emotional responses. Once she has attained a frame of mind receptive to the possibility, she is able to discern what the signs mean.

In noticing the way we are able to learn from such a story, Nussbaum is struck by the differences in the way we read stories and the way we approach philosophical texts. We read a story, she says, "suspending skepticism; we allow ourselves to be touched by the text, by the characters as they converse with us over time. We could be wrong, but we allow ourselves to believe."[11] By contrast she characterizes the attitude we take toward philosophy texts as "retentive and unloving." She says, "Before a literary work … we are humble, open, active, yet porous. Before a philosophical work … we are active, controlling, aiming to leave no flank undefended and no mystery undispelled."[12] While Nussbaum recognizes a place for the characteristic philosophic attitude, she thinks that some truths are available only if approached in a way that parallels our approach to literary works.

Nussbaum's example of coming to understand things in terms of a narrative of love might be expanded to other instances in which an individual shifts his or her understanding of the meaning of things. One context where this sometimes occurs is therapy. A patient comes in with a particular narrative of self-understanding and sometimes through the process emerges with a different narrative. For example, one might give up the picture of an idyllic childhood and come to accept an account in which neglect or abuse are prominent. Or one might come to an understanding that includes much more ambivalent attitudes toward a significant other than the romanticized official version allows. Such a shift in narrative can involve painful acknowledgment, and it may take overcoming resistance to be able to accept it, but ideally it can result in a shift in interpretation of meanings that leads to a healthier pattern of life.

The question of whether to accept an alternative narrative of self-understanding in such a context involves a consideration of evidence, but the kind of consideration needed relies on powers of imagination and emotional resonance as much as on logical inference. In fact treating the issue as if it were a purely intellectual matter can be a means of self-deception. If I treat the suggestion that I have a pattern of manipulative behavior toward others as a hypothesis, I may virtually always be able to dismiss the signs of this pattern and cling to an alternative account. But if I allow myself to put aside my aversion to the possibility and enter into the suggestion with a suspension of disbelief, I may discover that the pattern described in the narrative of manipulation rings true. Of course, I might be wrong, but the possibility of mistake need not rule out the possibility of genuine insight.

Life-orienting stories, like therapeutic narratives, purport to show us particular meanings. A theistic narrative invites us to consider our lives in relation to a benevolent deity who seeks our fulfillment. An atheistic narrative tells us that the only good we can hope for is one that doesn't depend on purposes or powers beyond the human community. We can look for signs that either kind of narrative is true. Cases of senseless and indiscriminate suffering might be taken as signs that an atheistic narrative is correct. Cases of redemptive transformation or experiences of a numinous presence might be taken as signs of a transcendent power and purpose. But our reading of the signs in either case won't be a matter of standing back in a detached kind of way to evaluate evidence. It will more akin to the situation of the person in a therapeutic encounter who is trying to make sense of her life. In that sort of context questions of whether we are in a frame of mind to be receptive to a particular meaning are often more central than questions about our ability to make logical inferences.

Russell assumes that if the right kind of evidence is available, he will be able to draw the proper conclusion, but Nussbaum calls our attention to cases in which we might fail to recognize a truth because of failing to attend to it in the right way. You can fail to recognize the signs that you love someone (or that someone loves you). You can fail to understand that you are excessively greedy or that your conception of yourself as an honest person is illusory. All of these are cases in which our ability to discern correctly is potentially affected by concerns or interests that might block us from attending to relevant features. But finding the right meaning often depends as well on having a set of concepts or a narrative that allows you to make connections that could otherwise be missed. A narrative is sometimes a vehicle for finding a meaning that becomes evident after you have recognized it.

So perhaps instead of assuming, as Russell does, that the appropriate way to think about God is to wait for evidence that we can evaluate from a detached perspective, we should think of our position as being presented alternative narratives, instructing us to think in different ways about the human context and as a result live different sorts of lives. One kind of narrative tells us to understand our world in relation to the purposes of a creator whom we might oppose or join. Another kind tells us that humans are alone in a universe that is unaware of and unconcerned about their values. Russell finds the second kind of story convincing and advocates living in accordance with it. He does not raise the question of whether there is enough evidence for the truth of this story, apparently assuming that only a god story would call for the kind of evidence he requires. Perhaps then we can imagine God in the afterlife scenario asking Russell, "What evidence did you have that the only reality is what humans can certify through empirical testing?" Or alternatively, "Why did you fail to recognize the signs that were available?"

Priority of the Story

Discussions of standard arguments for God's existence proceed on the assumption that the appropriate way to consider theistic belief is to decide first about whether or not God exists and only after a positive verdict on that question move on to evaluate particular accounts of divine activity. However, genuine belief in God moves in the opposite direction. People don't first become convinced of God's existence and then look around to determine whether there is an acceptable revelation of God. They respond to a revelatory story and in the process acquire a belief in God. While accepting such a story involves a predisposition to find the idea of God plausible, it is in the context of considering a developed story that the idea can come to seem compelling.

Life-orienting stories are not immune from critical evaluation. We can test various narratives from the perspective of what we think we know about the world, and this kind of testing allows us to rule out or reinterpret particular stories as potential objects of belief. It is noteworthy that over time many religious ideas about the human condition and the nature of reality cease to be viable. We may not be able to test religious ideas in quite the same way as we do scientific ideas, but looking at religions historically reveals that some claims endure while others are discarded. Holmes Rolston has suggested that only a few of the many claims made in religions "have survived the sifting of experience."[13]

Traditions that have thrived have learned to rethink what is central to their story. An important case study in this regard is the way Christian thinkers have made efforts to come to terms with understandings developed by various empirical disciplines and articulated their core story in the light of new ways of thinking. Many contemporary Christians would find superstitious the enchanted world full of spirits that their medieval predecessors took for granted. They live instead in a world that is permeated by assumptions derived from scientific ways of thinking and understand their faith in ways that presuppose scientific outlooks. New ways of thinking about the natural world or human nature or history can render some ways of articulating a life-orienting story unacceptable, but they often motivate adherents to reconsider the meaning of their story. In the process of rethinking what is fundamental and what is not adherents sometimes discover what they judge to be important insights into the story's meaning that were not previously apparent.[14]

However, while empirical testing can reveal the need for altering and refining the understandings of traditions or even for abandoning particular traditions, such testing alone is insufficient to establish that a particular religious or nonreligious story is correct. Unless we smuggle in assumptions that are disputable, we are unlikely by appeal to obvious facts to be able to rule out some alternatives that persuade other reasonable and informed people. There is, however, another sort of testing that is relevant. We can ask whether a particular story or a particular type of story fits with and motivates a life in accordance with our reflective judgments of what is good or worthy. In Chapter 5 I will describe how Tolstoy rejects a certain kind of life-orienting story on the grounds that it cannot motivate him to take his own life seriously. Whether he is correct or mistaken about that assessment, it would be a major defect of a life-orienting story to undermine a person's ability to be moved by her best reflective judgments of what is worthy.

We may lament that we can't find some indisputable test to settle issues like God's existence, but the option of sitting on the fence is unavailable. Our actions and our priorities will make sense only against the backdrop of an assumed understanding of what is real and what is important. We will show by the way we live whether we believe in God or whether we assume a world without a divine source. We can reason about it, but the kind of reasoning we need to do is different from searching for indisputable facts that might allow inferences to God. Instead we need to reason about the available stories that purport to make sense of our lives with or without God, and in the end we need to find some story believable enough to live by.

Notes

1   C. Stephen Evans, *Faith Beyond Reason: A Kierkegaardian Account* (Grand Rapids, MI: William B. Eerdmans Publishing Company, 1998), 94. The use of this quotation as an epigraph is by permission of Eerdmans Publishing Company.
2   Michael McGhee, "Seeke True Religion. Oh, Where?" in *The Meaning of Theism*, ed. John Cottingham (Maldon, MA: Blackwell Publishing, 2007), 85. The use of this quotation as an epigraph has been accepted as fair dealing by Wiley-Blackwell.
3   Ludwig Wittgenstein, *On Certainty*, eds. G. E. M. Anscombe and G. H. von Wright (New York: Harper and Row, 1969), #141, 21e.
4   Jane Austen, *Emma* (New York: Alfred A. Knopf, Inc., 1991), 418.
5   John Cottingham, "*The Spiritual Dimension: Religion, Philosophy and Human Value* (New York: Cambridge University Press, 2005), 2.
6   Justin L. Barrett, *Why Would Anyone Believe in God?* (New York: Altamira Press, 2004), 95–105.
7   Barrett, 107–18.
8   Alvin Plantinga speaks of dispositions to form beliefs that presuppose God, which are triggered under certain conditions, calling the experiential context that gives rise to the beliefs grounds. See, for example, "Reason and Belief in God," in *Faith and Rationality*, eds. Alvin Plantinga and Nicholas Wolterstorff (Notre Dame: University of Notre Dame Press, 1983), 80.
9   Immanuel Kant, *Critique of Pure Reason*, trans. Norman Kemp Smith (New York: St. Martin's Press, 1965), 520 (A 623 B651).
10   Kant, 520 (A 624, B652).
11   Martha Nussbaum, "Love's Knowledge," in *Love's Knowledge: Essays on Philosophy and Literature* (Oxford: Oxford University Press, 1990), 282.
12   Nussbaum, 282.
13   Holmes Rolston, *Science and Religion: A Critical Survey* (New York: Random House, 1987), 7.
14   Charles Taylor chronicles the complexity of historical changes in the West that have resulted in revised understandings of Christian faith and conditions in which religious unbelief became a viable possibility in *A Secular Age* (Cambridge, MA: Harvard University Press, 2007).

4

Resistance and Receptivity

"… judgements about what is true are affected by our moral nature; this nature is sometimes needed to evaluate evidence properly, and particularly situations in which there is evidence that is moral in character." (Paul Helm[1])

"… when we are dealing with the central truths of our human experience … the truth yields itself only to those who are already to some extent in a state of receptivity and trust." (John Cottingham[2])

Victor Hugo's *Les Misérables* contains a striking fictional illustration of a shift from a way of life dominated by hatred, which is precipitated by the collapse of a narrative of revenge. Hugo tells the somewhat melodramatic tale of how Jean Valjean in an act of desperation steals a loaf of bread to help feed his sister and her children. He is caught and sentenced to five years of hard labor, but because of repeated escape attempts, he serves a total of 19 years. In the process he becomes a bitter and hardened man. Hugo tells us picturesquely that during his imprisonment Valjean condemned society and sentenced it to his hatred. "He had no weapon but his hate. He resolved to sharpen it in the galleys and take it with him when he went out."[3]

On his release Valjean's papers label him as a criminal and a dangerous man. Respectable citizens keep their distance, and he struggles to find work and lodging. Welcomed into the home of a saintly bishop, he repays the kindness by stealing the silver dinnerware. When police drag him back to the house, the bishop unexpectedly claims that the silver was a gift, and not only that, he offers silver candlesticks, which Valjean had neglected to take. After he is released by the police, Valjean hears the bishop say, "Forget not that you have promised me to use this silver to become an honest man."[4]

Then the bishop pronounces solemnly, "Jean Valjean, It is your soul that I am buying for you. I withdraw it from the dark thoughts and from the spirit of perdition and I give it to God."[5]

The bishop's actions and declarations leave Valjean in an agitated state of mind. As he travels on, he steals from a small boy, and then unsuccessfully tries to find him to return the money. Collapsing in emotional exhaustion, Valjean begins to weep for the first time in 19 years. Hugo tells us that he had set himself stubbornly to resist the bishop's words and deeds.

> He felt dimly that the pardon of this priest was the hardest assault, and the most formidable attack which he had yet sustained; that his hardness of heart would be complete, if it resisted this kindness; that if he yielded, he must renounce that hatred with which the acts of other men had for so many years filled his soul, and in which he found satisfaction …[6]

Valjean's narrative of revenge, which sustained his hatred, had no room for the kindness and forgiveness the bishop had displayed. He needed to think of the world he had sentenced to his hatred as deserving of his vengeance. Encountering someone who willingly returned good for evil was difficult to process. Hugo describes the bishop's act as like an intense light that hurt Valjean's eyes. When he looks at himself next to this incomprehensible kind of goodness, he finds his own nature revealed. Hugo says at one point that Valjean could either have become the best of men or the worst. He could either accept the bishop's sacramental declaration or withdraw further into the prison of his own hatred. In the end Hugo describes the experience of a symbolic shrinking of the old self, which is overwhelmed by the reality of an entirely different way of living, exemplified by the bishop.

Hugo is obviously telling a conversion story. The narrative of revenge is replaced by a narrative capable of sustaining a way of life characterized by loving and forgiving acts. There is little doubt about the shape of this alternative narrative. The bishop speaks of buying back Valjean's soul and giving it to God. Valjean has been bound in darkness, and now he is set free to become what God intends. The question of whether Valjean will accept this new possibility hinges on whether he will give in to the bishop's kindness or resist it. It's not just a question of whether he can acknowledge the bishop's actions as a fact. It's whether he can allow himself to experience an emotionally charged awareness of a way of living that makes his own look shabby by comparison. The bishop's unexpected action is the shock that produces uncomfortable self-knowledge, and Valjean is described as realizing that allowing this forgiving love to penetrate his awareness would mean giving up the hatred to which he clings.

One point this story illustrates is the possibility of being resistant to truths that threaten our way of understanding the world and responding to it. When it comes to narratives that structure a way of life, we don't approach things as disinterested evaluators, but as people who are invested in particular ways of living. Our investment is not merely a matter of having certain beliefs we are reluctant to part with. Our way of life will be characterized by attitudes and emotionally charged motivations that are closely connected to a moral vision that provides support for a self-image. Truth claims that make that self-image precarious are difficult to entertain.

Hugo's account also illustrates the role of moral awareness in coming to see an alternative way of life as a viable possibility. When Valjean becomes aware of a goodness that does not fit into his own narrative, but seems to exert a claim on him, he has a reason to find his own story deficient and to seek one that can accommodate this awareness. While it might have been possible to give a cynical interpretation of the way of life he had encountered, he perceives in the bishop's actions a goodness he does not comprehend, yet recognizes as superior to his own mode of life. In recognizing it, and in recognizing his own deficiency, he is in a position to be receptive to the background story that makes this alternative way of life intelligible.

Truth and Receptivity

There are truths that ought to be accessible to anyone who possesses the right kind of intellectual skills. However, the closer we get to matters that are of central significance for how we think about ourselves and how we live our lives, the more it becomes apparent that intellectual skills are not enough. Some insights depend on our moral, aesthetic, or emotional sensibilities. These truths are not, as it were, lying clearly in the open for anyone to recognize, but require attentiveness from someone who approaches them with an appropriate state of mind and a willingness to respond to them.

When we ask scientific questions, we are interested in the kind of truth that anyone with the relevant kind of understanding of scientific procedures and ability to do scientific thinking would have reason to accept. But often in life we are guided by the kind of truth that comes as we learn to discern various kinds of significance that may not be apparent to just anyone. While it is obvious to most people that cruelty is a bad thing, it may take moral insight to recognize some practices that are generally accepted in our culture as cruel. While we can all read other people's intentions to some extent, some have highly developed skills of interpersonal sensitivity that allow them to notice in others what most of us would miss and recognize its meaning.

In the case of Jean Valjean it is the discernment of goodness that triggers a transforming kind of self-knowledge. In one sense the goodness is so obvious that it seems hard to miss. But the discernment involved is more than affirming a true proposition about the bishop's behavior. Grasping the significance of the bishop's act requires the engagement of moral and emotional sensibilities that can be suppressed. We can imagine a different individual, or even the same individual, refusing to be touched by the experience. But in this case the awakening of Valjean's conscience plays a vital role in his ability to recognize and accept unpleasant truths about his own life.

We can often resist the kind of understanding that arises through the engagement of our moral and emotional capacities, and often we have motivation to resist such understanding. Our motivation to avoid uncomfortable self-appraisals and to maintain comfortable rationalizations can block the recognition of moral meanings. We are capable of suppressing even a minimal awareness of those meanings when we fail to notice that what we are doing is what we easily condemn in others. At higher levels of love and concern, it takes not only determination, but practices akin to the spiritual disciplines of religious traditions to see clearly and consistently what needs to be done.

Iris Murdoch portrays the moral life as an attempt to see reality as it is, an effort that is opposed by "the fat relentless ego."[7] Instead of seeing the situations we face with clarity, we become caught up in "self-aggrandizing and consoling wishes and dreams."[8] Our self-serving fantasies make it difficult to gain an empathetic awareness of the value of others and act accordingly. But when we are seeing clearly, we will discern that others have "needs and wishes as demanding as one's own," making it "harder to treat a person as a thing."[9] Murdoch suggests that what is needed are "techniques for purification and reorientation" of what is "naturally selfish."[10] She proposes an appropriation of the spiritual activity of prayer for people who no longer believe in God. On her account prayer is fundamentally a kind of "attention to God which is a form of love."[11] In place of God she calls for attentiveness to the Good, which becomes a "source of light" revealing "things as they really are."[12]

In Murdoch's phenomenology of the moral life the Good is perceived both as authoritative in relation to us and as an object of attraction. The authority is connected with our experience of the Good as an awareness of something real. Perceptions of the Good have an authority like our awareness of facts independent of us to which we submit. But the Good is not merely something that we acknowledge intellectually; it is an object of love. Following Plato, Murdoch sees the desire for anything as a desire for that object as good, even though some desires are "distorted shadows of goodness."[13] Hence, "Good exerts a magnetism which runs through the whole contingent world, and the response to that magnetism is love."[14] In perceiving the real value of things in an undistorted way, we give expression to our love of goodness.

Being drawn to what is good is a key factor in becoming aware of the truth about things when that truth includes moral significance. The person who is most acutely aware of moral meanings will be one who has virtues that are structured by concerns for values that transcend a self-centered perspective. These concerns affect what such an individual attends to as well as how receptive that person is to noticing what is called for. While even someone who cares little about anything that doesn't fit into an egoistic frame of reference can have revelatory moments, the habitual avoidance of the pull of goodness makes it increasingly difficult to notice that pull. It is when we love goodness and make efforts to live in accordance with our awareness of it that we recognize most clearly its meaning in specific circumstances.

Receptivity and God

If our state of mind and our willingness to respond are crucial factors in the moral insight we attain, might receptivity also play a role with regard to religious truth claims? Murdoch's Good is after all a secular substitute for God. The vital difference between the two is that while the Good is an object of love, it is not something capable of returning our love. By contrast God is conceived as a Goodness that acts for our benefit. If we have the kind of difficulty viewing our world in the light of the Good that Murdoch describes, it would not be surprising if there were similar difficulties viewing our lives in the light of an active Goodness. If insight into moral meanings depends on our receptivity, we might suspect that recognizing an authoritative voice that calls us to a higher level of perfection could depend on our receptivity as well.

Religious traditions often emphasize the importance of receptivity as a precondition for receiving some truths. Only the pure in heart, we are told, may see God. Not just anyone can expect disclosures of God; they will come to those who are seeking in the right way or to those who are adequately prepared. While such claims may make sense for someone who accepts a religious system, they can seem circular to the person who approaches such systems with doubt. They make it sound as if getting into the right frame of mind to receive confirmations of God involves attitudes and patterns of thought that already presuppose God.

Well, not quite. While it is certainly true that theistic religious traditions portray some truths as only for the spiritually advanced and describe spiritual advancement in a way that already presupposes belief, they do not need to say that one must already believe in God to get any kind of assurance of God's existence. The kind of receptivity involved in finding a theistic narrative convincing presumably involves some degree of openness to the possibility of God and to what that possibility might mean for one's self-understanding. But it need not involve the confident trust or demonstrated obedience that might be required for fuller revelation.

But why should any level of receptivity be important for being convinced by a story of divine action? If God does anything in the world, shouldn't the signs of divine agency be clear enough for anyone to recognize? How could it make sense for a revelation of God to be given in such a way that we might miss it if we are not in the right frame of mind?

Overwhelming Evidence

We can imagine a world where unmistakable displays of the divine made denial of the existence of God unthinkable. We can conceive of the kind of evidence that would make it crystal clear to everyone that we are living under divine power and authority. In such a world the existence of God would be an obvious fact that everyone would acknowledge, and with the right kind of enforcement, everyone could be brought to act in accordance with divine requirements.

By contrast our kind of world is one in which the existence of God can be doubted or rejected altogether. While believers find reasons to affirm God's existence and signs of God's activity, they have to acknowledge that the presence of God is not an undeniable fact. Compared to the overwhelming awareness of God they may expect in the afterlife, human beings are situated at what John Hick calls an epistemic distance.[15] Even those who believe in God can have periods of doubt, and those who don't believe are unconvinced by alleged signs of God's existence.

Believers have sometimes puzzled over why the reality of God is not more obvious. Why don't we have the kind of evidence that would make the existence and activity of God hard to deny? One approach to such questions is to reflect on the nature of divine purposes. If the God spoken of in theistic religious traditions is real, then genuine encounter with God means involvement with a Love that seeks our good by demanding a great deal of us. But recognizing such a Love for what it is calls for a moral and personal insight akin to Jean Valjean's recognition of a superior goodness. The kind of recognition that might have a transforming effect involves an attraction to and submission to divine goodness. The kind of response that would benefit us is a welcoming of this active Love and a willing surrender of our egocentric way of life. If we think of God's concern as primarily getting us to accept a fact and conforming to particular behavioral requirements, overwhelming displays might be effective means, but if the kind of acknowledgment sought is a potentially transforming response, what will be needed is something that evokes our love.

Ordinarily having indisputable evidence that another person exists is not a barrier to giving or withholding a welcoming response. While the fact of another person's existence can place us under obligation, we can generally choose to limit our involvement with a particular individual. But such a choice seems unavailable with a creator who sustains our existence and asserts authority over us. To recognize the existence of such a being is to find ourselves involved in a relationship that overturns aspirations we might have to assert our own authority over how we live. If it is an undeniable fact that God exists, we will have to make the best of it. However, a situation in which we are compelled to adjust to the reality of God does not seem particularly conducive to winning our hearts.

Søren Kierkegaard tells the parable of a king who sought to win the heart of one of his subjects.[16] He could appear before her in his regal splendor, but such a display would be so overwhelming as to call into question the possibility of a freely given love. If the young woman consents to marry him, will it be because of his riches and power, or worse, the fact of his authority to claim what he wants? The king in Kierkegaard's parable decides that he must seek to win the love of this woman without external displays of his position. He must go incognito, as a common man. If she responds to him in this form, he will have what he seeks. Of course, Kierkegaard's parable is a representation of the Christian doctrine of incarnation. But the idea could be applied more generally to the kinds of displays that might be compatible with an uncompelled welcoming of God.

Theistic religions generally portray God as challenging our egocentric ways. To welcome this kind of God, we need to be able to recognize the bankruptcy of those ways and feel the attraction of a different way of life, one characterized by submission to a will that is seen as calling us to a higher good. We need to freely embrace that good as our own. If God could be presented to us, not as an undeniable fact, but as a possible good to which we might be drawn, the question of whether we could love such a reality might be raised without coercion. If we could come to love the kind of reality represented by God under these conditions, then we might well be in a position to benefit from any signs confirming God as a fact.

Sufficient Evidence

J. L. Schellenberg has claimed that while there need not be overwhelming evidence of a spectacular nature, we should expect that God (if God exists) would provide enough evidence to ensure that no one could inculpably fail to believe.[17] He argues that if we start with the idea of a perfectly loving God, we can conclude that God would seek a relationship with any creatures capable of relationship. Hence, creatures who are not resisting a relationship with God will always be in a position to have one. Since such a relationship depends on the belief that God exists, Schellenberg asserts that they must always have evidence that is causally sufficient to produce this belief. Unless creatures freely resist the evidence that would have produced belief, it ought to be evident to them that God exists. Hence, the presence of any nonresistant or inculpable nonbelief is reason for concluding that a perfectly loving God does not exist.

This argument resembles a type of argument from evil against the existence of God. Some arguments pick out a kind of evil that exists in our world and assert that if there were a loving and all-powerful deity, this kind of evil would not exist. So, for example, one might claim that if God exists, there could be no reason for allowing the brutal killing of a young child. Since such things occur, we can conclude that God doesn't (or probably doesn't) exist. Schellenberg's argument concentrates not on such despicable evils, but on a kind of ignorance that he thinks a loving God would not allow. His argument could be viewed as developing an intuition about the kind of world that a loving God would create.

Why wouldn't God allow inculpable nonbelief? Such nonbelief, claims Schellenberg, would interfere with providing an important good for human beings (meaningful relationship with God), and if God desires the wellbeing of creatures and values such relationships for their own sake, God will certainly provide that good if possible. However, by a similar line of thought we could notice that there are numerous goods that creatures might have, which through no fault of their own they do not have. Some of these are even goods that are of central importance for survival and minimal flourishing. People sometimes lack adequate food and security. They live precarious and sometimes very short lives that could have been much better. So if the love of God is to be understood in such a way as to allow us to predict what goods will be provided, we don't have to look far at all to find numerous phenomena that lead to the conclusion that God doesn't exist. Strikingly, however, when Schellenberg imagines a scenario in which God prevents inculpable nonbelief, he claims that the evidence he describes would not be overturned by the facts of evil we observe in the actual world.[18] He wants to allow that there could be reasons for the various evils we actually experience, but deny that there could be a good enough reason for God to allow an inculpable failure to believe that God exists. Such a view seems surprising. If there are such justifying reasons for the vast range of evils, it would be remarkable if there were no such reason to justify the occurrence of inculpable nonbelief.

Schellenberg claims that God could have prevented inculpable nonbelief by providing everyone with sufficiently powerful experiences of God's presence, beginning at an early age.[19] The evidence would be private, rather than public, but it would be universal and sufficiently strong that not believing could only be the result of some blameworthy resistance on the part of the individual. Since having this belief is needed for the good of an explicit and meaningful relationship with God, Schellenberg thinks that reflection on divine love should convince us that God would have a bias toward producing such belief and that reflection on possible reasons for not producing it should convince us that God would not permit any nonresistant nonbelief.

One problem with this argument arises from an ambiguity with regard to the meaning of "nonresistant nonbelief." (The ambiguity is somewhat hidden when "reasonable nonbelief" is used as a stand-in for inculpable or nonresistant nonbelief.) One meaning of the term has to do with whether there is resistance to accepting the proposition that God exists. However, it is possible to be willing to accept the proposition if sufficient evidence should be apparent while being resistant to committing oneself to a way of life involving submission to divine authority and fundamental life changes. Schellenberg's defense of the existence of nonresistant nonbelief focuses on the first kind of resistance, pointing out that there are unbelievers who seem exemplary in their willingness to examine evidence and make appropriate inferences. However, it is the second type of resistance that conflicts more centrally with achieving a transforming relationship to God, and it would be much more difficult to determine whether nonbelief lacking this kind of resistance occurred.

If we knew that someone who would willingly make the kind of sacrifices involved in submitting to divine authority failed to discover sufficient reason to believe, we might wonder why. But there is no similar puzzle for someone who is nonresistant in the first sense, but not the second. For such an individual coming to believe could be an epistemic advance without being an advance toward a meaningful relationship with God. After all, many people who do acknowledge the existence of God have not responded to something they understand as challenging their egocentric way of life. The belief that God exists can be another part of a structure that insulates a person from serious confrontation with a divine call to change.

Furthermore, lack of belief need not be thought of as an impassible barrier to any kind of significant relationship with God. If we think of God as issuing an authoritative call that we may experience through conscience, challenging our self-centered ways, a person might respond positively to this call without conceiving it to come from God. Many theists would be willing to acknowledge that an atheist can be responding to God without knowing it. In other words they would accept that one may have a developing relationship with God without having an explicit belief that God exists.

Of course, there are advantages to recognizing God's existence (if God does exist), but if we imagine God's primary goal to be the kind of relationship requiring willing submission to a transformative process, should we conceive this as a two-stage process in which the first stage is to produce a belief that God exists and the second is to bring about conditions conducive to developing appropriate attitudes toward God? An alternative possibility is to view the invitation to relationship as occurring within an encounter with a larger story about God that raises the question of these attitudes directly by conveying practical instruction about what it means to respond to God. Typically, people who respond positively to a theistic life-orienting story acquire a belief that God exists in an almost incidental way as a byproduct of being convinced by the story. The story conveys the need to surrender resistant impulses as part of what it means to accept a relationship with God.

A relatively thin theism leaves unspecified what kind of response is called for unless we smuggle into it features that actually come from historical religious traditions in which God's action toward us is understood in terms of paradigmatic events, which reveal God's intentions. Schellenberg imagines that there could be something like individual religious practices that lead to a rich personal relationship with God.[20] But what he describes seems parasitic on developed theistic traditions in which religious practices are rooted in reflective communal understandings of what God has revealed.

Schellenberg recognizes that his thesis would be considerably weakened if he had to assert that God would ensure belief in a whole range of propositions, not just the limited claim about God's existence. So he portrays that claim as sufficient for getting one started down the road to a rich personal relationship. But this is a fantasy. It substitutes an imaginative possibility of how people might develop such a relationship for what we learn from people who claim such a relationship in the actual world. Furthermore, had we no knowledge of actual religious traditions, it would be difficult even to comprehend the fantasy. We can make sense of it only by implicitly imagining the revelation of something analogous to a religious life-orienting story, but the closer we get to that, the less important it seems to secure a belief that God exists, which is independent of the larger revelation.

Pascal and the Search for God

Pascal claimed that in order for knowledge of God to benefit us, that knowledge must be accompanied by an awareness of our own need for radical change. He writes that it would be "dangerous for man to know God without knowing our own wretchedness."[21] Presumably the danger is that awareness of God would be just another vehicle for pursuing our egocentric aims. If God has power and enforces certain restrictions, we can take these into account in our strategic planning, but if we think of ourselves as fundamentally in good shape, such a response might very well solidify the sort of life we need to give up. To benefit from knowledge of God, Pascal thought, we need to be able to receive that knowledge from a position of humility in which we recognize our need to have our misdirected aims put right.

Pascal's reflections about the need for being in the proper state of mind to benefit from evidence of God led him to the conclusion that God needed to walk a tightrope between being too obscure and too obvious. He writes,

> It was not right that he should appear in a manner manifestly divine and completely capable of convincing all men. But it was also not right that he should come in a manner so hidden that those who sincerely seek him should not know him. He has wanted to make himself perfectly knowable by them. Thus willing to appear openly to those who seek him with all their heart and hidden from those who flee from him with all their heart, God has tempered the knowledge of himself by giving signs of himself that are visible to those who seek him and not to those who do not seek him. There is enough light for those who desire only to see and enough darkness for those of a contrary disposition.[22]

Hence, from Pascal's point of view the failure to find sufficient evidence of God from a position of detached objectivity is less an indication of the lack of evidence and more an indication of approaching the issue in the wrong way. It is in awareness of our need that we are prepared to ask the question of whether there is something to meet that need. Seeing that we have the kind of need that God might answer does not resolve the question of whether God exists. But someone who is thinking of God as a potential answer to a pressing problem might well be open to signs of God that someone who is dispassionately considering evidence might miss. While some might worry that looking hopefully for signs of God can result in the illusion of discovery, Pascal warns that the attitude of not caring whether God exists is an almost guaranteed way to miss the signs that may be available.

The signs in question for Pascal are signs of divine love. There is something a little odd about looking for signs of love, yet not caring whether we find them. But there is nothing odd about looking intently for a love that we hope to find. We can deceive ourselves about what we have found, but the fact that we care about finding something we recognize as a possible good is not a reason for searching as if we lacked any interest in the matter. In fact caring greatly is a reason, not only for searching diligently, but for refusing to be satisfied with anything other than the genuine article.

Pascal was not averse to offering arguments to move someone in the direction of belief. But he was skeptical about the value of metaphysical arguments from the natural world to God. When offered to believers, he thought that such arguments could be recognized as saying the obvious – that the world is God's work. But when offered to unbelievers, he worried that they divert attention from the real sources of belief. It is through encounter with a full religious story that people are motivated to examine both their own nature and the purported answer to their predicament. So Pascal's arguments often take the form of pointing unbelievers toward the Christian story or pushing them to confront themselves.

Finding God for Pascal depends on a willingness to repudiate our distorted self-love and the passions that defend it. In a famous passage he enters into an imaginary conversation with an unbeliever who says he cannot believe. What Pascal recommends is a procedure for overcoming the passions that are keeping him from believing. He suggests participating in the practices of a religious community. Through trying out practices such as prayer and scripture reading and worship with an open mind, the passions supporting unbelief can be calmed, opening the door to experiential confirmations of belief.

Brainwashing Yourself?

Pascal's recommendation for coming to belief will strike some people as contemptible. What he suggests can sound like a proposal for brainwashing yourself. Perhaps acting like a believer would eventually produce belief for some people, but isn't there something dishonest and not quite rational about coming to belief in this way?

If we think so, it is probably because we imagine that there is an alternative procedure that is properly rational and that the suggested procedure deviates from the rational alternative. But what exactly is the alternative supposed to be? If it is suggested that the proper way is to form beliefs only in accordance with explicit reasoning about evidence, such a procedure is much too strict. None of us form all our beliefs in this way. Our ability to rationally evaluate evidence is a skill that we develop through being inducted into the thought forms and practices of particular communities. We learn to accept some things, not because we have gone through a procedure of evaluating evidence, but because we have been taught to think in certain ways. Sometimes we come to reject aspects of what we have been taught, but the ability to do so is dependent on using what we have accepted through processes that involve some level of trust. If we worry about having any beliefs that are affected by processes we cannot certify in advance, we are worrying about what is an inescapable part of the human condition.

Of course, there are plenty of processes that we will deem it unwise to subject ourselves to. We may discern or suspect that some of them will turn us into people we don't want to be. We have reason to shy away from procedures with the potential to turn us into blindly obedient minions or fanatical zealots who have left their critical faculties behind. There are surely a great many religious groups that we might avoid for this very reason, worrying that our concern for truth and for virtue might be compromised. There are also affiliations with political groups, both of the Right and the Left, which we might judge conducive to producing thoughtless parrots of the party line.

But none of these considerations tell us in advance not to submit ourselves to ways of thinking and acting that could alter us. Furthermore, sometimes we have reason to suspect that certain potential transformations, which are likely to alter our beliefs, will do us some good. Many of us think that way about getting a liberal arts education or about going through psychotherapy. In such cases, even if we don't fully comprehend in advance what a process might do to us, we often have at least a vague idea of an end result we find attractive.

Pierre Hadot has argued that studying philosophy in the ancient world is best understood as embarking on a path whose goal was transformation of the individual's life. All of the major philosophical schools of antiquity, he writes, conceived our problems as arising from "unregulated desires and exaggerated fears."[23] The solution to our misdirected passions was wisdom, consisting in a proper vision of the way things are and leading to a mode of being and living corresponding to the vision.[24] Acquiring such wisdom meant submitting to practices that were designed to bring about a transformation of our vision of things and a corresponding transformation of the personality. Hadot describes these practices as spiritual exercises, intended to produce "a return to the self, in which the self is liberated from the state of alienation into which it has been plunged by worries, passions, and desires."[25]

The end result of undertaking such study included alteration of an individual's beliefs and concerns. Presumably people who were attracted to a particular school of philosophy and submitted themselves to its disciplines understood that their values and mode of life would be changed by the process. That, of course, was the point. They would abandon the false values that dominated most people's lives and acquire a superior way of living. Their attraction to a particular vision and a particular way of life led them to embark on a path presumed to cultivate the attitudes and experiences needed for internalizing the kind of wisdom required by that way of life.

When Pascal proposes the procedure of affiliating with a religious community and engaging in their practices, he is addressing individuals who are considering the beliefs of people they find admirable and who have been convinced that it would be reasonable to have these beliefs. But these inquirers protest that they do not in fact believe in God and can't see how they could come to believe. Pascal's response notes that belief may in some cases be regarded as the result of a process that prepares an individual to develop a state of receptivity. One who is attracted by the way of life supported by the Christian narrative and who regards it as possibly true can embark on a path that cultivates a state of mind conducive to becoming convinced.

Pascal offers a theory about what such a process will do that is reminiscent of the way ancient philosophical schools conceived their programs. Just as they thought of philosophic work as redirecting passions that have been misdirected, Pascal suggests that what keeps a person from belief are passions that interfere with recognizing the signs of God. This theory of unbelief is not an argument for the truth of God's existence. Rather, it assumes that God exists and offers an account of why not everyone recognizes it. As such, it is analogous to explanations of belief in God by people who assume that there is no rational basis for believing such a thing. Freud, for example, has already decided that there is no good reason to think God exists when he offers wish fulfillment as a mechanism for explaining why anybody has such a belief.

Pascal's explanation of unbelief suggests that when we ask about reasons for thinking that God exists, we need to consider whether we are in a position to appreciate the kinds of reasons that might be given. He claims that certain passions can interfere with being able to seriously consider a religious narrative, particularly passions connected with egoistic attachments that might be challenged by the god of a religious story. The therapy he suggests is to engage in practices that will enable people to let down their guard with a suspension of disbelief that may open them to the persuasive power of the narrative.

The Practice of Atheism

Pascal's suggestion that practice may help to produce conditions under which belief can flourish is likely to raise suspicion if we imagine that without any systematic practice we would all naturally be atheists. If we assume that we have to work ourselves up to entertain a theistic narrative, but that clear-headed thinking about the evidence will result in acceptance of an atheistic narrative, then it may seem as if the activities that might be conducive to acquiring belief involve a kind of cooking of the books. Recent work in cognitive psychology, however, suggests that the reverse of this picture is closer to the truth. The tendency to believe in supernatural agency is closely connected with the way the human brain processes experience, and if we don't resist the tendency to think in such terms, we are likely find ourselves believing some kind of narrative about supernatural agency. To be atheists, we need to adopt practices that are conducive to maintaining atheistic belief.

Cognitive psychologists point out that most of our beliefs are nonreflective. In contrast with beliefs that we arrive at through deliberate reflection or explicit instruction, nonreflective beliefs come to us automatically and instantaneously. These beliefs derive from the operation of what psychologists call mental tools that work without our conscious awareness. Our reflective beliefs are bound up with what we believe at a nonreflective level in a variety of ways. First, nonreflective beliefs function as defaults for beliefs we consider reflectively. Second, our judgment of the plausibility of reflective beliefs depends on how well they resonate with our nonreflective beliefs. Finally, nonreflective beliefs shape what we experience and remember.[26] Because of our dependence on nonreflective beliefs, the reasons that we come up with for beliefs that we consider reflectively often have little to do with why we actually believe them. In many cases they "amount to justification after the fact."[27]

After a discussion explaining how our mental tools produce belief in God in particular environments, psychologist Justin Barrett summarizes, "Thus, believing in God is a natural, almost inevitable consequence of the types of minds we have living in the sort of world we inhabit ...."[28] Overriding this belief is certainly possible, but it takes effort and needs to be supported by practices conducive to maintaining atheism. Barrett lists strategies for maintaining unbelief that include developing explanatory patterns that can replace supernatural agency, living in an environment where the triggers for belief occur less frequently, finding ways to filter accounts of others' experience to avoid evidence that seems to support supernatural agency, and cultivating opportunities for disinterested reflection with likeminded people.[29]

The point is not that atheism is false, but that believing it involves a kind of going against the grain that needs the support of certain habits of reflection and environmental conditions conducive to overriding human tendencies toward theistic belief. An individual might think that there is good reason to regard the tendencies producing belief in God as unreliable and that there should be concerted efforts to override certain beliefs deriving from these tendencies. But that is a far cry from the pretence that rejecting belief is simply the product of how we would think if we just consider things uncorrupted by particular practices. It may be how we would think if we have learned to maintain a suspicion toward certain operations of our mental tools, but to develop and maintain that suspicion we need to engage in the practices conducive to overriding beliefs these tools would otherwise produce.

Resisting Belief

For obvious reasons Pascal did not know about the conclusions of contemporary cognitive psychologists, but if we imagine informing him, he might have thought that they confirm his claim that failing to believe in God involves a kind of resistance to a tendency that naturally leads to belief. Perhaps he would have seen this resistance as a manifestation of pride. We become confident enough in our reflective reasoning that we think ourselves able to selectively overturn the nonreflective sources on which that reasoning depends. In his own terminology Pascal contrasts knowing the truth through reason and knowing it through the heart. He claims that the first principles upon which reason operates are discerned through the heart. "Reason must use this knowledge from the heart and instinct, and base all its arguments on it."[30] The failure of reason to be able to validate its starting points, thinks Pascal, serves to humble reason. Reason tends to assert itself beyond its limits, while submitting to those limits means accepting some beliefs deriving from sources that reason cannot certify.

The inclination to find the idea of supernatural agency a plausible way of thinking about the meaning of purposive phenomena is one factor involved in being receptive to a theistic story. This inclination derives from the way our mental tools work, and it is the sort of response that Pascal might have identified with something instinctual. We can raise the question of whether this inclination ought to be trusted. However, we are ordinarily inclined to trust beliefs produced by the operation of our mental tools, and from an attitude of trust we would need explicit reasons for thinking that a particular use should be overruled. We can substitute for trust a suspicion of the inclination to think in terms of supernatural agency, but that is the sort of attitude that Pascal would likely have judged to indicate a prideful attempt to resist what we cannot certify through reflective rationality.

Pascal's use of the term "heart" in connection with what he calls instinctual responses is only one of the ways he uses this term. Another is connected with what we love or care about. On his view one might resist the truth (or suppress the heart) by failing to trust certain instinctual sources of belief, but we can also fail to find the truth because of misdirected love. In a famous passage Pascal says, "The heart has its reasons, which reason does not know."[31] In this passage he speaks of the heart as a source of what we love, claiming that the heart is drawn in two directions, toward the self and toward God (the universal being). Pascal thinks that believing in God requires a hardening of the heart toward the self and an opening of the heart to God. The alternative of hardening the heart toward God and an opening toward the self, he connects with unbelief.

What does it mean to harden the heart toward self and to open it to God? In a film called *Stranger Than Fiction* a certain character begins to hear a voice that is providing a narration of his life.[32] After some investigation, he discovers that he is actually a character in a novel and that the voice he has been hearing is his creator, the author of his story. Unfortunately, he learns, this author's heroes tend to die tragic and early deaths. So he meets with the author and tries to persuade her to change the story. She provides him with a draft of the novel, and he reads the story of his life, including the part where he dies while saving a child from being hit by a bus. He has the freedom either to act out the story he has read or to reject it and substitute his own story. In the end he becomes convinced that the way the story has been written is the way it needs to go. He gives up whatever inclinations he might have had to resist the author and willingly goes to his death.

While many writers have emphasized the idea that belief in God can help satisfy our needs for comfort and security, it takes only a little acquaintance with theistic religious traditions to reveal ways that belief in God, when taken seriously, takes away much that might make us comfortable and secure. Without the kind of authoritative demand represented by God, it is tempting for all of us to view our lives in terms of our individual projects and plans. When God enters the picture, those projects and plans are displaced. Only when they fit into divine purposes to which we need to submit can these individual aims be recognized as legitimate. A central part of theistic religious life is learning to submit to a good that can be constraining and can thwart strong desires, including desires for comfort and security.

The theistic vision of life is a matter of giving up a more limited perspective and identifying ourselves with a superior perspective. This vision is expressed in varying ways. Devara Dasimayya of the *bhakti* tradition of Hinduism aspires to a unity of will with the divine when he prays,

> I'll not place my feet
> but where your feet
> have stood before:
> I've no feet
> of my own.[33]

Evelyn Underhill characterizes the spiritual life as being drawn "to the place where He wants us to be; not the place we fancied for ourselves."[34] She describes a process of "first turning to Reality, and then getting our tangled, half-real psychic lives – so tightly coiled about ourselves and our own interests, including our spiritual interests – into harmony with the great movement of Reality."[35] This process involves "… killing the very roots of self-love; pride and possessiveness, anger and violence, ambition and greed in all their disguises, however respectable these disguises may be …."[36]

A theistic life-orienting story that leads us to view our own thoughts and desires as distorted and misdirected and calls us to love a transcendent good is something we have motives to resist. If we can deny the authority of a higher perspective that calls our own aims into question, we might be able to find a less demanding story. Of course, there are other ways to resist. Plenty of people who claim to accept a theistic story seem pretty skilled at interpreting its meaning in ways that minimize the demands. There is a continuing temptation to translate what is difficult into something more palatable.

But for those less inclined to such devices, responding to a theistic story means aspiring to replace the kind of self-love that comes easily to us with a love for something that transcends and overrides our individual interests. It means giving up a narrowly conceived idea of our good in favor of something that is affirmed to be our true good. What is involved here is not just an affirmation, but submission to a process of spiritual formation through which one ideally becomes increasingly able to internalize the beliefs and concerns that define a way of life.

Hugo said that the good Jean Valjean became aware of was like a light that hurt his eyes. It was at once something compelling, but also something that was difficult to attend to. In becoming aware of a manifestation of the kind of goodness that a particular theistic story portrays, Valjean experiences a disclosure of a possible way of living. It is something he can dismiss or something he can come to embrace. In embracing it he acquires a story that enables him to say why and how such a way is his good and motivates him to shape his life accordingly.

Pascal's appeal to reasons of the heart suggests that in being drawn to love a good that transcends our love of self, we unlock our capacity to respond to God. Theistic religious stories describe for us a way of life that is in harmony with an ultimate goodness. When such an account awakens in us a longing for the kind of good it portrays, we have a compelling reason to take seriously the picture of reality the account presupposes. While it is possible to view such a longing with suspicion, it is also possible to see in it, as Pascal did, a part of our nature that puts us in touch with reality, opening our eyes to the signs of a Goodness that seeks to transform us.

Notes

1   Paul Helm, *Faith With Reason* (Oxford: Oxford University Press, 2000), 96. The use of this quotation as an epigraph is by permission of Oxford University Press.
2   John Cottingham, *The Spiritual Dimension: Religion, Philosophy and Human Value* (Cambridge: Cambridge University Press, 2005), 139. The use of this quotation as an epigraph has been accepted as fair dealing by Cambridge University Press.
3   Victor Hugo, *Les Misérables* (New York: The Modern Library, 1992), 78.
4   Hugo, 92.
5   Hugo, 92.
6   Hugo, 96.
7   Iris Murdoch, "On 'God' and 'Good,'" in *The Sovereignty of Good* (London: Routledge & Kegan Paul, 1970), 52.
8   Murdoch, 59.
9   Murdoch, 66.
10   Murdoch, 54.
11   Murdoch, 55.

12 Murdoch, 70.
13 Iris Murdoch, *Metaphysics As A Guide To Morals* (New York: Penguin Books, 1993), 343.
14 Murdoch, *Metaphysics*, 343.
15 John Hick, *Evil and the God of Love* (New York: Harper and Row, 1977), 280–91.
16 Johannes Climacus, *Philosophical Fragments*, ed. and trans. Howard V. Hong and Edna H. Hong (Princeton: Princeton University Press, 1985), I, 26ff.
17 Schellenberg's thesis is developed in *Divine Hiddenness and Human Reason* (Ithaca, NY: Cornell University Press, 1993). He has defended and expanded his ideas against various critics in numerous subsequent publications. A useful collection of responses may be found in *Divine Hiddenness: New Essays*, eds. Daniel Howard-Snyder and Paul Moser (Cambridge: Cambridge University Press, 2002).
18 Schellenberg, 52.
19 Schellenberg, 48ff.
20 Schellenberg, 40–1.
21 Blaise Pascal, *Pensées*, ed. and trans. Roger Ariew (Indianapolis: Hackett Publishing Company, 2005), 225 (S690, L446).
22 Pascal, 49–50 (S182, L189).
23 Pierre Hadot, *Philosophy As A Way of Life*, ed. Arnold Davidson, trans. Michael Chase (Maldon, MA: Blackwell Publishing, 1995), 83.
24 Hadot, 58.
25 Hadot, 103.
26 Justin Barrett, *Why Would Anyone Believe in God?* (New York: AltaMira Press, 2004), 1–19.
27 Barrett, 16.
28 Barrett, 108.
29 Barrett, 112–15.
30 Pascal, 31 (S142, L110).
31 Pascal, 216 (S680, L423).
32 Crick Pictures LLC, 2006.
33 In *Speaking of Siva*, trans. A. K. Ramanuja (London: Penguin Books, 1973), 106.
34 Evelyn Underhill, *The Spiritual Life* (Harrisburg, PA: Morehouse Publishing, 1996), 35.
35 Underhill, 53.
36 Underhill, 53–4.

5

Belief As a Practical Issue

"... *religion is a* forced option ... *We cannot escape the issue by remaining skeptical and waiting for more light, because, although we do avoid error in that way* if religion be untrue, *we lose the good,* if it is true, *just as certainly as if we positively chose to disbelieve.*" (William James[1])

"*When someone complains ... that his or her life is meaningless, he or she is often and perhaps characteristically complaining that the narrative of their life has become unintelligible to them ... .*" (Alasdair MacIntyre[2])

In a clever series of commercials an investment company associates itself with decisive action. One ad pictures a bride and groom standing in front of the minister to give their wedding vows. When the man is asked whether he will take this woman, he launches into an extended soliloquy about the difficulty of making a definitive commitment because of the uncertainties and risks involved. While the bride stands open-mouthed, a man from the audience comes up to take the groom's place and cutting through the verbiage, says "I will." The commercial ends with the company's signature phrase, "Less talk, more action."

While action can obviously be poorly planned and ill-considered, the point of the ad is well taken. There comes a time when decisions need to be made one way or another, and waffling indefinitely can have risks of its own. Another of the company's ads shows a man sinking in quicksand while others in his party convene a meeting to discuss a plan of action.

Belief in God is sometimes treated as a theoretical matter about which we can indefinitely weigh the pros and cons without ever reaching a conclusion. However, if we are talking about the kind of belief that makes a significant difference in our lives, there are practical limits to indecision. Trying to put off a commitment until we resolve all the uncertainties will not actually shelter us from risks because we will consciously or unconsciously live on the basis of some understanding that contains assumptions about what is ultimately real and ultimately important. If we don't live by a story that affirms the reality of a benevolent creator, we will live on the basis of one that denies such a reality or one that treats the issue as unimportant for shaping a way of life.

In addition to considerations connected with the need to settle on a life-orienting story, practical concerns become relevant in another way as well. A life-orienting story that includes or excludes God is not merely an object of belief that could be adopted dispassionately; it needs to engage our motivational impulses and moral sensitivities. Toward the end of this chapter I will describe how one writer's quest for a livable narrative moves from the rejection of some stories on the grounds that they fail to motivate a worthwhile life to the serious consideration of the kind of narrative judged capable of motivating such a life.

Examining Presuppositions?

Some people regard the intrusion of any practical considerations into thinking about God's existence as illicit. They hold that we ought to be able to decide about whether God exists prior to considering any life-orienting story that presupposes God. The main problem with this suggestion is that it is not at all clear how to examine the presupposition that God exists when we separate it from religious narratives.

We have a pretty clear idea of how to make judgments about the existence of various kinds of things. We understand what sort of evidence is relevant to the question of whether there are oil reserves in a particular area or whether someone who claims to be the long-lost heir to a fortune is genuine. But God does not fit into any of the usual paradigms for evidence gathering. It is not as if we might look for God at some particular location and verify whether God had been there or not. God is represented, not as a physical reality, but as a reality on which the whole material order of things is supposed to depend. How can you judge whether that sort of reality exists?

Some would propose thinking of God as an explanation for the natural world and proceed to consider whether such an explanation is needed.

But focusing on the role of God in explaining the natural order diverts our attention from considerations that are more centrally related to belief in theistic traditions. These traditions portray God as an agent who acts within the world and who may be encountered by human beings. If we want to know whether this kind of god exists, the focus of our attention should be on signs of the kind of deity who enters into the human story in a meaningful way.

But if we try to consider whether there is a transcendent agent who may be encountered by human beings, it makes little sense to think that we can do so independently of considering religious traditions in which people have believed in divine actions and human interactions with the divine. The primary evidence for thinking that a god of this kind exists comes from the experience and testimony of religious communities whose narratives and practices are offered as vehicles for discovering God.

Hence, the proposal that we should first decide whether God exists and then consider whether any particular theistic account of divine activities should be accepted is a misguided way to proceed. You can't believe in a deity who acts historically and with whom humans may interact without believing specific things about what God has done and how people make contact with God. To find the specifics, you have to consider the claims of particular traditions in which some story about God's acts is told.

The point is not that we are unable to think about God in a generic sort of way that encompasses ideas of God from a variety of traditions. It is rather that when we exclude specific claims of revelatory encounter, we risk screening out the kind of considerations that people within religious traditions find most significant. The stories of religious traditions that describe God's actions and the testimony of people within those traditions to have some experience of divine disclosure are of central relevance. It is to those stories and testimonies in all their particularity that people respond either with belief or unbelief.

However, when we consider the question of whether God exists in terms of whether some community's interpretations of its experiences are correct, the prospect of arriving at an answer that everyone will agree upon seems remote. How can we decide whether anyone has experienced a divine disclosure or not? How can we judge whether the paradigmatic stories on which a tradition bases its faith are fact or fiction? If a story seems to us very convincing, how do we know whether to trust our inclination to believe it? If it seems unconvincing, can we be sure that we are not considering it with an overly skeptical attitude? Faced with the task of weeding out potential confusion and superstition from genuine encounter, we might be tempted to give up and declare the issue of whether God exists to be impossible to decide. However, to think of that as an option is to forget that the question is a matter of practical consequence.

Forced Choices

When we think about the question of God's existence as arising from a practical point of view, in relation to our concerns about how to order our lives, the issue seems more pressing than when viewed as arising in a more theoretical context. We do, after all, have to find some way to understand our experiences and activities, and if an understanding that involves the idea of God has different practical implications about how to live from understandings that omit God, our judgment about whether to accept or reject an account involving God is subject to some of the necessities that we face as agents who must sometimes choose what to do.

Sometimes we find ourselves in a situation where we have a *forced choice*.[3] I call a choice forced for someone in a case where there are important practical consequences that depend on what that person does and when refraining from deciding what to do is the practical equivalent of deciding on a particular course of action. If your supervisor directs you to do something that is unethical and illegal, you might respond in various ways, but at a fairly basic level, your options are to follow the order, not to follow it, or to try to get the order changed. If you try and fail to get the order changed (say by discussing it with the supervisor or going to a superior), then your choice becomes doing what you have been told or not doing it. There are, of course, many ways that you might do a thing or not do it. Not being able to decide what to do in such a case is one way of not doing what you have been told and subjects you to consequences equivalent to having decided not to do it. It is, thus, a kind of practical equivalent of making the decision not to follow the order.

Forced choices occur not only in situations where some potential negative consequence is involved. They also arise when some positive consequence is at stake. Imagine that you have been offered a job opportunity in your field. It is the chance to do something very challenging and potentially very satisfying. But it would also involve giving up the relative security and stability of your current job, a job that you don't particularly like. You weigh the pros and cons of taking the plunge, but you can't quite make up your mind what to do. Each time you are asked, you put off the decision, and in the end the opportunity disappears. Your inability to commit yourself one way or the other is the practical equivalent of deciding against the opportunity.

Some forced choices are cases in which the way we respond is tied up with how we understand or interpret something. That is, different understandings would make alternative responses reasonable. For example, suppose that you are a single woman who for about a year has been dating a man to whom you are strongly attracted. He has indicated that he wants to marry you, and you are open to the prospect until you learn something about his past. You learn that in a previous relationship years ago he treated a woman very badly. He admits that his behavior was despicable, but he claims to have changed, and your experience of the last year gives you some reason to think that the change is genuine. A close friend tells you that you would be a fool to let him get away. Another friend tells you that you would be foolish to continue in the relationship. When your coolness toward him leads to an ultimatum to decide one way or the other, you can't make up your mind, and your indecision becomes the practical equivalent of rejecting him.

In this last case the way you act is intimately tied up with your judgment about whether the man has genuinely changed. If you interpret things one way, you risk failing to recognize a real change and losing out on a relationship that seemed to have great potential. If you interpret things another way, you risk not taking seriously enough a significant character flaw and making a choice that could prove disastrous in the future. Not being able to judge and act on your judgment is just another way of opting for one of these risks over the other. Of course, you are not trying to decide just by considering risks; you want to interpret things in a way that is true. But in life we do not always have the luxury of having decisive evidence of what is true. Sometimes we have to go with our best judgment.

When we view the question of God's existence as a practical matter, it looks very much like a forced choice. What is at issue is some way of understanding the nature of the human situation that will enable you to interpret the meaning of your experiences and adopt an appropriate mode of life. You are presented with a variety of narratives that purport to tell you what human life means and how you should live. Some of these narratives describe the significance of everyday events in terms that relate these events to a transcendent reality and offer instructions on how to live a life in harmony with that reality. Some of these stories characterize the transcendent as a personal reality called God, and others characterize it in different ways. Still other narratives deny any transcendence of the physical realm and tell you how to live in the absence of any such belief.

It is easy to imagine being overwhelmed by the variety of accounts and unable to choose between them, but if we think of these accounts as defining potential ways of life, not being able to decide does not exempt you from the need to have your own way of life. You will either live as if there were a transcendent reality called God or you will live as if there was no such reality. You can be a theoretical agnostic, but if you try to be a practical agnostic, it will be unavoidable that you come down on one side or another. Not being able to decide is a way of deciding against the kind of life in which a relation to God is a central feature.

It is important to recognize that the actual options for an individual are not at the level of generality of thinking that God exists or God does not exist. They are rather particular theistic or naturalistic or monistic accounts that are constitutive of a way of life. The forced choice is not between some generic form of god and some generic form of atheism. It is rather between alternative life-orienting stories that are developed in sufficient detail that a person could actually live in accordance with them.

Recognizing that there is a kind of practical necessity at work does not, of course, tell you what way of life to adopt. Nevertheless, if we see this as a case where failure to decide amounts to a decision, we might judge that it would be preferable to explicitly endorse one of the available options rather than allowing indecision to determine a way of life. But from what perspective should an individual think about whether to consider an account that includes God. One possibility would be to approach accounts that bring in God with an attitude of skepticism, to assume that God does not exist until clear-cut evidence shows otherwise.

Burden of Proof and Default Positions

It has been argued that one who believes in God bears a burden of proof and that in the absence of the right kind of proof or evidence, disbelief is the proper default position.[4] We are familiar with the idea of a burden of proof from contexts such as debates or legal trials. In a criminal trial it is up to the prosecution to establish the guilt of the defendant, and when the prosecution fails we justifiably treat the defendant as not guilty. Whether or not the defendant is actually guilty, we have a method for arriving at judgments of guilt or innocence that allows us to reach a definitive conclusion and act in accordance with it.

It can seem as if the issue of God's existence should be dealt with in an analogous manner. After all, when someone asserts the existence of something, we ordinarily think the person should have reasons for making such a claim, and we do not generally require reasons from someone who does not accept an existence claim. If, for example, someone does not believe that there is a conspiracy to overthrow the President that extends to the highest levels of government, it would be sufficient to cite the lack of evidence for such a conspiracy. So we might judge that our default position should be to assume nonexistence until we are given enough evidence to move us to belief.

But perhaps such a conclusion is too hasty. The method of assuming the nonexistence of something until it is established by the evidence clearly makes sense in certain cases, but how much should we generalize this method? Three considerations seem relevant. First, a presumption of nonexistence makes most sense in cases where we can assume that if something existed, we would be able to find clear and recognizable evidence that would establish its existence. In cases where that condition is not met, the presumption is more questionable. Second, whether the best policy is to presume nonexistence depends in some cases on practical considerations. Sometimes our aims are better fulfilled by presuming the existence of something or by not making any presumption one way or the other. Third, in some cases we are already convinced of the existence of something, but may not be able to show why in terms of publicly accessible evidence. Yet we would find it difficult to follow a policy that tells us to disbelieve what we in fact believe.

With regard to the first consideration, the idea that it makes sense to presume nonexistence until existence is established generally seems acceptable in cases where we are imagining a claim about something whose existence we are in a position to verify observationally. It seems less clear that it is the appropriate attitude to take with regard to something when the relevant evidence is not available or when we don't know how to evaluate potential evidence. Should one believe or disbelieve in the existence of intelligent extraterrestrial life in the universe? There are reasons that might lead us to think that such life probably exists, but we have no definitive evidence of it. Would it be improper for someone to believe that there is such life without evidence that establishes it with a high degree of probability? But why should that be unless we assume that the lack of evidence is really a kind of evidence against? Someone might say that it would be better to withhold judgment on the grounds that you can avoid having an erroneous belief, but why is it better in this kind of case to be more concerned with avoiding error than with accepting what might be true? Of course, if the idea is proposed as a scientific hypothesis, the proper approach would be to withhold judgment on it until the evidence meets scientific standards. But whether something is established scientifically is different from whether it might reasonably be believed.

Sometimes a lack of compelling evidence is combined with a practical need to decide what to do. In some cases a possibility that something is true gives us strong reason to take preventive action. You might think that the sound you heard is not very strong evidence for judging that there is a bear around the corner, yet act as if there were one by moving swiftly in the other direction. You might have very minimal reasons for thinking that your spouse intends to leave you, but in some circumstances it could make good sense to act as if this possibility were true and take steps to prevent it. Of course, acting as if something were true is not the same as believing it. You could act to prevent something that you think is a remote possibility. But while one might take preventative action in the case of the bear or the spouse without actually believing, in the case of God the kind of action called for would be a whole way of life. While a person might live as if God exists without being sure, it is at least problematic to think that one can both assume that God does not exist while living as if God does exist.[5]

How are practical considerations relevant to thinking about God's existence? In the paradigmatic burden of proof situation we are told to presume innocence in a criminal trial until guilt is established. This assumption is connected with our concern to avoid the very bad consequence of treating an innocent person as if that person were guilty. The risk of inappropriately punishing an innocent person is seen as sufficiently bad that avoiding this possibility calls for adopting the default position of assuming innocence, even if we thereby increase the risk of not punishing someone who is actually guilty. We seek to minimize the risk of punishing the innocent by putting ourselves into the frame of mind where we are willing to think of a guilty verdict as false until convinced otherwise. If we were to begin by assuming guilt or by making no assumptions about guilt or innocence, we would evaluate the evidence differently.

If the reason for assuming that God does not exist until we are given enough evidence to convince us otherwise is like the paradigmatic "innocent until proven guilty" presumption, it is presumably because believing in God when God does not exist is thought undesirable. We can avoid such a state by assuming that God does not exist until the evidence becomes decisive. However, such a strategy opens us to another possible risk that looks at least as bad. We might fail to believe in God when God does exist. By making disbelief the default position, we are treating the error of mistakenly believing in God as if it were more undesirable than the error of failing to believe when God does exist. Many people have thought that failing to believe in God and being wrong is a much greater risk.[6] But let us suppose that the risks are roughly equivalent. In that case why should we assume that the proper default position is to start by assuming the nonexistence of God? If you run a significant risk either way and are genuinely undecided, then why not say that there is no default position? If our primary concern is to get the truth, focusing exclusively on the kind of evidence that would require us to move from disbelief to belief could mean missing considerations that might have convinced us from a starting point that is more open to the possibility of God.

Whether or not we are persuaded that disbelief ought to be the default position probably hinges on how plausible we find the existence of God. Some people start with the view that the existence of God is extremely unlikely, and for someone who thinks that way it seems natural to adopt the position of treating the belief as guilty until proven innocent. But others start with a strong inclination to believe. For them adopting the default position of disbelief would mean overriding a strong sense that God very likely does exist. So when it is proposed that we should assess evidence by starting with the assumption that God does not exist, is this proposal intended to apply to everyone?

We do not start any assessments of evidence with blank slates, but begin with beliefs that we actually have. Some of these beliefs can be rationally examined and discarded, but we will always have plenty of beliefs left with which others might disagree. So where should we start? Descartes explored the possibility of withholding judgment about anything we could not establish with certainty, but that is clearly a recipe for ending up in a skeptical quagmire. An alternative strategy is suggested by Charles Peirce. He writes,

> We cannot begin with complete doubt. We must begin with all the prejudices which we actually have . …. These prejudices are not to be dispelled by a maxim, for there are things which it does not occur to us *can* be questioned. Hence this initial skepticism will be a mere self-deception, and not

real doubt . ... A person may, it is true, in the course of his studies, find reason to doubt what he began by believing; but in that case he doubts because he has a positive reason for it, and not on account of the Cartesian maxim.[7]

Peirce's alternative is for an individual to start with her actual beliefs. In some cases these beliefs will be so firmly a part of that individual's belief structure that she finds it difficult even to entertain a question about them. In such cases doubt is artificial. Where you start need not, of course, be where you end up. Reasonable people modify their beliefs over time, and they hope that in so doing they get closer to truth. But the default position for someone who firmly believes in the existence of something is more realistically continuing to believe it until convinced otherwise. One can suggest a general maxim with regard to new beliefs that there be a caution about adopting a certain kind of belief too quickly, but in many cases beliefs are deeply rooted and an individual with such beliefs is typically better off treating them as innocent until convincing reasons are provided to establish their guilt.

For someone who lives his life treating obligations to others as realities, the suggestion that the proper position is to refrain from believing that there really are obligations unless such a thing can be established by evidence is hard to take seriously. However, the belief came about, it is there. Similarly, someone who starts with a firm belief in the god of a particular religious tradition has a de facto default position of belief. Such a person might have various reasons for doubting the belief, but reasons that require assuming its falsity until shown otherwise need not be among them.

A Misleading Picture

The idea of a special burden of proof for someone who believes in God is connected with a way of construing our situation that is often assumed. If we think of the idea of God as a hypothesis that is posited to explain agreed-upon observational data, then it is a reasonable expectation that someone who proposes the hypothesis has a burden of proof of showing that it is actually needed. The atheist by contrast might be thought of as one who accepts the observational data, but presumes that there is no need to posit anything beyond the natural order to explain it unless sufficient reason is offered to show such a need.

However, that picture of things misconstrues the way belief in God works. One who is persuaded of God in the process of being persuaded by a life-orienting story in which God plays a central role is not starting with a problem of explaining publicly available observational data and then bringing in God to solve the problem. The starting point is more like a situation in which it is unclear how to construe the meaning of what we experience until some story is offered through which a particular meaning can be discerned. A story that proposes a potential meaning gains plausibility by rendering experience intelligible, cohering with accepted facts, ordering judgments of value, and providing effective guidance. But in such a situation an atheistic story enjoys no favored epistemological status over a theistic story. The question is which kind of meaning we find more convincing.

Rather than thinking about acceptance of a life-orienting story as making an inference from established data, we need to think of it as trying on a way of putting the experiential world into a meaningful order that can function as a guide to living. We can look at the stories that guide us with the eye of an objective investigator, but we should not imagine that this perspective will allow us to construct a life-orienting story from obvious facts or establish that a particular story is uniquely rational. No doubt we can rule out some stories as failing to cohere with what we know or strongly believe. But any life-orienting story posits ways of thinking that go beyond what can be verified empirically.

What persuades us of a particular story's truth may well involve such things as dispositions to regard particular elements of experience as vital clues to the nature of things, an imaginative willingness to enter into a particular story's meanings, an emotional resonance with an understanding of moral order a story portrays, or receptivity to a particular self-assessment that might have been resisted. In other words the question of what we judge true will depend on factors other than our ability to give a relatively detached assessment of evidence. What we discern the relevant evidence to be and how we weigh it depends on features of our nature that we try to keep under a tighter rein in situations involving matters that are decidable by straightforward empirical testing.

To recognize that our assessments of life-orienting stories involve a kind of participative and even passionate rationality is not to discount the importance of reflecting on these stories. Being convinced by a life-orienting story involves holding on to a vision of meaningful order in which various elements are seen as fitting into a pattern. In any such vision there will be some things that are in tension with recognizing the pattern. In subsequent chapters I will discuss things that challenge the coherence of naturalistic stories and things that challenge the coherence of theistic stories. Reflective rationality calls for meeting potential challenges, and doing so involves more than showing that logical contradiction can be avoided. Some challenges, when taken seriously, will damage our ability to find the meaningful order portrayed by a story at all plausible.

In the end we will find one story more convincing than alternatives, and the strongest argument for a story that persuades us is often to articulate it in a way that shows its attractions. It's often because we can't quite grasp what it would mean to accept a particular story that we can't take it seriously. So when someone can show what it means to think and live in accordance with a story that we have dismissed because of considering only simplistic versions, we may be able to entertain imaginatively the possibility of making such a story our own. To be persuasive the narrative needs to be told in a way that won't simply be dismissed out of hand and that will highlight the kinds of experience and patterns of thought that draw people in. To be fully drawn in is to be engaged by the story at a motivational level.

We miss the mark when we imagine the process of considering a life-orienting story as something we can do from a position of detached rationality. We consider these stories not just as thinkers, but as agents who need a story to live by. The story we judge true must connect with our judgments of what is worthy in order to engage us in a way of life. As we imaginatively enter into a particular story, attending to the meanings it offers and structuring our lives in terms of these meanings, we may experience the way of life the story shapes as full of motivating power, or we can be relatively unmoved by it. The failure of a story to move us can be an important reason for rejecting a potential story and for seeking one that can move us, as the following case study illustrates.

Thinking About A Way of Life: A Case Study

In an autobiographical account entitled *A Confession*, Leo Tolstoy describes a crisis in his life that occurred in his late forties. He tells us that he had been brought up in the Christian faith but, by the time he was 18, he had ceased to believe it. In retrospect he wonders whether he had ever seriously believed. He recalls a discussion when he was 11 in which a high school boy announced with excitement that the idea of God and religious accounts were pure invention and remembers that he regarded these claims as a possibility. He tells of an attitude he absorbed from his elders that it was important to learn the catechism, but one did not need to attend church or take the matter all that seriously.

Tolstoy reports that for him and others in his social class, religious doctrines had virtually nothing to do with the way people lived. It was easy for someone to profess religious belief without recognizing that these beliefs were not the understandings that actually guided behavior. When Tolstoy came to realize the lack of connections in his own case, he simply laid aside any pretension of belief.

His early life, he reports, involved a kind of faith in perfection. But his determination to perfect himself soon disintegrated into a wish to be more powerful, more famous, and more important than others. Tolstoy confesses to giving in to various base desires, and yet still being regarded by others as a relatively moral man. Eventually he began to absorb a view of life that was held by fellow writers:

> The view of life adopted by these people, my literary associates, was that generally speaking life is a process of development in the course of which the most important role is played by us, the thinkers; and that among the thinkers it is we, the artists and poets, who have the most influence. Our vocation is to educate people.[8]

Tolstoy says that he did not know what he had to teach, but adopted this account nevertheless. He observes, "This faith in the meaning of poetry and in the evolution of life was a religion and I was one of its priests."[9] But noticing disagreements among writers about the true doctrine to be taught and observing the immoral lives they led resulted in a renunciation of this religion.

At a more general level Tolstoy reports that he accepted a view of educated people of his time that could be summarized as a belief in progress. What this belief amounted to was never clearly specified, but it involved a sense that things were evolving toward a greater end and that individuals could somehow participate in the advance. However, Tolstoy says, there were events that challenged his belief in progress, and he recognized that his own activities were motivated more by a concern to secure financial prosperity for his family than toward some wider end.

Then came the crisis. Tolstoy describes the crisis as initially involving moments of bewilderment when he began to consider the meaning of what he was doing. He tried to dismiss the questions of why, but found himself increasingly obsessed with them. When he thought about his concerns for his family or his writing, he came to view his own actions with a sense of futility. Whether he became a famous writer or educated his children, he found it increasingly difficult to think of what he was doing as worthwhile. Tolstoy reports,

> My life came to a standstill. I could breathe, eat, drink, and sleep and I could not help breathing, eating, drinking and sleeping; but there was no life in me because I had no desires whose gratification I would have deemed it reasonable to fulfill. If I wanted something I knew in advance that whether I satisfied my desires nothing would come of it.[10]

Tolstoy's disengagement with life and his consequent despair centered around his thoughts about death. When he considered his life from an external, more objective perspective, it looked very small and inconsequential. He could work toward various goals, but whatever he might accomplish would eventually be gone and forgotten. This way of thinking had a subversive effect on the internal perspective from which he could view the concerns of his life as important and devote himself to passionately pursuing them. The things that he enjoyed, his family and his writings, could distract him from this sense of futility and meaninglessness for a while, but he kept coming back to the thought that any sense of meaning was only a delusion.

When he looked to the sciences, Tolstoy says he could find precise answers to a variety of questions, but no answers to the puzzle about how to live that had obsessed him. Science could provide him with a picture of material particles undergoing various changes in space and time. Within this picture an individual person is a "temporary, incidental accumulation of particles." But such a picture provided no answers to Tolstoy's concern to find a point to his activities, except perhaps to suggest that there was no point to be found.

Nor could Tolstoy find an answer in philosophical thought. He found views that accepted the meaninglessness of existence and advocated an escape from it or a resignation to it, but nothing that could provide a framework supporting the concerns required for deep engagement with life. Tolstoy came to the conclusion that the only kind of answer that would satisfy him would situate his life in relation to something infinite. Religious traditions offered such answers, but to Tolstoy their appeal to faith seemed to posit an irrational kind of belief. He says, "Faith remained as irrational to me as before, but I could not fail to recognize that it alone provides mankind with the answers to the question of life . ...."[11]

Convinced that only religious traditions provided answers to the questions he was asking, Tolstoy began to study them in earnest. His studies included the Christian faith he had been taught as a child. But he was unimpressed with the forms Christianity took among the educated class of his country. It was not genuinely a part of their lives, as it was among the poor and uneducated. Unlike the elite, the uneducated masses were able to live in a way that allowed them to accept suffering, hardship, and death without lamenting their fate. Their faith was woven into the fabric of their lives.

So Tolstoy set out on a quest for God. He sought God with a sense of his need and of hope that he could find help. Convinced that without God no real life was to be found, Tolstoy eventually came to a conviction of the reality of God:

> And I was saved from suicide. When and how this change occurred in me I could not say . ... I returned to all those things that had been part of my childhood and youth. I returned to a belief in that will that had given birth to me and which asked something of me ... I returned to the conviction that I could find the manifestation of this will in something that had been hidden from me for a long time in what humanity had worked out long ago for its own guidance. In other words I returned to a belief in God, in moral perfection, and to that tradition which had given life a meaning. Only the difference was that before I had accepted all this unconsciously, I now knew that I could not live without it.[12]

Tolstoy's account of his abandonment and recovery of faith can easily be misunderstood. If we try to understand the shift from unbelief to renewed belief under the paradigm of building up evidence until a conclusion becomes apparent, the account is bound to seem puzzling. Instead of considering evidence, he seems to be focused on the benefits of belief. He seems to move from a need to believe that there is meaning to life to the conclusion that whatever it takes to give life meaning is a reality. In terms of the evidence accumulation paradigm, such a move is clearly illicit.

But how else could this story be understood? It may help to notice how Tolstoy lost his childhood faith. He accepted what he had been taught at an early age and imagined he believed it, but what he had been taught never took root. It had little or nothing to do with how he lived. Dropping it was not a matter of discovering that some evidence he thought he had was not sufficient. It was a matter of recognizing that the religious beliefs he imagined he had were too disconnected from practical living to do any real work. Something else functioned to guide the way he lived.

Tolstoy attempts to describe what was performing the function of religion in his life. He looks first to a faith in perfection. But however attractive this might seem as an ideal, his actual life was dominated by other motives. He describes a vague picture of how the role of creative artists such as him was to educate the masses. But this ideal seemed to disintegrate on close examination. Asking what the artists had to teach or trying to view them as exemplars made the view difficult to sustain. Similarly when he thought critically about the belief in progress that permeated the culture, the idea seemed flimsy. Besides, Tolstoy admits, as with his early religious belief, it was not that idea which actually governed his life. Concern with securing the financial interests of his family was the real motivator.

Tolstoy's crisis was a loss of confidence in any of the narratives that might have convinced him he was doing anything of worth. He found nothing in science that could support a way of life that could engage him. In fact when he looked at the narratives science had to offer, they seemed only to confirm what he suspected – that nothing he might do was genuinely important. Tolstoy's awareness of life-denying philosophies made him even more skeptical of the possibility of finding an understanding of the human situation that would enable him to sustain a life of passionate concerns.

In the end he concludes that as far as finding an understanding that can make sense of a life of genuine engagement, it will be a religious story or nothing.[13] The kind of meaning he thinks necessary would require linking his limited existence with a larger whole that made the values and concerns that might engage him more than human projections. Religious stories portraying a transcendent order provide what he is looking for. So he begins to explore these stories with the thought that there may be one he could believe.

He is disgusted with the kind of Christianity those in his social class exhibit, but intrigued by the way the peasant class actually live out their religion. Given the possibility of a genuine religion, he begins to seek God, and when he reconsiders the tradition he had been taught in his youth, he finds that it provides an account of what is valuable in life that resonates with his sense of what is worthwhile. When he thinks in terms of this narrative, his suicidal despair goes away and what he calls the "life force" returns "gradually and imperceptibly."

Tolstoy had been seeking an understanding sufficient to guide his life and energize his motivations. When he gave up the Christianity of his youth, it was because the doctrines failed to engage him at a practical level. When he returned to the tradition, it was with a belief that alternatives he has tried have also failed to do the job. In the end he approaches the Christian narrative as a needy individual who has become convinced that the kind of understanding of life it provides is what he needs to live again. It seems to him a good that can make sense of his life, and when he entertains this possible good, he comes to believe it is true.[14]

What is involved here is less a weighing of evidence and more a matter of looking with fresh eyes at a narrative that provides a particular way of ordering his understanding of himself and his world. While it might appear to be a case of thinking "I need it, so it's true" it is, I think, better to see it as a case of "Something that meets a vital need is offered to me. Should I trust the urge to believe in the genuineness of what is offered?" The vital need is to have a story about what is real that can make compelling the concerns and values by which we order our lives. When an account is able to do this, and alternatives of which we are aware cannot, then we have some reason to suspect that this account is true.

One can find fault with Tolstoy for dismissing too easily alternative narratives that might have enabled him to reconnect with life. Perhaps there are nonreligious stories or alternative religious stories that could have played the role of guiding and engaging him. But he should not be faulted for the way he approaches the question of God. For him the question of whether to believe is intimately connected with the question of how to live. He explores the question of whether to believe in God as a question of whether an account that leaves God out could provide a context in which his sense of what is worthwhile does not collapse into unintelligibility. The conclusion that only a religious account could make sense of his strivings gives him a significant incentive to reexamine the possibility of belief.[15]

In contrast to approaching the question of God as an intellectual puzzle, Tolstoy approaches it as the practical issue of whether there is a transcendent reality that he must confront in order to take his own life seriously. The question of God for him is whether there is a will higher than his own that demands something of him, a will that calls him to moral perfection and to a way of life that is more than the fulfillment of selfish desires. He finds an account of such a will in an ancient tradition, and when he considers his own life in the light of that tradition's story, he acquires the guide to life he was seeking. Whether Tolstoy gets the right answer or not, his way of thinking about whether to believe in God shows the importance of considering the issue from a practical point of view. To be acceptable, a life-orienting story must effectively engage us in a way of life we can judge worthy.

Notes

1   William James, "The Will to Believe," in *The Writings of William James: A Comprehensive Edition*, ed. John J. McDermott (Chicago: The University of Chicago Press, 1977), 732.

2   Alasdair MacIntyre, *After Virtue*, 3rd edn. (Notre Dame: University of Notre Dame Press, 1981), 217. The use of this quotation as an epigraph is by permission of University of Notre Dame Press.

3   The concept of a forced choice is indebted to William James's classic discussion in "The Will to Believe." However, my concept combines his notions of forced choice with what he calls momentous choice. My discussion of practical necessity in this chapter is inspired by James's approach.

4   For example, Antony Flew defends this view in "The Presumption of Atheism," in *The Presumption of Atheism, and Other Philosophical Essays on God, Freedom and Immortality* (New York: Barnes and Noble, 1976).

5   John Bishop argues that we can take something as true in practical reasoning without believing it. But that would be different from assuming it was not true, yet acting in accordance with it. See John Bishop, *Believing By Faith: An Essay in the Epistemology and Ethics of Religious Belief* (Oxford: Oxford University Press, 2007), 33–5.

6   Pascal's famous wager argument depends on this judgment.

7   Charles Peirce, "Some Consequences of the Four Incapacities," in *Philosophical Writings of Peirce*, ed. Justus Buchler (New York: Dover Publications, 1955), 228–9.

8   Leo Tolstoy, *A Confession and Other Religious Writings* (New York: Penguin Books, 1987), 23.

9   Tolstoy, 23.

10   Tolstoy, 30.

11   Tolstoy, 53.

12   Tolstoy, 65–6.

13   I will return to a discussion of Tolstoy and the meaning of life in Chapter 9.

14   Austin Farrer thinks of faith as a matter of approaching evidence with a subjective attitude that allows for the appreciation of evidence. An important

feature of the attitude he identifies is having a positive response to the possibility of God. See *Saving Belief* (Harrisburg, Pennsylvania: Morehouse Publishing, 1994), 1–24.

15 Charles Taylor offers a strong defense of the claim that what we say about reality must account for the categories we employ in articulating what we are doing as agents. See his *Sources of the Self: The Making of the Modern Identity* (Cambridge: Harvard University Press, 1989), 3–107.

6

Anthropomorphism and Mystery

"To whom then will you liken God,
Or what likeness compare with him?"

Isaiah 40:18[1]

"… the only absolutely critical and unquestionably ubiquitous human-like attribute ascribed to gods is that they have minds." (Todd Tremlin[2])

In the television series *Joan of Arcadia*[3] the lead character is a teenager who begins to receive visits from God. God appears in human form, but in various bodies, sometimes male, sometimes female, sometimes as an adult, sometimes as a child. Joan takes some convincing that it is really God she is meeting, and after she gets used to these meetings she sometimes mistakenly takes a stranger who strikes up a conversation to be another divine manifestation. But the confusions are sorted out quickly, and Joan is left with little doubt when she is receiving God's message for her. Often with considerable reluctance, she learns to accept God's instructions and act on them, typically with unexpected results.

In one early encounter Joan irreverently says to God, "I didn't think you would be so snippy." In reply she is told, "I'm snippy because you understand snippy." Apparently God's revelation to Joan is adjusted to her powers of conceptualization and to modes of interaction she is comfortable with. We get hints in the show that there is much about God that would be absolutely incomprehensible to Joan, and God's project appears to be less focused on giving her information or satisfying her curiosity and more on showing her enough to get her moving in a desired direction. Her various revelations may allow her to draw some conclusions about God, but whatever conclusions she draws will be those of someone who has a very limited understanding of something far beyond her depth.

If there could be such a thing as a revelation of God's nature to humans, it would presumably have to be adjusted to human capacities to comprehend and expressed in some human language in forms intelligible to people who have the understandings of a particular culture and era. What we say about God needs to be articulated in terms that make sense to us, and what makes sense to us is closely tied to the kinds of experience and modes of interpretation that are familiar to creatures in our kind of world. It would be arrogant to assume that our experiences and thought processes put us in a position to comprehend much about dimensions of reality that differ significantly from our own.

Edwin Abbott's *Flatland*, an imaginative book of the nineteenth century, suggests some of the difficulties.[4] The narrator of the story is a two-dimensional square who lives in a two-dimensional world. Much of the story gives an account of how that two-dimensional world works and how its characters live. But in the second part of the story the narrator tells how he encounters a sphere from a three-dimensional world. Of course, he can perceive the sphere only as a two-dimensional circle with anomalous features. For example, the circle, which appears in his plane, keeps changing sizes and occasionally disappears. The square rejects the strange account given by the sphere, which describes things the square cannot fit into his frame of reference. He rejects all the arguments used by the sphere to convince him that he is dealing with something from a dimension beyond his own. He is convinced only when the sphere lifts him out of his world and enables him to experience the three-dimensional world firsthand.

Trying to speak about God involves using terms suited for the world of ordinary sense experience to conceive of a different kind of reality. Even if we manage to say things that are true, our understanding of the significance of what we say is likely to be so minimal that from a higher point of view it would reveal more ignorance than insight. However, even if there is a point of view from which our understanding amounts to very little, its adequacy depends on what purposes this understanding achieves for us and whether a superior account is available. A limited understanding that is suited to our level of comprehension and is conducive to the formation of appropriate attitudes and actions in relation to a supreme reality may be sufficient for our needs.

Consider a case in which an answer to a question is framed to fit a particular level of understanding and to achieve certain purposes. A father is attempting to explain the mysteries of reproduction to a child who has asked where babies come from, but is too young to understand much. Rather than giving a biology lesson, the father says something like this: "When two people like your mother and I love each other very much, they can come together in a way that makes their love overflow. When that happens, a new life starts to grow in the mother, and after a while a baby is born." From one point of view such a story is clearly inadequate. But from another point of view the story is just right. It gives the child a poetic kind of picture that conveys a value-laden understanding of a way to think about the birth of a child. It takes a tin ear to simply dismiss such a story as false. The poetry conveys a type of truth that might be well suited for the child's level of understanding. Furthermore, this sort of account may be more conducive to cultivating appropriate attitudes toward new life than a purely biological story would.

The use of metaphorical ways of speaking about God is a pervasive feature of theistic language. The various poetic images used in the scriptures of theistic religions to refer to God elaborate a controlling idea. God is to be thought of as a personal agent. This mode of thought builds on our knowledge of personal agency derived from everyday experiences of dealing with human beings. When the analogy is developed, there are numerous qualifications of differences between God and the human agents we encounter, but the attitudes and actions we learn to be appropriate in human interactions become the basis for recognizing the appropriate attitudes and actions in relation to God. For example, the teaching that God is like a parent who brought you up and cares for you conveys a certain understanding of how to respond to God.

Reflective believers are aware that the images they use are ways of thinking about something that is beyond human comprehension. They may regard certain ways of thinking as divinely revealed, but a revelation of God in terms that humans can use cannot be expected to convey what is beyond the limits of human understanding about these matters. Reflective belief involves a kind of balancing act between affirmations about God and acknowledgment that these affirmations don't do justice to the reality.

Thomas Aquinas claimed that we can use words to make true statements about God, but that we do not fully understand what we are saying: We use words that we understand in relation to creatures to talk about perfections that are far beyond the kinds of perfections any creatures possess.[5] Like the square in *Flatland* (or like Joan of Arcadia) we are starting with the conceptual resources we have available and using them to point toward something we can only obliquely represent. Even so, such language may be sufficient for the practical purpose of directing a person into a way of life in which belief in the transcendent plays a vital role.

Mental Toolkits

In recent years cognitive psychologists have offered persuasive accounts of the importance of human thinking that occurs at levels below conscious awareness. According to their accounts, the human mind has "mental workshops" that utilize various "tools" to put our world in order. Among our mental tools are ways of categorizing different types of reality. For example, we are able very quickly to distinguish between living things and objects that are not alive, and in recognizing something as living we have an understanding, sometimes called "intuitive biology," that allows us to make a wide range of inferences appropriate to this kind of thing. When a living thing is recognized as an animal, we naturally apply a range of knowledge about its nature. We know, for example, that it needs to eat, that it can die, and that it has a nature that is specific to its species. Similarly, we have an "intuitive physics" that allows us to form a variety of expectations about the behavior of physical objects. Some research with children reveals how early various aspects of this intuitive physics, such as the assumption of object permanency, are activated.

One of the most important kinds of categorization for our practical purposes is the recognition of something as an agent. Agents are beings capable of initiating action on the basis of mental states. This category includes nonhuman animals, as well as other human beings. We naturally think of a tiger as feeling hungry and acting to satisfy that desire. We think of a mother goose as recognizing danger and acting to protect her young. We notice when the family pet is indicating she wants to go out. In evolutionary terms the ability to detect agency and to interpret the purposes of another agent are clearly vital to survival. So we are equipped with what might be called "agency detection devices" and the kind of "intuitive psychology" that we utilize to judge mental states when we attribute agency.

Our intuitive psychology comes into play in an important way when we are dealing with human agents. We need to be able to understand other people in order to deal with potential conflict and develop various modes of cooperation. We need to be able to recognize states such as suspicion or resentment or anger. We also need to be able to make judgments about the receptiveness and trustworthiness of others in cooperative ventures. As one cognitive psychologist puts it, "… we are all consummate psychologists who spend large amounts of time and energy attempting to read the minds of others, especially as their beliefs and desires pertain to us."[6]

When we apply a concept, such as "agent," we are using what Pascal Boyer calls an ontological template that contains large amounts of information about something, as well as rules for generating inferences relevant to its behavior.[7] We attribute beliefs and desires and intentions to agents and use these attributions in determining how to respond or relate to them. The mental tools that allow us to make these attributions do not result in infallible judgments. We are sometimes wildly wrong in our attempts to understand others, but our intuitive psychology often allows us to act quickly and effectively to achieve our purposes, and the processes operate at a level that is typically below conscious awareness.

God as Personal Agent

The agency template provides the basic structure in theistic religions for thinking about and relating to God. The orienting stories these religions tell invite us implicitly to think about God as a person with beliefs, desires, and intentions and to respond accordingly. Learning to think of God as a personal agent involves transferring features that we naturally attribute to human persons to the divine. We are told, for example, that God knows things, that God can perform actions, that God has purposes and can communicate these purposes. Thinking in this way is a matter of applying the person template we use with human beings and in the process activating a number of standard inferences that we make with human agents. However, in the case of God learning to use the template appropriately also means recognizing ways in which some of the standard expectations and inferences that apply to our dealings with other people do not apply to God.

For example, we can be confident that a human person will be at a particular location in a particular bodily form. But God, we are told, is not to be thought of as limited to a particular location or requiring any physical embodiment. In fact theistic traditions often warn against representing God in art or in imagination as having some physical appearance. So through a process of using the person template and qualifying its use, an individual learns what can be said and what cannot be said about God and, equally important, what attitudes and actions are appropriate in relation to God.

It's not all that difficult to teach a child how to talk about God. Children learn the idea in the way they learn most uses of language: through the examples of older speakers. Sometimes there is explicit instruction about theological ideas, but much of a child's ability to use theological language involves a transfer of patterns of thought that are learned in nontheological modes of discourse. Occasionally a child will get something wrong or make inferences that are off the beaten path but, as with other concepts, the child eventually gets a feel for what can be said and what kinds of questions will be taken seriously.

If we try to describe this sort of teaching as if it were an explicit instruction, an example of words to a child might go something like this: God is very wise and good. God made the whole world and has told us about how to live. You should be grateful to God and seek to follow the ways God has laid out for us. God is with you wherever you go; you may not see God with your eyes, but you can talk to God in prayer. Don't expect God to answer with a voice you can hear. God speaks inside your mind when you listen very carefully.

Obviously such instruction could be expanded at great length, but it is clearly an attempt to provide the child with the basic template of personal agency for thinking about God, but at the same time to block some inferences that would be appropriate with regard to human interactions, while authorizing others. For example, you can't think of God as limited to one place, but you should think of God as responding to your needs and giving you guidance. Different traditions give different accounts, but in any theistic religion what is communicated enables a child to engage in religious practices and seek to exemplify the way of life that tradition upholds.

Robert Coles describes an interview with an 11-year-old Muslim boy (Haroun) who described his religious life in these terms: "I talk with Allah, and He listens. I pray to him and Mohammed, and they speak to me." Coles pressed the boy about how Allah speaks, and the boy replied, "With words for me to remember." Later the boy offered an example of the words he heard. "I ask Allah to give me strength and He says I already have strength. All that day I heard Him: 'You already have strength.'"[8]

In a later interview the topic turned to evil in the world. Haroun referred to the teaching he had been given that the world would only be saved from trouble when Allah finally intervenes to save it. But apparently not fully satisfied with that answer, he described his own prayer experience from that morning. While at prayer, he says that Allah had told him, "Pray to be worried all your life as you are now. Pray that you don't put your worries in some closet." The worries referred to were apparently about the wrongs in the world. Haroun understood the voice of Allah to be telling him not to be complacent about those wrongs, but to continue to bring them to mind (and presumably to do his own part to combat the wrongs).

Haroun clearly thinks of prayer as a two-way conversation between himself and Allah. Although Allah is incomparably great, that does not preclude giving personal guidance to those who seek it. Humans, however, have to be attentive to the guidance provided and ready to put it into practice. Quite clearly, Haroun learned to think in the ways he does by example and by instruction, but he has taken what he has been taught to heart in such a way that for him Allah is an experiential reality that clearly makes a difference with regard to how he lives.

Anthropomorphism

Using the template of personal agency to think about God can result in significant anthropomorphism. However, the extent to which God is thought of as humanlike depends on how this template is qualified. Over time a theistic tradition develops some more or less agreed-upon ways of qualifying the agency template. Many of these can be thought of as developing from the internal logic of the practices and paradigmatic experiences of the religious community. But there are also external influences, arising from attempts to accommodate modes of discourse that come from other contexts, such as the scientific or philosophical thought of a particular era.

One qualification of the agency template that represents a move away from anthropomorphic deities is the idea that God does not have a body. In ancient Greece Xenophanes criticized the polytheistic religion of his day on the grounds that the gods of each country resembled the citizens of that country. He notes that "Aethiopians have gods with snub noses and black hair, Thracians have gods with gray eyes and red hair."[9] He suggests that if animals such as horses or lions or oxen had gods, they would portray their gods with bodies like their own. Xenophanes urges a move away from the kind of representation of deity that pictures gods as having the sort of bodies that humans do and living the kinds of lives we live.

Monotheistic religions replace the deities who physically resemble human beings with a deity who has psychological traits, but not physical ones. In standard uses of the agency template we are dealing with agents who exist at a particular place in a particular bodily form. But God is to be conceived as an agent who does not require a physical form to act.

In Judaism the prohibition against graven images is presumably a way of moving people away from conceiving of God as being like polytheistic deities. If God cannot be given a visual representation, God must be very different from the gods.

The urge to represent the deity as having a physical form can, nevertheless, be found, even in the scriptural texts of monotheistic religions. Consider, for example, the story in Hebrew Scriptures in which Moses asks to see the glory of God (Exodus 33). He is told that he cannot see God's face, but only God's back. It is certainly possible to read the reference to bodily parts in a metaphorical way, and later members of the tradition will do so. But this story and similar accounts suggest that the writers of these texts found it natural to think of God as having a bodily form, even if the form involved something very different from and more magnificent than ordinary human appearance (since it would kill a human being to see God's form directly).

In Xenophanes' critique of polytheism it is not merely the physical resemblances between the gods and human beings that he finds objectionable. It is also the representation of deity as subject to human failings. He specifically cites stories of the gods engaged in behavior that deserves blame when humans do it, such as theft, adultery, and deception. Within monotheistic traditions the principle that God lacks what humans can recognize as defects is the basis for a number of qualifications of the agency template. The principle can be used to reject not only moral deficiencies, but cognitive or volitional deficiencies as well. Hence, God should not be conceived as acting impulsively or with short-sightedness.

It is hard to avoid the conclusion that the God of the Hebrew Scriptures is sometimes portrayed in ways that reveal what we can recognize as human deficiencies. Consider, for example, the story of Exodus 32 in which God is portrayed as becoming angry with the Israelite people. God says to Moses, "… let me alone that my wrath may burn hot against them and I may consume them; but of you I will make a great nation."[10] What follows is an extraordinary account in which Moses attempts to talk God down from this angry state and change God's mind about such a plan. Moses offers specific reasons why it would be better not to do what God has suggested. The end result is that God "repented of the evil which he thought to do to his people."[11]

For a reader who has become familiar with the concept of God as developed in this tradition, it seems astonishing that God could be portrayed as being overcome by anger, having an impulse to act out of that anger, needing to be talked down, and in the end being persuaded by a human being to change plans. Yet it would be natural for someone using the personal agency template to think in these terms, and it requires some training to learn to use the template in a more qualified way. As the tradition learns to critique its own anthropomorphic tendencies, readers can say that whatever it means to attribute wrath to God, it cannot mean that God loses control and flies off the handle. What we recognize as a weakness in ourselves surely cannot be a trait of the being of greatest worth. Furthermore, the portrayal of God as needing to be reminded of information or acting impulsively suggests a God who is conceived in our image. Over time monotheistic traditions develop qualifications of the personal agency template to remove such obvious imperfections.

Of course, it can sometimes be unclear what should be removed. While a God who loses control due to anger in the way that humans do seems to exhibit a defect, does the possession of emotion constitute a defect? The ancient conception of emotions as passions to which a rational being is subject might suggest this conclusion. It might also be suggested by thinking about the role of the body in emotional reactions. However, eliminating emotions from God would appear to eliminate the significance of a great deal of religious teaching about God. Is it not quite true that God loves people or has compassion for them? Does God's opposition to injustice or concern for the poor lack the passion that scriptural accounts might suggest? Theologians who think emotions of any kind unworthy of God can reinterpret these attributions as picturesque ways of describing behavior that from a human being would indicate a certain type of emotion. But the point is that there is some room for reasonable disagreement within a tradition about exactly what qualifications need to be made to the agency template when it is applied to God.

Perfect Being Theology

Part of the force of critiques based on the charge of anthropomorphism arises from the internal logic of theistic belief and practice. If God is to be conceived as worthy of absolute devotion and of worship, then it won't do at all to think of God as too close to the level of human beings. I might have a kind of admiration, even adoration, of a human being who exhibited extraordinary powers and virtues, but worship is out of the question.

Portraying God as worthy of worship calls for emphasizing a significant gap between God and human beings.

One expression of a fairly systematic way of explicating the gap can be found in the methods of perfect being theology. Anselm gives a classic exposition of this approach when he defines God as "a being than which nothing greater can be conceived,"[12] and proceeds to draw a number of conclusions about God by reflecting on what traits can make a being greater. God, he thinks, will lack nothing desirable and will be "whatever it is better to be than not to be."[13] With this guiding principle in mind Anselm proceeds to reflect on the nature of God's knowledge and power, God's compassion and justice, God's relation to time, and so on.

A number of contemporary theists have found the idea of God as a maximally perfect being intuitively satisfying. It furnishes a way to reflect on various characteristics that have been traditionally applied to God and develop a fairly determinate account of what they mean. Consider, for example, knowledge. It seems obvious that a personal being, possessing all traits that contribute to perfection, would have knowledge. How much knowledge? Since lacking any knowledge might be regarded as a defect, we might postulate knowledge of every truth. Similarly, possession of power is presumably a desirable thing. So how much power would an absolutely perfect being have? Perhaps it would be the power to accomplish any task that being could coherently choose. How much goodness? Obviously such a being must have an unlimited degree of goodness.

While this sort of process can yield traits such as omnipotence, omniscience, perfect goodness, etc., it raises several questions. One is the question of whether a very determinate account of such traits is overly speculative from a religious point of view. Ideas of God originate in religious traditions, and the accounts developed by those traditions can be regarded as ways of articulating understandings that make sense of the paradigmatic experiences and practices of religious communities. A being who is worthy of worship must clearly be unimaginably great and have qualities that leave finite humans with a sense of awe. It makes sense to postulate a knowledge that dwarfs human knowledge, a power that is unsurpassably great, and a goodness that is on a different level from our own. But trying to nail these qualities down as if we knew exactly what it means to have perfect knowledge or power or goodness seems suspect.

When it is suggested, for example that God must know every true proposition, the assumption is that God's knowledge can be characterized in the way we might try to characterize ours – in terms of linguistic claims. When it is said that God must have maximal power, we probably imagine the kinds of things we call power, such as the power to build a skyscraper or the power to change the course of a river. Some events in sacred texts might suggest that God can do things that seem very remarkable to us, but surely the nature of God's power is more mysterious than any determinate formulas might suggest. Thinking that God can do anything or anything logically possible and consistent with other divine attributes gives the impression that we are in a position to define the scope of divine power. But perhaps there is room for a more humble agnosticism about the nature of power that operates at a different level from our own.

When asked whether God could prevent a tsunami or cure any cancer patient, it is tempting to answer yes. But giving an affirmative answer seems to presuppose an understanding of the nature and context of the use of divine power that is beyond what most believers could claim to know. There is no problem in claiming that God's power will be sufficient to accomplish God's purposes, but claiming to know exactly what God could or could not do without understanding how a creator acts in a created order is suspect.[14] Similarly, while it seems pious to say that God knows everything, we have very little idea of what such a formula even means. A believer might rest assured that no knowledge needed to fulfill God's purposes is lacking or that divine knowledge is vaster and greater than we can imagine, but such affirmations do not require a precise account of how far divine knowledge extends.

The use of perfect being theology puts considerable weight on various intuitions about what perfection means. For example, ancient and medieval Christian theologians were convinced that since God was perfect, God must be impassible. That is, God must be incapable of feeling any sorrow or suffering. To them it seemed clear that a perfect being would not be vulnerable to the kind of distress that the events of life often bring to us. But the assumption that the sort of invulnerability we might wish for is what a perfect being possesses is clearly speculative. It is also a conclusion that requires considerable tampering with accounts in a tradition with teachings about divine love. Can a being who cannot suffer really care about another in the way God is said to care?

The point is that our intuitions about perfection tempt us to form very determinate ideas about what God must be like, yet there is good reason to be cautious about thinking we can form a fully determinate account of divine attributes. In some cases we can recognize talk about God as unacceptably anthropomorphic when it involves a questionable projection of our own mode of life onto God. But that does not mean we can form an idea of God that clears away the puzzles about what such a being would be. It would be better to admit that when we talk about divine attributes, such as knowledge or power or goodness, we are not in a position to be very precise.

Do Words Apply?

David Hume uses the religious motivations for avoiding anthropomorphism in his attack on the portrayal of God implicit in some versions of the design argument for God's existence. His character, Philo, endorses the view that when we take into account the vast gap between the human and the divine, words that we understand well enough in the human case lose any real meaning when applied to God. Philo says,

> … we ought never to imagine, that we comprehend the attributes of this divine Being, or suppose, that his perfections have any analogy or likeness to the perfections of a human creature. Wisdom, thought, design, knowledge; these we justly ascribe to him; because these words are honourable among men, and we have no other language or other conceptions by which we can express our adoration of him. But let us beware, lest we think, that our ideas any wise correspond to his perfections, or that his attributes have any resemblance to these qualities among men. He is infinitely superior to our limited view and comprehension ….[15]

Philo's account makes clear that there is a kind of tension between the concern to magnify the difference between the human and the divine and the need for some cognitive content to the idea. Using the agency template to talk about God requires the use of terms that we understand from our dealings with human agency. Yet when these terms are applied to God, many of the human associations will have to drop out. If we think of God as having beliefs, those beliefs are surely not much like human beliefs. If we think of God as designing a world, surely we are not thinking about something with much of a resemblance to cases of human design. The suggested conclusion is that words applied to God do not convey any real information. They are only ways of expressing certain attitudes.

The religious appeal of such an account may be seen in the way it expresses a concern to magnify the greatness of God. The greater God is, the less adequate any language might seem to speak about God. The theological tradition of negative theology parallels Philo's insistence by claiming that affirmations about God should not be understood as conveying any positive knowledge, but only as pointing us away from some inadequate understanding of the divine nature. However, to understand all theological claims as conveying only negations seems to undermine the religious intuitions it sets out to protect. If a believer can say nothing positive about God, then how could any way of talking about God be preferable to any other? If our experience of some things as indicating perfection or value to a higher degree tells us nothing about God, then it is puzzling how God could be an object of attitudes such as reverence or respect. Attitudes of this kind are not devoid of cognitive content. They make sense only if one can think of the object of these attitudes as worthy of reverence and respect, and if we know nothing at all about that object, such attitudes are difficult to sustain.

Hume's Philo appears to think that unless we can posit an identifiable similarity between a word, such as "wisdom," applied to a human case and "wisdom" applied to God, we are using the word only to express an attitude. But what is going on in the case of divine attributes is a bit more complicated. The category of agency that is applied to God is not identical with human agency. It is more general, encompassing any entity capable of purposive action. Responding to God as an initiator of purposive action involves using the terminology we have available for purposive agents. But we are capable of using that terminology with the realization that its meaning will be different when applied to a kind of intelligence that is far beyond human comprehension.

When a being of incommensurable intelligence is described as wise, there is, of course, a range of implied positive attitudes. But the appropriateness of those attitudes depends on the judgment that divine purposiveness is not arbitrary or capricious, but is the product of a comprehensive understanding that takes into account relevant facts and values. Such a judgment is not a claim to comprehend divine wisdom or to explain how it is exemplified in every circumstance. But neither is it entirely devoid of cognitive content. When believers apply the concept of agency, they use terminology that has specific meanings when applied to human agency, but is less clear when extended to a superhuman agent. But underlying all this language are some cognitive claims about a being who is capable of purposive behavior.

Philosophers have proposed theories of the nature of language about psychological attributes that are applied to God. Aquinas proposed the theory of analogy, as a way of saying that the words communicate something, even if their meanings differ significantly from their meaning in a human application. William Alston invokes the theory of functionalism to suggest that psychological terms when applied to human beings can be understood in terms of a function played in regulating behavior. He suggests that when applied to God words like "knowledge," "love," or "forgiveness" should be understood as referring to whatever performs an equivalent function in relation to divine behavior.[16] Such theories can be challenged, but whether or not one has a particular account of the nature of theistic language, it is important to recognize that these theories are attempts to steer a course between saying that the words have no cognitive content at all and saying that they give a precise and determinate understanding of the divine nature. Such a course is necessary for the coherence of a viable theistic religious outlook.

Even Kant, who was a major opponent of the idea that we can apply our concepts to God to gain understanding, finds himself invoking God as an agent who is able to discern what needs to be done to bring about a harmony between virtue and happiness and has the power to bring about the appropriate correlation. Kant claims that we can "think a supersensible being, without at the same time meaning to cognize it theoretically …."[17] Apparently he wants to deny a certain kind of knowledge about the divine nature, but he wants to keep the template of personal agency, and even commend some of its uses in thinking about how to live. It appears that in his own way he is trying to steer a similar course between overconfidence and a flat denial of the possibility of theological claims.

But isn't any application of terms from human psychology to God anthropomorphic? Furthermore, since our thinking about agency inevitably makes use of human psychology, isn't it anthropomorphic to think of God as an agent? Admittedly the qualifications that a theistic tradition develops will move the idea of God away from a very close comparison to human beings, but when we think of God as having knowledge or purposes, doesn't that necessarily mean thinking of God as in some way like us? Perhaps it does, and it is understandable that the wish to cleanse our language of inappropriate anthropomorphism might lead us to question the idea of God as an agent. On the other hand, the claim that God is not an agent because such an attribution is too anthropomorphic amounts to a rejection of the idea that God is capable of purposive activity. If God is capable of purposive activity, then using the agency template may be more appropriate than any alternative way we have of speaking about God.

Alternatives to God as Agent

There are, of course, alternatives to conceiving the ultimate reality by means of the template of personal agency. But insofar as God is thought of as a higher order of perfection, our resources for representing that perfection without the agency model are limited. The typical approach is to represent the perfect by way of contrast with some aspect of the experiential order that is thought of as inferior. Hence, for example, God might be thought of as a Unity underlying the diversity of our world. The nature of a unifying source is something we might get hints of in a mystical experience in which phenomenal features of our world drop away, but what is glimpsed is usually thought to be beyond our capacities to describe.

Plotinus calls the ultimate reality the One or the Good. The world is a product of an emanation from this perfect source, described in terms of analogies like the overflow of water or the radiation of light. The farther away from the source, the less of divine perfection anything possesses, but insofar as human beings possess something of the divine in their souls, they can recognize that their true destiny is to turn away from the world and toward the source. When the higher order of perfection is thought of by way of contrast with our kind of existence, it is tempting to disvalue the lower order. A theistic account that proclaims the created order to be purposively produced by a good agent may declare that order to be good, even if flawed. By contrast Plotinus' thought would lead us to think of embodied existence as a relatively unfortunate condition from which we need to escape.[18]

The tendency to disvalue embodied existence is also apparent in the Advaita Vedanta form of Hinduism. Shankara distinguishes between an ultimate (Brahman) with qualities (*saguna*) and without qualities (*nirguna*). He acknowledges the legitimacy of characterizing God with the personal language of agency, but claims that there is a deeper reality or a fuller truth in which all attributions are superseded. The truly ultimate is something to which none of the distinctions that arise in our thinking or experience apply. Furthermore, the level at which we think of ourselves as individual beings reflects a kind of confusion. The fuller truth is that Brahman without qualities is the only reality and the appearance of separate existence in an independent world is an illusion from which we need to be freed. The world is neither God's creation, nor is it an emanation from God. It is instead a kind of appearance that we can recognize as such by discovering a meditative experience in which the distinction between subject and object melts away. God might be compared to an infinite ocean of being in which apparent individuality dissolves.[19]

For both views the question could be raised as to whether the ultimate source should be characterized as impersonal. Both views are clearly attempts to get to a level of reality more ultimate than agency, but it is misleading to say that this level should be characterized as impersonal in contrast to something personal. Rather the point of both views is that there is a level of reality at which distinctions of this sort fail. At this level it is a certain kind of experience that points to something beyond what our language equips us to describe, but which we can nevertheless recognize as the perfect or fully real source.

Perhaps there is a thin line between refusing to use the language of personal agency because any conception of an agent we could have would not do justice to the divine reality and using the language of agency, but invoking qualifications that serve as reminders of the inadequacy of human terms and conceptions. But there is an important practical difference. Rejection of the language of agency tends toward the kind of religion in which one may make the ultimate an object of aspiration and seek to be united with it (or recognize a union that already exists). The use of the language of agency supports the kind of religion in which the divine can be understood as a subject to which one may respond in ways analogous to responses to other persons.

God as Object and Subject

The question of whether to think of the ultimate in more personal terms or as something that can be an object of aspiration, but not of interpersonal response, is closely related to the question of what sort of religious experience should be given primacy. The kind of mystical experience in which the individual is swallowed up into a larger whole might suggest an ultimate that is beyond the personal. Numinous experiences in which a person confronts something overwhelming, but apparently purposive, suggest a personal reality.[20] A view that rejects agency language can accommodate numinous experience by assigning it to a lower level. A view that uses agency language can accommodate monistic mystical experience as an indication of depths of the divine reality that are beyond comprehension.

Either a divine agent or an ultimate thought of without the language of agency would be beyond comprehension. But with a personal ultimate there is an additional layer of complexity. It's not just that God does not fit well into any category we have for descriptive purposes. It is that trying to conceive of God as a subject alters the project of trying to gain an understanding of God. Whatever understanding I might gain will be in the wider context of interpersonal relationship. I can study a rock formation purely as an object. But when I try to understand something that I recognize as exhibiting personal agency that way, I am no longer just a knower. My pursuit of knowledge is in a context in which factors other than my concern to know become relevant.

One such factor is that I may myself be an object of knowledge in relation to the other person. Hence, understanding another person may mean grasping that person's beliefs, attitudes, and desires in relation to me. I may not be able to take myself out of the equation and assume that the understanding I gain is unrelated to whether the person regards me as a threat or desires to impress me or hopes to get something from me. Another important consideration is the relevance of an ethical relation between me and the other person. That person may have justifiable claims on me with regard to how I act or fail to act. What I am aware of when I understand the other person is bound up with what I recognize about what attitudes to adopt and what I should do.

Some writers in theistic traditions have suggested that God cannot be an object of knowledge at all. The idea is that humans encounter God as a subject and can know God only as a subject to whom they relate in particular activities such as prayer and worship. Abraham Heschel, developing the thought of Martin Buber, contrasts a philosophical approach to God in which the goal is to comprehend some object with a prophetic approach in which one becomes aware of being an object of another's knowledge and concern. Given such a situation, Heschel claims that to think of God as an object of investigation is both futile and presumptuous. Alternatively, to think of yourself as being known by God and to be the recipient of God's demands is to discover a kind of knowledge that is available to human beings. Heschel goes so far as to say that what humans can know about God is limited to knowing what God asks of us.[21]

Heschel might be viewed as exaggerating in order to make a point. In order to respond to God's demands, one must presuppose that they are authoritative demands. To respond to God in worship presupposes that God is worthy of worship. Heschel clearly wants to guard against thinking that humans can comprehend the divine nature, but he needs to be able to accept some characterizations of God as better, or more legitimate, than other characterizations. He emphasizes himself that humans are the objects of God's passionate concern, and saying this involves a portrayal of God. Nevertheless, even if there can be limited and fairly abstract ways of characterizing God, thinking of God as a proper object for theorizing might be viewed as a way of missing the point. If we think of God as an agent who knows all about us and has purposes in relation to us, we do not show our comprehension of these truths by using them to form a theory, but by our attitudes and actions. If knowing about God means recognizing a relationship to God that is best characterized in interpersonal terms, the kind of knowledge that takes center stage is a practical knowledge of how to respond to God.

Responding to God as a personal agent does not eliminate the need to have some ways of thinking about God's nature. But when the task at hand is viewed in relational terms, the form of thought needed looks more like the poetic images of scriptural traditions than the typical categories of a metaphysical system. A term such as "creator" may seem hopelessly imprecise and anthropomorphic to a metaphysician, who might seek to translate it into some more abstract category. But the likely result of the translation process is to lose much of the religious significance of the term. It is the capacity of the poetic terminology to engage an individual in a way that is conducive to experiential responses that is vital. If the metaphysical terminology is subordinated to a religious understanding that preserves the primacy of personal language, it can have its place. But when metaphysical language displaces the personal and poetic, the purposes and concerns underlying religious language are altered.

For someone who is primarily concerned to describe God in precise and straightforward language, it may be frustrating to hear anthropomorphic characterizations of God that by countless qualifications appear to melt away into an acknowledgment of a mystery that is beyond human understanding. But from the point of view of one who becomes aware of a divine other, a response of praise and obedience does not depend on getting past metaphorical and figurative ways of understanding to an understanding in which elements of mystery are resolved. In the *Confessions* Augustine asks, "What then is the God I worship?"[22] In answer he recites a number of traditional characterizations of God, many of which he puts in paradoxical form. Addressing God in prayer he says,

> You love, but are not inflamed with passion; you are jealous, yet free from care; you repent, but do not sorrow; you grow angry, but remain tranquil. You change your works, but do not change your plan: you take back what you

find, although you never lost it: you are never in want, but you rejoice in gain; you are never covetous, yet you exact usury; … You pay debts, although you owe no man anything; you cancel debts, and lose nothing.[23]

Augustine is acutely aware that the scriptural tradition he is utilizing generates countless puzzles, but he regards the paradoxical nature of the language as a not altogether surprising result of the fact that he is speaking about a reality that no language is adequate to describe.

Within a relational context there is room for acknowledging that human representations of a transcendent agent are partial, rough, and even simplistic. In fact gaining an appreciation of the inadequacy of human representations may itself contribute to the humility needed for a proper response. Augustine freely confesses his inability to grasp the divine nature, yet what he is seeking is less a matter of precise terminology and more a matter of having the impediments within him removed so that he may experientially know and respond appropriately to a reality that is the object of his desires, even if it is beyond his comprehension.

If the legitimacy of using the agency template is allowed and is combined with instructions from a tradition in which paradigmatic experiences are taken to reveal something of the nature of God, believers have a great deal of guidance about how to respond to God. In relying on particular ways of thinking and particular practices to connect them to the ultimate, reflective believers may recognize that their understanding of the nature of God is very limited. But the name of the game is not understanding for its own sake. It is gaining enough understanding to harmonize one's life with an ultimate reality of highest value. It might be imagined that a belief in something that is not fully understood would have little effect on a person's life. But in fact belief in the kind of transcendence we call God has a major practical significance for how we experience the world and how we live our lives.

Notes

1   Revised Standard Version.
2   Todd Tremlin, *Minds and Gods: The Cognitive Foundations of Religion* (Oxford: Oxford University Press, 2006), 101. The use of this quotation as an epigraph is by permission of Oxford University Press.
3   CBS Television, 2003–5
4   Edwin Abbott, *Flatland* (Princeton: Princeton University Press, 1991).

5   Thomas Aquinas, *Summa Theologiae* (London: Blackfriars, 1964), vol. 3, 57 (Ia q.13 a 3).
6   Tremlin, 68.
7   Pascal Boyer, *Religion Explained: The Evolutionary Origins of Religious Thought* (New York: Basic Books, 2001).
8   Robert Coles, *The Spiritual Life of Children* (Boston: Houghton Mifflin Company, 1990), 69ff.
9   Xenophanes, in Philip Wheelwright, *The Presocratics* (New York: The Odyssey Press, Inc., 1966), 33 (Fragment 7).
10   Exodus 32:10, Revised Standard Version.
11   Exodus 32:14, Revised Standard Version.
12   Anselm, *Proslogium* in *St Anselm: Basic Writings*, 2nd edn. and trans. S. N. Deane (La Salle, IL: Open Court Publishing Company, 1962), 7.
13   Anselm, 11.
14   I take up the question of divine power in relation to evil in Chapter 9.
15   David Hume, *Dialogues Concerning Natural Religion*, ed. Norman Kemp Smith (Indianapolis: The Bobbs-Merrill Company, 1947), 142.
16   William P. Alston, "Functionalism and Theological Language," reprinted in William P. Alston, *Divine Nature and Human Language* (Ithaca: Cornell University Press, 1989), 64–80.
17   Immanuel Kant, *Critique of Judgment*, in *Kant Selections*, trans. J. H. Bernard, ed. Theodore Greene (New York: Charles Scribner's Sons, 1929), 523–4.
18   Plotinus, *Enneads*, in *The Essential Plotinus: Representative Treatises from the Enneads*, 2nd edn., ed. and trans. Elmer O'Brien (Indianapolis: Hackett Publishing Company, 1975).
19   Shankara, *Brahmasutrabhasya*, in *A Sourceboook of Advaita Vedanta*, ed. Eliot Deutsch and J. A. B. van Buitenen (Honolulu: University of Hawaii Press, 1971).
20   The classic discussion of numinous experience is in Rudolf Otto, *The Idea of the Holy*, trans. John W. Harvey (Oxford: Oxford University Press, 1923).
21   Abraham Heschel, *Man Is Not Alone: A Philosophy of Religion* (New York: Farrar, Straus, and Giroux, 1951), 128–9.
22   Augustine, *The Confessions of St. Augustine*, trans. John K. Ryan (New York: Doubleday and Company, 1960), 45 (I, 4).
23   Augustine, 45, (I, 4).

7

Naturalistic Stories

"When I became convinced that the Universe is natural – that all ghosts and gods are myths, there entered into my brain ... the joy of freedom ... I was free – free to think, to express my thoughts ... free to live for myself and those I loved ... free to investigate, to guess and dream and hope – free to judge and determine for myself – free to reject all ignorant and cruel creeds, all the 'inspired' books that savages have produced ... free from the fear of eternal pain ... I stood erect and fearlessly, joyously, faced all worlds." (Robert Ingersoll[1])

"... religious people have a thirst for things that are against reason ... We ... who thirst for reason want to look our experiences as straight in the eye as if they represented a scientific experiment, hour after hour, day after day." (Friedrich Nietzsche[2])

It can be a profound relief to discover that you can reject the existence of something that you view as a source of worry. Imagine spending much of your time trying to protect yourself against acts of witchcraft by your neighbors, believing that they have magical powers to do you harm. Coming to believe that none of your neighbors actually have such powers might be a powerfully liberating experience. Now you can dispense with a great deal of what you have come to view as wasted activity. You can devote yourself to better things.

Some people think about belief in God in a similar way. To one who has become skeptical about God, the belief can seem like a source of unnecessary anxiety that distracts our attention from improving our lives individually and collectively, wasting enormous amounts of time and energy. Even worse, it can support dogmatic forms of intolerance and oppressive power structures. It is understandable why some might conclude that people would be better off if they could lay aside any beliefs about supernatural beings and free themselves from obsessions about a realm beyond.

The ancient philosopher Epicurus reveals a concern to liberate people from the anxiety-producing religious beliefs of his time when he lists fear of death and fear of the gods as primary obstacles to achieving peace of mind. With regard to fear of death, he offers arguments to show that when we are thinking clearly, we will realize that death (nonexistence) is not something to be feared. As for the gods, he claims that they have their own concerns and no real interest in human life. They are not at all like the beings described in religious stories who send blessings and punishments to humans. Instead they are happy, immortal beings who live wonderful, trouble-free lives. They have better things to do than bother with creatures like us.[3]

Epicurus' philosophy is a good example of a naturalistic life-orienting story. The story he tells combines an account of what is real with a teaching about what is important in life and how we should live. The account of ultimate reality is adopted from the presocratic philosopher Democritus. Reality consists of atoms in empty space. Our world was formed through a process of motion, resulting in various combinations of atoms, some of which have a relative stability. People have souls, but the souls are a special kind of atoms. Even the gods, like everything else, are composed of atoms. It might seem that in allowing the existence of gods, Epicurus should be thought of as telling a supernaturalistic story. However, the gods do not transcend the natural order. They are material beings like us, only made of better material. The ultimate nature of things is revealed by a story about atoms joining together in various random combinations through a natural process to form the familiar world.

Epicurus uses his picture of reality to liberate us to pursue something we are interested in anyway: our own pleasure. Given our existence as temporary combinations of atoms, there is no higher end to be sought than seeking pleasure and avoiding pain and no need to trouble ourselves with tales of realms beyond our own. So we are released to find whatever enjoyments arc available; however, we are advised to do it intelligently. Some pleasures should be avoided because they lead to more suffering in the long run. Generally Epicurus advocates a life of simple pleasures, including the pleasures of friendly conversation with a few like-minded people. He advises against a life of immoderation and against those involvements that are likely to bring excessive trouble and worry along with any pleasures. Instead we should learn to appreciate the enjoyments that are readily available and carry with them less risk.

Naturalistic life-orienting stories, like religious life-orienting stories, portray a way of life that connects with our motivations. In the case of Epicurus the motivation to seek pleasure and peace of mind are prominent. But a naturalistic story might appeal to other motivations. Naturalists typically see themselves as facing up to the truth and rejecting comforting illusions or superstitions, hence, the courage to accept the truth, whether comforting or not, is often an undercurrent in the appeal of a naturalistic story. Sometimes naturalists appeal to our desire for independence from authority and the freedom to shape our own way of life. In contrast with Epicurus' self-centered emphasis, some naturalists appeal to concerns to build a better society or live in harmony with the natural world. As with religious stories, a naturalistic portrayal of the kind of life that is desirable is understood against the backdrop of an account of the way things are that is supposed to make the desired way of living seem sensible and attractive.

Naturalism, Science, and Scientism

A life-orienting story that is recognizably naturalistic both affirms and denies something. It affirms the existence of a realm called nature, and it denies the existence of any transcendent order beyond the natural realm. Of course, what exactly is affirmed and what is denied depends on how nature is conceived. If we are told that there is no supernatural realm, we should understand that to mean the elimination of paradigmatic supernatural entities, such as God. But could nature include immaterial minds or could there be the sort of freedom that produces events that are not fully explainable in causal terms? Might nature allow for strange phenomena such as telepathy or psychokinesis? It all depends on what a particular naturalist is willing to recognize as a part of nature.

Many naturalists are reductionists who think that only what can be accounted for in terms of law-like regularities describing the behavior of elementary material entities should be recognized as real. But a naturalist could allow for the possibility of emergent properties that were not manifest until objects reached a certain level of complexity. In complex entities like brains, it might be thought, we see something fully natural, but capable of physical effects that are not fully accountable in terms of regularities we can attribute to the behavior of component parts. To understand what is happening in a creature capable of conscious experience and choice, a naturalist might judge, we have to utilize higher-level concepts appropriate to the kind of reality in question.

Whether one gives a reductive or a nonreductive account, naturalism calls for some specification of the limits of the realm of nature. Contemporary naturalists tend to delineate the limits by appealing to science. Nature is composed of the kinds of entities and powers that are recognized in the explanations of natural science. One puzzle about appealing to science as the arbiter of the limits of nature is whether the scientific norm is supposed to be what science currently teaches or perhaps a hypothetical more advanced science of the future. It is well known that scientific findings are subject to change, and while some changes amount to gradual accretions of new information, there are also cases of radical upheaval in scientific understandings. One with confidence in scientific method is likely to believe that over time science produces results that get nearer to the truth, but identifying the scientific conclusions of any particular era with the ultimate conclusions of science ignores the possibility of further significant advance.

On the other hand, identifying the limits of nature by appealing to some hypothetical future account to which we have no access means leaving the account of nature to be accepted as indeterminate. Perhaps the best policy for a naturalist to follow would be to accept the findings of contemporary science as a tentative account of what nature is and is capable of, but to recognize that the account may have to be modified in the future. A naturalist might be fairly confident that future modifications will leave some core understandings untouched and use current understandings as a guide to what to believe about the natural world. So, for example, a naturalist might note that there is no way that a phenomenon like telepathy could be accounted for, given our current understanding of how the physical world operates, and reject the possibility on those grounds.

For related reasons a naturalist might be confident that science is not going to establish the existence of God. Given our understandings of what counts as an acceptable scientific explanation, God is not the kind of entity that would qualify. This conclusion does not seem particularly striking. God is not generally conceived to be a physical entity within the system of nature. Trying to understand the operation of that system would not be enhanced by positing a transcendent being whose effects are not predictable or testable. However, for a scientific naturalist the conclusion that God is not something within the natural order to be tested by the empirical methods of science means that God must be relegated to the class of nonexistent things, since naturalists recognize nothing beyond the natural order.

The idea that only nature exists and that science decides what is within the realm of nature suggests an affinity between naturalism and scientism. The term "scientism" has been used in a variety of ways, but on one account scientism is the view that the only acceptable truth claims about reality are those that are justified by the methods of science.[4] Although someone who accepts this form of scientism would presumably be accepting naturalism, it is entirely possible to be a naturalist and reject scientism. Thinking that there is no reality beyond nature does not commit one to thinking that only science can give us truth about reality.

Furthermore, the most plausible versions of naturalism will be those that reject scientism (as defined above). As Mary Midgley puts it,

> Science cannot stand alone. We cannot believe its propositions without first believing in a great many other startling things, such as the existence of the external world, the reliability of our senses, memory and informants, and the validity of logic. If we do believe in these things, we already have a world far wider than that of science.[5]

We learn to trust our senses and form introspective judgments well before we acquire the specialized skills involved in scientific procedure. We learn how to operate in the physical world as well as within our cultural and interpersonal world. Much of the knowledge we are able to acquire depends upon learning to recognize and interpret meaning as expressed in a variety of cultural forms. Included in the knowledge that is logically prior to scientific investigation is an awareness of value that enables us to pick out what is relevant in various contexts and make choices about what to do. While some of our prescientific beliefs can be revised in the light of scientific discovery, the project of forming beliefs entirely on the basis of science is misguided and futile.

So if the strongest form of naturalism is not based on the scientistic idea that science is the only way to know, why think that naturalism is true? Perhaps the best way to understand the inclination to think naturalistically is to see it as rooted in a distrust or suspicion of sources of belief other than empirical investigation of the kind paradigmatically exemplified in the natural sciences. Some sources may be rejected altogether, and others may be accepted insofar as they cohere with the results of empirical investigation. One naturalist writes,

> At the heart of naturalism is a commitment to a way of knowing about the world, a way of deciding what exists and how things fit together. This is the way of science and evidence – a rational, empirical stance about belief that requires us to question faith, tradition, authority, revelation and intuition as reliable guides to reality.[6]

Similarly, Michael Rea has suggested that the most charitable understanding of naturalism is to view it as a research program involving acceptance of a set of methodological dispositions.[7] The naturalistic research program treats the methods of natural science as a basic source of knowledge and rejects or at least devalues other potential sources.

But depending on what weight is given to other sources, this approach can lead us back to scientism. In order to judge whether the methodological commitment is really different from scientism, we need to know the extent to which sources other than empirical investigation might be allowed to operate. Naturalists clearly want to give a kind of primacy to the results of scientific study, but allowing that primacy to have substantive significance, while giving some room for ways of knowing other than empirical testability can be a difficult balancing act. When the primacy of science is overemphasized, naturalism collapses into a self-refuting scientism or into a view that is unable to account for much of what we believe with a high degree of confidence.

Furthermore, it is not quite accurate to characterize the naturalist view as involving a rejection of faith, tradition, or authority, for naturalism involves a trust in the authority of communally accepted modes of empirical investigation. One who learns to do science is initiated into a tradition that relies on a set of beliefs, skills, practices, and values that are passed on to aspiring scientists. Much of what is scientifically acceptable is determined by judgments in accordance with standards that respected members of the scientific community have applied in paradigmatic ways and that are internalized by those who are socialized into scientific ways of thinking. The idea that science is a way to bypass tradition entirely fails to take into account how science itself is a human activity that depends on fundamental assumptions, as well as paradigmatic practices and values. Rather than thinking of naturalism as rejecting tradition as a source of knowledge, it would be better to think of it as affirming one kind of tradition over others.

Since naturalists rely heavily on science, they sometimes mistakenly assume that their views of reality carry the authority of science. However, it is a logical leap to move from the account of the world given by science to the conclusion that the categories and explanations of science are sufficient for understanding reality. Science itself cannot make this kind of claim, since it has no way to investigate it through scientific methods. Science studies the natural world insofar as that world can be thought of as a physical system, and scientific success in thinking in this way about the natural order may tempt one to conclude that reality is no more than a physical system. But whatever the status of that conclusion, it is not a conclusion of science. We can easily imagine a theist accepting the full range of scientific procedures and conclusions and understanding what science says within the context of a theistic account of reality.

While a naturalistic view of reality can be defended as a metaphysical hypothesis, the confidence with which it is believed often exceeds what we might expect such theorizing to produce. It is often a loss of confidence in any available religious story that convinces people that some naturalistic story must be correct. Needing some functional equivalent for a religious life-orienting story, one might view a naturalistic account to be the best available. Not to be underestimated as well is the way naturalism can come to seem plausible to someone who learns to practice intellectual disciplines that bracket ways of thinking other than naturalistic ones. The habits of thought acquired by someone who is inducted into a methodological naturalism, utilized in scientific work, can facilitate the shift to thinking of naturalism not just as a method that is useful for certain purposes, but as the truth.

The Naturalist Vision

Trusting science to provide a comprehensive account of reality does not by itself give one a life-orienting story, since science does not teach us how to live. What science teaches is, of course, relevant to thinking about what to do, but there are many ways of life compatible with understanding the world in scientific terms, and the naturalist addition that those terms are ultimate and complete is still compatible with many possible understandings about how to live. Some account of what attitudes to take toward the naturalist vision, as well as an account of the significance of the naturalist view for practical conduct, is needed before a naturalistic understanding can be shaped into a way of life.

What are we to make of a world naturalistically described? Some naturalists view the announcement that nature is all there is with unequivocal exhilaration. It is incredibly good news that there is nothing beyond the natural order and that we may view ourselves simply as part of that order. In contrast to religious stories of the nature of things a naturalistic story, for example, might present the prospect of rejecting authoritarian structures or purposes that we don't embrace. It might be thought conducive to achieving real autonomy and creativity. The exhilaration that some naturalists feel is often the reverse side of a significant antipathy for a theistic picture of things. Thomas Nagel confesses,

> I want atheism to be true and am made uneasy by the fact that some of the most intelligent and well-informed people I know are religious believers. It isn't just that I don't believe in God and, naturally, hope I'm right in my belief. It's that I hope there is no God! I don't want there to be a God; I don't want the universe to be like that.[8]

On the other hand, there are naturalists who view their understanding of reality with a sense of disappointment or even tragedy. Camus thought that human existence in a universe that could not fulfill our inevitable passions produced absurdity. He urged a practice of consciously facing up to and maintaining awareness of the full absurdity of our lives, a stance requiring continual reminders to combat our strategies of avoidance.[9] Bertrand Russell described a sense of alienation from a natural order that had no congruence with or awareness of our human values. He thinks of humans as heroically clinging to their values in superiority to the mindless natural order that will ultimately wipe out any of our achievements.[10] Physicist Stephen Weinberg expresses a kind of nostalgia for a religious vision he is unable to accept. He writes,

> It would be wonderful to find in the laws of nature a plan prepared by a concerned creator in which human beings played some special role. I find sadness in doubting that we will. There are some among my scientific colleagues who say that the contemplation of nature gives them all the spiritual satisfaction that others have found in a belief in an interested God. Some of them may even feel that way. I do not.[11]

John Haught uses the term "sober naturalist" for naturalists who find their own vision of the way things are a pessimistic one. He calls those who find the naturalist vision to be fully satisfying "sunny naturalists."[12] Either attitude could be the basis for a life-orienting story. We might either be told that there is a harsh reality to which we must adjust or told that there is a wonderful truth about things that we can wholeheartedly embrace.

Sunny naturalists often contrast the desirable possibilities of their view with undesirable aspects of a religious story. One such naturalist speaks of the positive consequences for character and behavior of viewing ourselves as part of the natural order and thinking of all that happens as flowing from various natural causes:

> … since we understand we aren't the ultimate originators of ourselves or our behavior, we can't take credit or blame for who we are or what we do. This reduces unwarranted feelings of moral superiority, pride, shame and guilt, while encouraging self-acceptance. And since we see *others* as fully caused, for instance substance abusers, criminal offenders, the destitute and homeless, we might become less blaming, less punitive and more empathetic and understanding. People don't create themselves, so responsibility for their character and behavior isn't ultimately theirs, but is distributed over the many causal factors that shaped them.[13]

Understanding that we are products of genetics and environment, we are told, "grounds a naturalistic ethics of compassion that guides personal behavior and motivates progressive social policy. This is unapologetically *humanistic* naturalism."[14]

Two observations seem relevant to such an assessment. One is that it presupposes a fairly standard account of what constitutes good and bad character and behavior. Humility is good; prideful superiority is bad. Sympathetic understanding of others is good; smug condemnation is bad. Such an ethical understanding does not come from empirical investigation, but is acquired in some other way. A second observation is that the rosy picture of behavior that is thought to follow from naturalism is hopelessly incoherent. If I give up thinking of people as responsible agents, deserving of blame or credit, how is it that I will respond to others with sympathetic understanding? I might respond with understanding to someone when I come to realize how difficult it was for that person in that situation to behave well. But if I think that all behavior is equally excusable, the likely response seems more like indifference. It is less like responding to a person and more like responding to an inevitable force of nature. I can't blame him, but neither can I excuse him in the way we do with persons of diminished responsibility. It is only when we can think of human actions in ways that distinguish them from events in a causal chain that we can view some actions as unduly restricted by causal pressures.

Furthermore, if I give up thinking of myself as a responsible agent, subject to blame and praise and drop any guilt feelings, replacing these feelings with self-acceptance, is that supposed to make my behavior toward others better? Suppose I think of their interests as unimportant compared to my own. Perhaps I should just accept that this is the way I am and get on with pushing them aside. But if I think I should not accept just any attitude or behavior in myself, I have to regard my attitudes and behaviors as subject to appraisal that might result in judging them unworthy. In other words I have to be more selective in my self-acceptance.

Naturalists don't have to be saddled with the kind of incoherence displayed in using ethical appraisal in a way that undermines its use. But this sort of incoherence is likely to arise for any naturalist who thinks that scientific understanding is a replacement for nonscientific modes of thought through which we make sense of our lives as moral beings. We can think of ourselves as objects within the natural order, but when we live our lives, we need to think of ourselves and others in terms that have no place within scientific discourse. We are also subjects who find ourselves relying on moral sensibilities to determine what is worthy and what is required. The challenge for naturalists is to leave room for regarding those sensibilities as providing genuine insight, for any coherent account of a naturalistic way of life will depend upon treating as authoritative those sensibilities that allow us to recognize the worth of that way of life and live in accordance with the vision of the good it prescribes.

The Appeal of a Nonreligious Way of Life

One way to characterize a naturalistic way of life is to contrast it with a theistic religious way of life. Naturalists often take this approach, typically to show the value of dispensing with unproductive types of behavior. For example a naturalist might say that his way of life does not involve worship of a deity or ritualistic acts intended to gain the deity's blessings. It rejects solicitation of favors by means of prayer. It does not involve hope or preparation for a life beyond this one. More generally, a naturalist will repudiate any practices that would presuppose belief in a divine power beyond the natural order.

Appreciating a way of life that leaves off such activities would be an expected result of becoming convinced of their futility. If a naturalist vision of reality is true, then the futility of many religious activities should be apparent, but what convinces a person that there is no transcendent power in relation to which religious practices might make sense? Often it is a matter of coming to view religious beliefs in a way that makes them look implausible. Argument can have a role here, but more important than any direct argument against a deity is acquiring a story that puts the religious enterprise in an unflattering light. For example, naturalists typically think of religious beliefs as arising out of a primitive or immature way of thinking. In contrast to someone who has a scientific understanding, the religious person is relying on hypotheses that might have seemed reasonable in an age without much real knowledge of how the world actually works. But now that we know so much more about natural causes, we can dispense with appeals to supernatural phenomena. If religion can be seen as attempting to do poorly something that science does well, then giving up religious beliefs and practices is a matter of moving beyond primitive ignorance.

The power of such a story comes not from whether we can verify its truth, but from the way it can structure our perceptions in a form that provokes normative responses. What makes a naturalistic story of a reality without transcendence attractive is the sense that there is a rational way to know things that is exhibited in science and that religion exhibits something inferior that we ought to repudiate. Implicit in this account is an appeal to our moral sense that we should not just believe what suits us or what seems comforting, but that there are standards of believing that don't allow for the extravagant tales told by religion. Hence, rejecting religion is portrayed as an essential part of living in accordance with certain kinds of epistemological and ethical ideals. What is ironic is that the stories used to undermine religious views depend upon claims that a genuinely austere ideal of rationality would have to view with suspicion. If they seem plausible, it is surely not because they appeal to the kind of evidence evaluation characteristic of science. Rather we are convinced by looking through the lens these stories provide and finding a satisfying order. In other words the process looks suspiciously like the way people acquire religious faith.

Naturalist Values

While an account of a naturalistic way of life will certainly be developed in contrast with the religious activities that it repudiates, this kind of characterization by itself can sound as if a naturalist is chiefly concerned about avoiding certain types of activity. To get a fuller picture, we need to know what a naturalist thinks it worthwhile to do. A general answer that many naturalists could endorse is that accepting nature as the only reality leaves room for a variety of activities that humans can recognize as worthwhile. A naturalist might seek to acquire knowledge and contribute to human understanding. A naturalist might develop friendships and loving relationships. A naturalist could seek experiences of beauty and attempt to develop talents and skills. All these pursuits can be recognized as valuable or worthwhile from a human point of view. Some naturalists would want to add that their view allows for a type of spirituality or a sense of reverence, but with a this-worldly, rather than an other-worldly focus.

Part of the difficulty in spelling out a naturalistic way of life is that a commitment to a naturalistic account of reality does not by itself commit one to any particular understanding of how to live. The view of reality has to be grafted onto a set of intuitions about such things as what it is good to do or to avoid, what motivations are worthy or unworthy, and what character traits should be cultivated. It is hard to say much about naturalism as a life-orienting story until a fuller account is given of the particular value intuitions with which it is connected. A naturalistic way of life like Epicurus' egoistic hedonism will clearly be very different from one that involves a central concern for universal justice. The relatively bare core naturalist story of human emergence and human nature taken from natural science needs to be supplemented by other stories that can connect this account with the particular way of life a naturalist might advocate.

Consider, for example, a naturalist humanism that regards improvement of the human condition as the central commitment each of us ought to have. Underlying such a view is presumably some vision of the good that gives an idea of the individual and communal conditions to be sought. We can imagine that one who is moved by this vision might be motivated to devote a great deal of time and effort working toward this end. But being moved in the requisite way is not automatic. At minimum it seems to call for some degree of optimism about the possibilities. Such optimism is likely to require ways of thinking that cannot be justified on empirical grounds. For example, it might be nourished by stories projecting expected progress toward a classless society that would transform humanity as we find it or stories that portray human tendencies toward self-destructive behaviors as potentially altered by the proper therapy.[15]

Furthermore, the view calls for some background story that makes apparent to us why human lives have the value they are alleged to have. A story making vivid the value of each human life or portraying the nobility of a life devoted to relieving suffering could inspire devotion to the recommended good. But those kinds of stories, which are common in religious views, are harder to come by for a naturalist. There is no easy link between thinking of human life as a byproduct of a mindless natural order and the thought that human life is especially important.

Enlightenment stories that portrayed human beings as having a special kind of dignity because of their rational capacity or because of their capacity for autonomous choice have functioned as a kind of secular equivalent of religious stories about humans made in the image of God and having a high destiny. But it is difficult for naturalists to hold on to such a vision in the light of their commitment to the primacy of understanding human beings scientifically. If we think of ourselves as just another animal species or if we focus on pre-rational origins of our thought processes, there is little to inspire a sense of the particular worth or dignity of human life. The point here is not that a naturalist cannot tell a story about why it is important to be concerned about human life or achieve equal justice or build a better society. It is that such a story will have to be grounded in modes of thought other than those developed in natural science and that ideas derived in this way are likely to be in tension with recognizing the primacy of scientific understandings.

Naturalism and Moral Order

Any way of life that is recognizably human will be lived within a moral order. Moral orders structure our understanding of what is right and wrong, good and bad, worthy and unworthy. We experience these orders as objective norms that provide authoritative standards by which to judge our desires, motivations, actions, and character. We also experience them subjectively through beliefs, emotions, and desires that are shaped by the normative structure.[16] Our moral reactions can be regarded as subjective expressions of some sense of the moral order in which we live. When we feel shame at acting cowardly or pride at telling a costly truth, we give indirect evidence of our conception of a moral order. When we provide help for someone who is destitute or give excuses for not providing help, we show our awareness of an order that we recognize as having a binding authority. When we decline an opportunity that we judge to be beneath our dignity or hide an action we think disreputable, we reveal something of the moral order we acknowledge.

So to convey a naturalistic way of life we need to convey the moral order presupposed by that way of life. However, orders of this kind do not make sense when viewed as a list of abstract prohibitions or aspirations. To comprehend the norms, we need to be able to articulate why they are important. For example, suppose that you respond with revulsion to the idea of eating human flesh. In trying to explain why you might suggest that human life has a certain dignity that one disregards by treating the human body as food. In trying to explicate what you mean by dignity, you might appeal to some account of what gives human beings special worth. It becomes apparent from this sort of exercise that our experience of authoritative norms is closely related to some understanding of what we take to be real. Value reactions that make sense within one understanding of reality may not make sense in another.

To explicate a naturalistic way of life we need to describe the moral order recognized by that way of life in a way that makes sense within a naturalistic conception of reality. What makes this task particularly difficult is that many of our moral reactions were developed in contexts that involved religious assumptions. So, for example, the idea of the immeasurable value of each person had a place in theistic religious stories that included conceptions of divine creation of human life and a destiny that extends beyond earthly existence. When one replaces a religious story with a naturalistic story, it can't be assumed that the moral reactions that fit in the religious context remain the same. In the nineteenth century Nietzsche expressed contempt for his contemporaries who thought they could dispense with the Christian story, but keep Christian morality in place. In his famous "God is dead" passage, he shows his scorn for the comfortable atheist who does not realize that giving up the story about God meant giving up the horizon in which Christian values made sense.[17]

Nietzsche's own alternative was to junk belief in the value of each person in favor of recognizing the superiority or nobility of a few particularly gifted individuals. He brands Christian morality as an expression of resentment by the poor, the weak, and the oppressed that attempts to bind the natural self-expression of those individuals with the capacity for real nobility and creativity. Laying aside these slave moralities opens the door for a morality worthy of a noble life. One can question whether Nietzsche's vision of moral order should be accepted. But the point to notice is his recognition of the dependence of our moral reactions on a narrative that makes them intelligible.

It has been a deep faith for many philosophers that morality is independent of religion. When a defense of this faith is viewed as necessary, it has often been thought that a retelling of Plato's *Euthyphro* arguments does the job. If divine commands aren't sufficient to establish authoritative norms, we can consider the norms on their own merit. However, considering norms on their own merit doesn't just mean thinking about abstract principles that might be viewed as foundational in some moral system. Whatever principles we have get their meaning in part by our judgments in particular cases, and the moral terms we apply in particular cases are understandable only in relation to our beliefs about factual matters. To try to separate out moral claims as if they were independent of our views of reality is to misunderstand how they function.[18]

If God is removed from an understanding of moral order, there will need to be significant adjustments of how that order is conceived. Some reactions that made sense in a theistic view of the world will drop out altogether, and others will need to be reinterpreted in the light of the new context in which they are placed. If universal human rights were thought to be connected with an order of things that is divinely ordained, it needs to be explained how those rights fit into a naturalistic story.[19] If the idea of the sacred played a significant role in understanding certain norms, the question of whether there is an adequate secular equivalent becomes relevant. In such a process there might be adjustment of moral intuitions, but adjustment could go the other way as well. Someone who is confident of particular moral reactions, but unable to make sense of them within the confines of a naturalistic story, might view this as a good reason to look for a better story.

The Place of Authoritative Norms

In addition to questions that might arise about particular norms, there are puzzles for a naturalist about how to understand any authoritative norms. Naturalists tend to idealize a way of thinking about reality in which we put certain tendencies of our nature on hold in order to assume a more objective point of view. If there are features of our world that we recognize as a product of the particular ways human senses work, we pull back from the use of categories that depend on the particularities of those capacities. So, for example, seventeenth-century physics involved adopting a point of view in which secondary qualities, such as colors, smells, sounds, and textures are dismissed from the account of the way things really are. Nature had to be understood in terms that do without forms of description that represent the world in a mind-dependent way. Philosophical critics, such as Berkeley, questioned whether any account we could give could truly be mind-independent, and thinkers such as Kant argued that the world studied by science is necessarily tied to particular ways of conceiving that depend on structures of the human mind. Nevertheless, the ideal of what Bernard Williams has called an absolute conception in which we try to describe things as they are in themselves and not just as they appear to us became a fundamental aspiration in science.[20]

When we grant primacy to this disengaged form of thought about reality that characterizes this scientific ideal, the place of values, or at least some values, becomes problematic. J. L. Mackie, starting with a naturalistic picture of the world, judged objective moral values to be "queer." They would have to have a kind of mind-independent reality like that we attribute to physical objects, yet they would be such as to have a motivating force on behavior.[21] What makes such values seem queer from a naturalistic point of view is that the disengaged perspective we assume to think about reality scientifically involves pulling back from any responses that could be described as anthropocentric in an attempt to give an account of the world as it is apart from peculiarities of the human perspective. The usefulness of this exercise is undeniable, but when it comes to objective moral values, a commitment to disregarding the anthropocentric means disregarding the moral sensibilities by which we recognize moral standards as authoritative norms.

There is no problem with interpreting some values as having a kind of derivative reality that we can reduce to something factual. Some can be regarded as individual or collective desires or as agreements devised for achieving certain desires. That a particular animal desires something is from a scientific point of view just a fact about that animal. A problem arises, however, when we try to treat all our value responses as objects to be viewed from an external perspective, for the moral responses that govern our activity and largely define our identity have the authority they do for us from the perspective we take as agents. If I come to think of the disgust I feel at adults who exploit children for their sexual gratification as a quirk of my psychology or as a product of social indoctrination, it loses the power to function for me as an indicator of a moral norm. More generally, to take my moral reactions seriously, I need to regard at least some of them as giving me insight into truths that I acknowledge as authoritative.

How should a naturalist regard the notion that we treat some norms as truth claims? One approach is to acknowledge that from the point of view of agency our value claims can seem like authoritative truths, but to treat this appearance as a kind of illusion. Forms of subjectivism and relativism that attempt to eliminate objectivity from moral claims are one version of this approach. It only seems as if we are finding truth because we are not quite aware of the cultural diversity that such claims exhibit. Once we are aware of this diversity we can give up the pretension that we are saying anything that could be objectively true. The truths are about how things seem from various cultural standpoints and have no claim to be extended beyond those standpoints. Another version of the illusion view would be to posit an explanation of why we make these judgments that shows what is really going on. Sociobiological explanations of moral sensibilities as instruments for gene replication which cause us to think in a certain way are an example. Michael Ruse claims, "Darwinian theory shows that in fact morality is a function of (subjective) feelings, but it shows also that we have (and must have) the illusion of objectivity.... In a sense, therefore, morality is a collective illusion foisted upon us by our genes."[22]

Of course, it is open for someone to claim that the way things seem from the point of view of moral phenomenology is not the way they really are. But a central problem for one who wants to get rid of authoritative norms because they do not fit easily into a naturalist ontology is to explain them in a way that does not undermine our capacity to rely on them. If we come to see ourselves as dupes of our genes or of our culture, it becomes hard to treat the deliverances of our moral sensibilities with the same seriousness. All of us live our lives on the basis of some understandings of what matters and what is vitally important. To regard such thoughts as illusions is to cripple our capacity to live coherent lives. Furthermore, an illusion theory would not be a promising basis for a naturalistic life-orienting story. Stories of this kind have to appeal to such things as the value of seeking truth or of achieving autonomy, and an account that undermines our confidence in these values undermines our ability to respond to and live in accordance with such a story.

An alternative to the type of theory that would regard our moral sensibilities as illusory is to accept them as sources of legitimate truth claims, but to point out that they can still involve a kind of human projection onto a reality that lacks values. Just as there can be objective truth to our attributions of color or sound, even though color or sound perception depends on having the right sort of sense organs, there might be objective truths about goodness that depend on having particular ways of judging value that develop in a species like ours. We can strive for agreement on our judgments, but we should recognize that our agreements depend in a crucial way on how we are wired. The sort of truth involved here is a relational truth about how a particular type of mind will perceive things.

The crucial question to ask is whether this view is sufficient to preserve the authority of our reflective moral judgments. The analogy with color sensations appeals to truths about what human beings with a particular kind of sensory capacity will perceive under designated conditions. But to treat our moral intuitions that way would mean thinking of their truth as a matter of having a certain kind of reaction under designated conditions. So, for example, someone with appropriately trained moral sensibilities might react with outrage to accounts of women being forced into prostitution. But unlike the color case, moral reactions can't be thought simply to consist of some kind of subjective awareness. The moral awareness carries with it a judgment about how things ought to be. Someone who has a moral reaction, but regards any truth claim as a claim about the subjective awareness involved in that reaction would be discounting the sense that the reaction purports to be about how things fit or fail to fit within a moral order.

The idea that the moral order is not really there, but is a human projection on what is really there, is attractive for someone who thinks that we should try to remove from the picture anything that might be tainted by subjectivity in order to discern what is really there. But what if some real things are recognizable only when looked for with the right sort of instrument? Admittedly, if there were no agents with formed moral sensibilities, no one would detect any moral order that provided insight into how things ought to be. But should we conclude from this that there is no moral order to be found or that it takes a self-aware agent to be able to detect such a thing? In the end the question may be whether we trust what our moral sensibilities apparently reveal to us.

The sense that there is a way things should be that is not merely a function of human desires or cultural constructs and that we recognize as authoritative for us does not easily fit within a naturalistic understanding of reality. To recognize such a thing as an aspect of the natural world would mean positing something that natural science has no way to detect or test for. Hence, it is understandable why a committed naturalist would be skeptical about our apparent apprehension of a moral order. But one who is not committed to the view that reality can be exhaustively understood in scientific categories may suspect that the terminology by which we understand ourselves as agents and utilize to act reveals dimensions of reality that are hidden by scientific detachment.

Is Naturalism a Faith Position?

Naturalists typically bristle when someone suggests that their view is a faith position. Julian Baggini, who defends atheism as a form of naturalism, thinks that the assumption that atheism calls for faith arises from a failure to understand how beliefs are rationally justified. People imagine that in the absence of a definitive proof for atheism something like faith must be necessary to establish it. Baggini points out that even when absolute proof is lacking there can be overwhelming evidence for one explanation over another and that talking about faith in such a case is at least misleading. On his view naturalism and the atheism it implies are simply the best explanation of the evidence.[23]

What Baggini has in mind is something like the following picture: We begin with various facts for which we might seek explanations. In explaining these facts we can either appeal to something within the natural order or to something beyond the natural order. Appealing to something supernatural is extravagant and unnecessary, since explanations that refer to nature alone give us satisfying accounts of the recognized facts.

Many theists are more than willing to accept this picture and to defend theism as a better explanation for such things as why the universe exists or why an evolutionary process capable of producing intelligent beings exists. However, it is far from obvious that the appeal of theism is based primarily on success or failure at this kind of explanation. It is tempting for an atheist to imagine that coming to believe in God would mean adopting an explanatory hypothesis to account for facts that are already accepted. But it would be better to think of acquiring this belief as a restructuring of the horizons within which experiences are understood. Imagine the possibility of someone who does not believe in authoritative obligations coming to believe that there are such things. Such a shift would not be at all like adopting an explanation for what is already understood, but would involve a claim to discern a significance or meaning that was previously unacknowledged. Whatever experiential factors triggered the apparent insight would be misconstrued if viewed as evidence to be evaluated in terms of competing explanatory hypotheses. Translating them from the experiential mode to the explanatory mode is a good way to miss what is at issue.

Similarly, evaluating experiential claims about transcendence by considering these experiences from a third-person explanatory perspective misconstrues the nature of these claims. It treats the experiential conditions that give rise to revelatory claims as data to be explained from an external point of view where we consider whether to go beyond the psychological states to posit a transcendent cause. What is easily lost here is that claims to discern signs of transcendence arise in an experiential mode. Experiential claims can be overridden by contrary evidence, but one who reflects on an experiential understanding she finds convincing need not be claiming that this understanding can be validated from a supposedly superior objective standpoint.

In response to naturalistic limits on reality to what appears from a third-person theoretical perspective in which we divest ourselves of anthropocentric responses, Charles Taylor asks, "What better measure of reality do we have in human affairs than those terms which on critical reflection and after correction of the errors we can detect make the best sense of our lives?"[24] The "making sense" that Taylor has in mind is not explaining behavior from the viewpoint of an external observer. Taking that viewpoint excludes patterns of understanding that we can't do without in understanding ourselves as deliberative agents. The terms that we use to express our moral reactions or to try to understand them are recognizably anthropocentric in that they characterize the meanings things have for us. But when we pull back from these meanings, we arrive at a world that makes no sense from the perspective of deliberation.

Taylor thinks that our account of what is real needs to encompass both understandings that we arrive at in explanatory contexts and understandings that we find essential for living our lives. He notes, however, that allowing our thought about reality to proceed from a vision of the good that moves us would not preclude the possibility of "coming to see God or the Good as essential to our best account of the human moral world."[25] What is at issue is whether it is legitimate to view insights from the deliberative perspective as potential sources for determining what is real. The naturalistic denial of such an approach hinges on a commitment to a way of understanding that is thought to be superior.

So is naturalism a faith position? While an affirmative answer can certainly be misleading, it seems clear that underlying the naturalist's view of evidence evaluation is a trust in the primacy of scientific ways of understanding.

Framing such trust is typically a variety of images and stories about what it means to be rational that venerate knowledge achieved through empirical methods and call into question alternative patterns of belief formation. Ironically, the claim that nature, defined in scientific terms, is all that exists does not seem like a promising candidate for an empirically verifiable truth. However, seen through the lens of the framing stories about rationality, the naturalistic claim gives expression to the intention to give allegiance to particular standards of rationality that are regarded as normative. This kind of allegiance at least resembles religious faith.

While naturalists reject the kind of life-orienting stories found in religions, they offer their own stories. These stories support the need to accept a fairly austere epistemological ideal and show why we should treat with suspicion claims coming from sources like religious revelation. Implicit in the appeal of any naturalist vision is a loss of confidence in religious stories. It is as we lose faith in the accounts that situate us in relation to something that transcends the empirical order that we are able to entertain a story that tells us to rein in the kind of aspirations that religious stories appeal to. But as we try on naturalistic stories to see how they fit, we should not lose sight of how these stories also take us beyond the limits of what we can verify and of how they appeal to us as beings capable of recognizing and responding to the moral orders. It is as agents who need a way of life that we have to judge whether the orientation they provide is something we can believe in.

Notes

1 Robert Ingersoll, "Why I Am An Agnostic," in *The Works of Robert G. Ingersoll*, vol. 4, Dresdon Edition (New York: C. P. Farrell, 1900), 65–6.
2 Friedrich Nietzsche, *The Gay Science*, in *The Portable Nietzsche*, ed. Walter Kaufmann (New York: Viking Press, 1954), 101 (#319).
3 Epicurus, "Letter to Menoeceus," in *Greek and Roman Philosophy after Aristotle*, ed. Jason Saunders (Toronto: Collier-Macmillan Canada, Ltd, 1966), 49–52.
4 For various ways to define scientism see Mikael Stenmark, *Scientism: Science, Ethics and Religion* (Burlington, VT: Ashgate Publishing Limited, 2001), 1–17.
5 Mary Midgley, *Science as Salvation* (London: Routledge, 1992), 108.
6 Thomas W. Clark, *Encountering Naturalism: A Worldview and Its Uses* (Somerville, MA: Center for Naturalism, 2007), 5.
7 Michael Rea, *World Without Design: The Ontological Consequences of Naturalism* (Oxford: Oxford University Press, 2004).
8 Thomas Nagel, *The Last Word* (Oxford: Oxford University Press, 1997), 130.

9   Albert Camus, *The Myth of Sisyphus and Other Essays* (New York: Vintage Books, 1955).

10 Bertrand Russell, "A Free Man's Worship," in *The Meaning of Life*, 2nd edn., ed. E. D. Klemke (Oxford: Oxford University Press, 2000), 71–7.

11 Stephen Weinberg, *Dreams of a Final Theory* (New York: Pantheon Books, 1992), 256.

12 John Haught, *Is Nature Enough? Meaning and Truth in the Age of Science* (Cambridge: Cambridge University Press, 2006), 10.

13 Clark, 3.

14 Clark, 3.

15 Erik Wielenberg offers a naturalistic version of the virtue of hope, which appeals to the power of science to improve the human situation through pharmacology. See his *Virtue and Value in a Godless Universe* (Cambridge: Cambridge University Press, 2005), 139.

16 Christian Smith, *Moral, Believing Animals: Human Personhood and Culture* (Oxford: Oxford University Press, 2003), 7–43.

17 Friedrich Nietzsche, *The Gay Science*, in *The Portable Nietzsche*, 95–6 (#125).

18 Jeffrey Stout, *Ethics After Babel: The Languages of Morals and Their Discontents* (Princeton: Princeton University Press, 1988, new postscript 2001).

19 Nicholas Wolterstorff, *Justice: Rights and Wrongs* (Princeton: Princeton University Press, 2007).

20 Bernard Williams, *Ethics and the Limits of Philosophy* (Cambridge, MA: Harvard University Press, 1985), 111.

21 J. L. Mackie, *Ethics: Inventing Right and Wrong* (New York: Penguin, 1977).

22 Michael Ruse, *Taking Darwin Seriously* (Oxford: Blackwell Publishing, 1986), 253.

23 Julian Baggini, *Atheism: A Very Short Introduction* (Oxford: Oxford University Press, 2003), 30–1.

24 Charles Taylor, *Sources of the Self: The Making of Modern Identity* (Cambridge, MA: Harvard University Press, 1989), 57.

25 Taylor, 73.

8

Theistic and Naturalistic Morality

"The attempts to inculcate morality independent of religion are like the actions of children when, wishing to move a plant which pleases them, they tear off the root ... and plant it in the earth without the root." (Leo Tolstoy[1])

"Morality is more than possible without God, it is entirely independent of him. That means that atheists are not only more than capable of leading moral lives, they may even be able to lead more moral lives than religious believers who confuse divine law and punishment with right and wrong." (Julian Baggini[2])

You can get along without all sorts of things that might have seemed essential. Some backpackers do without tents, devising other means to shelter themselves from the elements. Some couples dispense with marriage, relying on less formal understandings of the nature of their relationship. Some people study academic disciplines on their own, rather than going through standard coursework. Dispensing with what others treat as vital alters the nature of what is experienced, sometimes in ways we find satisfying and sometimes in ways that thwart our aims. The realization that you *can* do without something does not by itself tell you whether doing without it would be a wise idea. That depends on how the item dispensed with might contribute to or hamper what you are trying to do.

Discussions of the relationship between God and morality tend to focus on the question of whether there can be a morality unconnected to belief in God. Believers whose moral experience is permeated with their thinking about God have often had difficulty conceiving of morality without God. One consequence is a widespread mistrust of anyone who explicitly claims to be an atheist. In response to such suspicion, atheists often take extreme care to defend the possibility of a viable moral life that is disconnected with any kind of religious belief.[3] But deciding that atheists can coherently have a moral life does not settle the question of how belief or disbelief in God might affect the moral life, positively or negatively. Even if it is possible to have a morality that dispenses with God, we can still wonder how such a morality might differ from one in which God played a central role and whether in removing God from moral thought anything of consequence would be lost.

Some advocates of naturalistic stories maintain that not only would nothing be lost, but that a great deal is gained by removing thoughts about God from moral reflection. They sometimes claim that God is irrelevant to determining what we ought to do and what we ought to be, pointing out that we can reflect on moral behavior and moral character perfectly well without considering divine commands or divine revelation. Furthermore, they urge, thoughts about such matters can only divert us from the real sources of moral understanding. Additionally, they often argue that bringing God in distorts morality by appealing to divine sanctions or rewards to motivate moral behavior. The result is to confuse genuinely moral action with self-interested behavior. I will discuss the relevance of God to determining right action in the first part of this chapter. In the latter part of the chapter I will deal with how belief in God might be related to moral motivation.

Is God Relevant to Determining What is Right or Wrong?

A great deal of philosophical discussion displays a lack of imagination about how God and morality might be connected. In introductory philosophy textbooks it is common to encounter the question of whether God is relevant to moral reflection reduced to a discussion of whether morality rests on divine commands. The focal question becomes whether God creates right and wrong by requiring or prohibiting certain things. Discussions that go back as far as Plato demonstrate a number of problems with simple versions of this view. Are there reasons why God approves of some actions and disapproves of others? If so, then those reasons would seem to be more basic than any commands, and we could conceivably understand why something was right or wrong by grasping the reasons. Furthermore, if we can imagine the possibility of God commanding actions that we confidently judge to be cruel or unjust, could commands make these into right actions? This kind of reflection supports the conclusion that what is right or wrong is not reducible to commands by a supreme power and that our judgments of right or wrong are not fundamentally judgments of what such a power has commanded.

However, even if it is true that there is something defective about the idea that right and wrong is just a matter of what has been commanded or forbidden by a supremely powerful being, that truth would hardly decide the relevance of God to moral thinking. That particular model of the connection between God and morality is only one way of conceiving the matter, and insofar as the model is interpreted to mean that morality arises out of facts that can be described independently of any moral significance, it fails to adequately represent a theistic vision of how things are. Fundamental to that vision is a sense that the kind of reality we can describe in factual terms is rooted in a more ultimate order, whose nature manifests something of supreme value. To apprehend the kind of reality God is said to be is to apprehend a dimension in which norms like rationality and goodness are as basic as anything we might call facts.

The project of explaining morality in terms of some set of facts that are themselves devoid of moral significance fits better within a naturalistic metaphysics where particular facts, which can be characterized without value components, are offered as an account of what is ultimately real. In a theistic understanding the truth about ultimate reality is misrepresented when the value dimension is omitted. To affirm God's existence is to affirm a supreme perfection that is experienced both as an object of aspiration and as a demanding requirement. Various models can be suggested for explaining the connection between the ultimate source of moral order and the particular judgments we make, but these models are ways of representing a view that sees ultimate reality as something laden with value.

In theistic stories human beings are created with the potential for fulfilling the purposes of a being of supreme benevolence and wisdom, but with the capacity to resist them as well. Cooperating fully with the divine project calls for recognizing it as something good, not just as something authoritatively imposed, and such a recognition means being able to think about the human good in ways that do not simply reduce to enforceable commands.[4] However, the need for this kind of understanding does not make divine commands irrelevant. One who thinks of God as having benevolently produced our nature and knowing what is good for us might be receptive to the possibility that divine revelation could provide corrective insight into how that nature is fulfilled. Hence, even if a simple version of divine command theory is rejected, the potential relevance of revelatory truth need not be.

An alternative to thinking of moral norms as arising purely from divine commands is to think of them as truths about how we must live to achieve flourishing lives. Such truths depend upon the nature of human beings and the kind of environment in which we live. That we are physical beings and social beings with specifiable needs is relevant to how we should treat each other. That we have emotions requiring cultivation and discipline is relevant to the kinds of habits we need to acquire. That we have capacities for social, intellectual, and aesthetic development is relevant to what we should care about and how we should structure our collective lives. In short the norms that govern human life arise from the desirability of fulfilling potentialities for flourishing that are built into our nature as it functions within the kind of environment we inhabit. To recognize that desirability and submit to it is to acknowledge a kind of moral order that could be thought of as divinely ordained.

We become aware of aspects of this moral order through the particular moral instruction that is passed on to us by our culture. But if we are reflective, this instruction is a vehicle for awareness of truths that can be used to judge the particular norms we have been taught. If, for example, we learn a morality that conveys to us a sense of the equal value of each person, we may come to judge some practices, which our culture takes for granted, to conflict with recognizing equal value. Our awareness may be clouded by many factors, including cultural conditioning that blinds us to the effects of our individual actions and our social practices. But in varying degrees we can come to discern moral norms that we recognize as having an authority to direct and structure our lives. Just as we learn through cultural instruction to acknowledge the authority of norms of rationality, we come to understand that particular modes of conduct and ways of being are built into grasping our place in the world.

Thomas Aquinas thought that human beings were capable of knowing a great deal about right and wrong, good and bad, through the exercise of their natural powers. We can discover something of how we must behave if social life is to go well and what is needed to develop our capacities for fulfillment of various potentials. In fact Aquinas thought that this natural knowledge was instrumental to understanding how we stand in relation to

God and why we need God. Without moral knowledge we could not understand the moral significance of God's status as creator and redeemer in relation to us. Nor could we comprehend a need for God, arising from our failure to behave in ways we recognize as binding on us.

The point here is that a theist does not have to imagine human beings to be entirely ignorant of morality until specific commands come from God. A theist might well imagine that God has put into human beings the capacity to become aware of a moral order through the use of such powers as reason and empathetic reactions. However, thinking that we have some level of moral understanding that does not depend on specific revelations need not mean viewing God as irrelevant to moral thinking. If some theistic life-orienting story is true, thinking about the context of our lives in relation to God will be essential to knowing how to apply our moral understanding correctly.

Our thinking about what is right or wrong, or what is good or bad, does not occur in isolation from our understanding of the human condition and human potentials. Believing that there is no such thing as life after death, that divine assistance is out of the question, that humans are a byproduct of a causal system devoid of any purposive intentionality, affects our judgment about what could constitute flourishing lives. So also does believing that we live in a created order that is structured to allow us to achieve ends we can recognize as worthy that transcend the empirical order. What we judge it good to do and good to be depends greatly on our conception of who we are and what is possible for us, so accepting a theistic or a naturalistic life-orienting story powerfully shapes our moral assessments.

There are clearly a great many matters that we can agree upon, regardless of the life-orienting story we find compelling, and when we operate in a pluralistic society it is important to be able to talk about matters of right and wrong at a level where the agreements are prominent. We can often agree in identifying general human rights or in finding particular rules of conduct necessary or regarding particular character traits as desirable. However, this level of agreement can hide important differences that do not become apparent until someone's moral thinking appeals to disputed ways of construing the human context. Different understandings of the human condition and the human good sometimes make communication on moral matters difficult. It is easy to misconstrue what the other person is saying when it presupposes patterns of understanding that are alien to your own.

Divine Revelation and Morality

One of the most difficult things for an adherent of a naturalistic story to take seriously is the idea that some truths about how to live have been divinely revealed. Part of the problem comes from simplistic pictures of what divine revelation of moral truths might involve. Any viable account of learning from divine revelation will have to involve something much more complicated than a broadcast of timeless moral truths to a passive human audience. Whatever is communicated would have to be adapted to the needs and level of understanding of humans of a particular era, and fuller comprehension might take shape only gradually. In Chapter 6 I discussed how accounts of God in theistic stories are subject to correction by a developing understanding of God's nature, which is used to reinterpret excessively anthropomorphic elements. There is a similar corrective tendency operative in the way theistic traditions view moral teaching.

Suppose, for example, that sacred documents describe God as urging "an eye for an eye and a tooth for a tooth." A historical reading of such a command might suggest that it be understood against the backdrop of a practice of blood vengeance in which a wrong done to one clan member could evoke massive retaliation against another clan. Without a reliable central governing authority, such clan justice might be the only credible deterrent to some threats. In such a context the command of an eye for an eye could be understood as a call to limit such vengeance to approximate the harm actually done. Viewed in context, such a move seems like moral progress, though still something less than ideal. A tradition that over time develops fuller moral insight might view it as a step along the way, perhaps as an accommodation to the historically conditioned context of recipients of revelation.

But if moral insight and historical perspective may be used to evaluate the authority and applicability of the moral teaching of particular texts, they might be used as well to treat some things in sacred texts as products of defective understandings of those who pass on the traditions. Hence, for example, an interpreter of Hebrew scripture might judge that if the Israelites thought they had a divine command to kill all men, women, and children of another tribe in their wars, they were mistaken. It is understandable, given moral and theological views of the time, that they might believe such a command had been given, but this kind of command would conflict with the tradition's developed understanding of morality and of God's nature.

In other words revelatory truths can be understood as coming to individuals who interpret their experience through the lens of their own moral and theological understanding, and over time a tradition can judge a report of divine communication as inconsistent with a fuller understanding of divine revelation.

Sometimes reinterpretations of a tradition by later adherents can transform it in significant ways. The Hebrew prophets challenged the center of Israelite religious practice when they claimed that God was not interested in animal sacrifices, but vitally concerned with righteousness in everyday living. Another theme in Hebrew prophetic literature is the claim that Israel had misunderstood the notion of being a chosen people by thinking that it meant some kind of divine favoritism, rather than a call to special service to humanity, which would involve significant sacrifice.

Rejecting apparently straightforward assertions in scriptural texts is the sort of move that fundamentalist interpreters can find problematic.[5] They want to know how anything in a sacred text can be regarded as authoritative unless everything is authoritative. However, even people who say such things exercise their own selective judgment, allowing what is said at one point to be overridden by something said at another point. Christian fundamentalists do not generally think that people should be stoned for all the offences that are given such a penalty in the ancient Hebrew code. They don't think the sacrificial system is still binding on everyone. They readily treat some instructions as appropriate for another cultural setting, but not for now (such as the holy kiss or women keeping their heads covered or not charging interest on loans). They rely on particular traditions of interpretation to decide what to take as binding and what to treat in some other way.

There is an important question, however, underlying the fundamentalist concern. How can one accept any truths as revelatory if it is permissible to understand revelation through the lens of particular control beliefs that allow some apparent revelations to be overridden? Part of the answer is that some of the control beliefs come from sacred texts that are regarded as having a higher authority. A Christian might recognize that the moral teachings of Jesus differ in some ways from the earlier Hebrew tradition, but think that there is a special authority or a fuller insight involved. This kind of overriding the teaching of some passages by viewing them in the light of what are judged to be revelatory high points goes on for all interpreters of a tradition, whether they recognize it or not.

Nevertheless, what can be troubling for someone who thinks particular truths to be authoritatively revealed is the realization that even if there is a revelation, there is no guarantee that it will be understood correctly in every respect. Judgments of importance and judgments of what should be understood as an expression of cultural or historical form or limited understanding enter the picture. People equally committed to a scriptural tradition may end up with significantly different theological and moral ideas. For example, some Christians are convinced that there can be some authorized use of violence and others are convinced that the only Christian way is complete pacifism.

The possible diversity can be overstated. Serious arguments about differing moral interpretations tend to take place in a context in which all parties recognize some things as fundamental. Hardly anyone committed to a Christian understanding thinks that forgiveness of others is unimportant or that love of neighbor is an optional undertaking. The point here is that one may believe in an authoritative revelation and appeal to it as a basis for substantive conclusions without thinking that such a revelation provides infallible moral understanding. A believer might think that in moral matters the revelation is clear enough on some things, even if there is room for dispute about others. But is such an attitude toward sacred scriptures consistent with accepting revelation about morality? If I can use the moral insight I think I have in judging what moral teaching scriptures are giving, how can I learn anything different from what I already think? Two considerations are relevant here. One is that the moral insight a member of a tradition brings to the task of interpretation is formed through the tradition. The judgment that something should be disregarded or weighed less heavily will typically appeal to an understanding of something in the tradition that is taken as reliable. The other is that for one who accepts a revelatory tradition, the mere fact that something conflicts with moral intuitions is not by itself a reason to dismiss it. A teaching such as "Love your enemies" may not have much to commend itself to moral common sense.[6] However, members of a tradition can come to view certain high demands as pulling them to a higher level of moral insight. When put into a theological context, they may even be able to articulate why such teaching is to be obeyed.

I have been claiming that acceptance of revelatory truth need not be understood in a way that makes the recipient a passive vessel, taking in any instruction blindly. However, there is a passage in Hebrew scripture that can evoke such an image. In a famous story Abraham is told by God to sacrifice his son and sets out to do it. At the last minute he is stopped, and the story has a happy ending, but what is portrayed as a deeply religious act has the appearance of a ghastly display of immorality. It is important to see, however, that the position of Abraham is not the same as the position of later members of the tradition. Later members of the tradition view the possibility of such a command in the light of what they take to be a revealed understanding of the divine nature, which limits what could be regarded as a divine command. Biblical scholars have pointed out that the text portrays a time when child sacrifice was an accepted practice, and it can be imagined that for someone of Abraham's era such a demand would not have been out of the question. It would instead be regarded as an extreme form of devotion. The developing tradition will make it clear that the God Abraham serves is not like the gods who permit such things as child sacrifice, and the story's account of divine intervention in stopping the act might be regarded as a foreshadowing of that fuller revelation. Abraham is portrayed as an ideal of obedience, even though with fuller understanding that obedience can be seen as proceeding from a very inadequate moral and theological perspective that later members of the tradition are expected to transcend.

Submission and Autonomy

An aspect of theistic ethics that seems most repugnant to naturalistic sensibilities is the notion of submission to divine authority. The believer bows to divine authority, allowing his or her own insight and judgment to be overridden by what the authority requires. Against any view that would allow for the legitimacy of such submission, philosophical critics have often asserted that it is irresponsible for mature moral agents to put aside their own moral judgment and follow the authority of another. Not only can such a procedure seem infantile, it can be recognized as potentially dangerous. The Abraham story is sometimes cited as an example of the kind of fanaticism that is thought to issue from a religious point of view.

Much depends, of course, on whether we view the practice of submission to divine authority as occurring in a moral context or not. Sometimes submission to the requirements of authority is a morally appropriate act. There are authorities that we recognize as legitimate, and that recognition itself involves moral judgment. Most of us think, for example, that citizens have some obligation to submit to the authority of the state. While that authority is not unlimited, it has a legitimate sphere of operation, and its claim to be obeyed is connected with the moral judgment that there are certain human goods that require the operation of some state authority. We may distinguish between states that are adequately performing their functions and those that are not, but when our own state has legitimate authority we acquire an obligation to obey its dictates, at least when they are within certain limits. Our autonomous judgment as moral agents and our submission to authority go together in such a case.

Similarly, it might be thought that if there is a benevolent creator who knows how we need to live to fulfill our nature, a certain submission to the will of that creator is called for. The grounds of submission would not be merely superior power. It would involve recognition of the legitimate role of the creator in enabling the achievement of the human good. Someone with a particular conception of who God is and what our relationship is to such a being might judge that there is an obligation of obedience.[7] Such an obligation need not be understood as a requirement to blindly follow any demand conflicting with our considered moral judgment. But it might sometimes mean doing what we would not otherwise choose to do.

Recall, for example, Socrates' conviction that the kind of life he was living was a response to a divine call. God, he thought, had given him a task, and the task wasn't something he was free to dismiss or ignore. He was like a soldier under the command of a higher authority. Socrates said that if the authorities of the state should tell him to abandon this call and pursue a life more like that of ordinary people, he would have to refuse. The higher authority trumps the lesser one. Notice that the orienting story Socrates tells affects greatly his sense of what he needs to be doing and how he needs to go about it. Someone who does not believe in divine calls might recognize a need and dedicate her life to fulfilling it, but seeing that you are suited to a particular task and taking it on is not quite the same as believing that you have been designated by a higher wisdom to fulfill a particular mission. The belief that there is a divine power who sometimes calls people for particular tasks and that there are ways to determine whether you have been chosen can play a significant role in your thinking about what is morally required and the seriousness with which it needs to be pursued.

Socrates clearly did not view being under divine authority as a substitute for moral reflection. In the famous prison scene in the dialogue *Crito* he reasons from various moral principles to which he is committed that it would be wrong for him to escape from prison, despite the injustice of his condemnation. He invokes no commands of God telling him to stay put, but at the end of the dialogue he says to Crito, "Then let me follow the intimations of the will of God."[8] The intimations apparently come from reasoning about the matter and considering possible objections to his conclusion. Similarly, most people who believe in God do not generally expect to have specific instructions that relieve them from the need to think about what to do. However, they may believe that certain general operating principles, confirmed by revelatory accounts, can be treated as authoritative, and like Socrates, they sometimes come to believe that they have been called to particular tasks.

Fanaticism

While it is one thing to imagine Socrates following what he understands as divine guidance without abandoning autonomous judgment about right and wrong, we may be uncomfortable when less reflective people appeal to what God has told them to do. Some of the worst evils have been produced by people who were convinced that they were doing the will of God. The awareness of religiously motivated evil makes adherents of naturalistic stories uneasy with the whole idea of divine guidance. What I have been urging, however, is that the activity of obedience to God for someone who accepts a theistic story needs to occur within a moral context. Not just any command in a religion that sees God as morally perfect should be regarded as coming from God or demanding obedience. Religious communities often point out the need to test subjective judgments about such matters against the judgment of the larger community. Such practices clearly do not guarantee that fanaticism cannot arise, but there are no guarantees in communities that reject divine guidance either.

While some naturalists have been inclined to blame religion for almost all cases of major immorality,[9] there are numerous examples of horrible atrocities committed in the name of nonreligious ideals. Secular ideals, such as the classless society or the pure race can be treated as "holy causes" that are thought to justify virtually any action in pursuit of the goal, and in the twentieth century the systematic use of state power to promote essentially secular ideals has rivaled, if not surpassed, any evils that have been done in the name of religion. The loss of moral constraints in pursing what is thought to be an all-important good is undeniably a danger when the good is construed in religious terms but, when we lack religious ideals, there are no assured safeguards preventing secular holy causes from taking their place. Many naturalists will no doubt judge nonreligious fanatics who think horrible actions to be justified in achieving their ends have a warped understanding. Those committed to a theistic story often think the same thing about fanatics who imagine great evils to be justified on religious grounds.

Religious motivations and quasi-religious motivations that take their place in many secular orienting stories can be powerful forces either for good or for evil. Their potential for corruption is in many ways the reverse side of their potential to strongly motivate one for good. Viewing some kind of good as supremely valuable can motivate a willingness to great personal sacrifice, characteristic of the religious saint (or the secular equivalent). But one may also pursue a vision of the good in a way that loses touch with the moral background needed for adequately comprehending that vision.

Rewards and Punishments

Thomas Nagel begins a discussion (for introductory students) of the idea that God might be needed for morality by describing a version of the idea that he characterizes as "crude":

> ... some people believe that even if you can get away with awful crimes on this earth, and are not punished by the law or your fellow men, such acts are forbidden by God, who will punish you after death (and reward you if you don't do wrong when you were tempted to). So even when it seems to be in our interest to do such a thing, it really isn't.[10]

Crude though it may be, something like this version probably represents the understanding of quite a few people who consider themselves religious. God is thought of as an enforcer of good behavior in cases where there are not enough rewards of good or punishments for evil to make good behavior pay off. When divine rewards and punishments are taken into account, doing what is right will always be in your interest. This way of thinking leads easily to the view that people who don't believe in God lack the kind of motivation they need to do right when it does not coincide with their interests.

One thing that makes this admittedly crude version of religious motivation seem problematic is that thinking of doing right and avoiding wrong in connection with rewards and punishments conjures up a picture of the moral life that seems to correspond to a relatively immature level of development. Children (and sometimes adults) need threats and entice-ments to get them to behave in desired ways. But when we offer rewards and threaten punishments to children, we hope that they will advance to a stage where external incentives are no longer needed. We hope that in time they may become people who recognize the importance of moral behav-ior, even when there is no reward to be gained or punishment to be avoided. Of course the expectation that a substantial portion of the human population will consistently be internally motivated to do right is more of an ideal than a basis for organizing society. Nevertheless, we might think that a system that relies fundamentally on external rewards and punish-ments perpetuates a kind of moral immaturity.

On the other hand, the idea that moral motivation should be free of incentives or disincentives altogether does not seem quite right either. Imagine instructing a child (or an adult), "The moral life will do nothing but make you miserable, but that is not important. You need to undertake it anyway." Thinking that acquiring virtue and avoiding vice makes no con-tribution to the quality of one's life is not much of an advertisement for it. However, appreciating just how it contributes depends on acquiring a point of view in which things valued from a moral perspective come to seem valuable to you. If you think that other people don't really matter or that contributing to society is unimportant, such a life won't make much sense, but if you can learn to have your thinking and feeling shaped by an aware-ness of moral significance, you may come to regard moral living as an indispensable component of the kind of happiness you seek.

For someone who thinks in this way, a compelling reason to avoid vicious behavior is that it will make you into a vicious person. Similarly, for some-one who has learned to appreciate what moral living is about, a central attraction of the moral life is becoming a person who exhibits admirable traits such as compassion, honesty, and generosity. The incentives most conducive to genuine moral motivation are those connected with an appre-ciation for moral values.

Nagel portrays religious motivation as a matter of being bribed by rewards or threatened by punishments to act in ways that go against what we might prefer. However, there are other ways to imagine the role of divine incentives. One possibility is to see the rewards as intimately con-nected with acquiring the concerns of a virtuous person. It is possible to think of heavenly rewards as being of this kind. For example, the heavenly reward for one who has learned the value of self-giving love might involve participation in a community where there are continued opportunities for practicing this kind of love. The reward for one who has learned to love God might be a fuller experience of the divine nature. But how are such long-range considerations supposed to be relevant to moral motivation? For a mature believer the possibility of a heavenly reward is not ordinarily an immediate motivation for action. It is not as if Mother Teresa calculated, "I will help this poor leper so that I can get a better heavenly reward." The relevance of such rewards arises at a different level, in reflecting on commitment to a way of life that may involve significant sacrifices of personal interests.

Morality and Happiness

It is well known that the righteous may suffer greatly for maintaining their integrity. Even if we are motivated to pursue the moral life, its demands may in certain circumstances be overwhelming, and the benefits of becoming the kind of person we aspire to be may seem too little. Kant argued that although virtuous action is not done to achieve happiness, the moral life becomes incoherent without the postulate that virtuous living ultimately leads to happiness.[11] Henry Sidgwick thought that without a way to connect virtue with self-interest there would be a fundamental contradiction in our intuitions of reasonable conduct.[12] At this level we are not talking about bribes to be good or threats to keep us from being bad. Rather the issue is whether being the kind of person with a commitment to moral living no matter what the cost is something that one with a strong interest in her own happiness can reflectively endorse.

Religious life-orienting stories tend to say that such a commitment makes sense because there is a moral order that harmonizes our concern for our own happiness with virtue. In some traditions the moral order is thought of as something like a natural law connecting what we do with what we get (the law of karma). In theistic traditions the moral order is bound up with divine purposes for human life. God provides a path that leads to fulfillment, and we can either embark on that path or follow another way. Following the path does not guarantee happiness in this life, but God's purposes for human fulfillment extend beyond this life, and what we do can contribute to achieving those purposes. Stories of this kind tell us that the observable order in which the righteous sometimes suffer greatly and the wicked sometimes prosper inordinately needs to be put into a larger context in which even great sacrifices need not to conflict with final fulfillment for the individual.

Naturalistic stories reject the larger context. They tell us to face up to the observable facts. The good sometimes suffer greatly and have few of the world's benefits, and the bad sometimes get away with horrible wrongs and enjoy their ill-gotten gains. There is no natural law or powerful agent to adjust the moral scales, and the hope for a fulfillment beyond this world is illusory. A naturalist can argue that while there are no guarantees, developing moral virtues may increase one's odds for happiness. But in specific circumstances it can be apparent that such a bet is not going to pay off. So for a naturalist an unconditional commitment to moral living will require a willingness to sacrifice some personal interests with no expectation that these sacrifices are somehow beneficial from an individual point of view. Compared to the adherent of a religious story, such a stance can seem heroic, affirming moral values in the absence of a wider order that supports them. But that raises the question of how naturalistic stories can motivate such heroism.

Some thinkers have doubted that they can. William James contrasts what he calls "materialistic theories" which claim that our sense of good and bad makes "no sense apart from subjective passions and interests" with views that claim our moral awareness puts us in touch with an order that exists independently of human reactions. In cases where there is a clash between individual interests and the requirements of morality, James thinks that the "subjective moralist" will feel freer to seek a resolution by "toning down the sensitivities of moral feelings."[13] James admits that most of the time both views can lead to similar behavior, but in what he calls the "lonely emergencies of life" our commitments are tested. In such cases he says we "fall back on our gods."[14] When the perspective we identify with ultimate reality is one in which human commitment or lack of commitment seems to lack importance, maintaining a commitment when it means significant sacrifice may seem less important than protecting personal interests.

James's claim is speculative. It would be very difficult to devise a reliable empirical test of his projections.[15] Nevertheless, what he suggests has an intuitive plausibility. It is noteworthy that virtually all religious moralities attempt to identify our deepest sense of value with the deep structures of reality. This kind of account is conducive to understanding moral demands as nonnegotiable requirements rooted in the nature of things. The question for a naturalistic system is whether viewing moral requirements as products of a human projection on a universe that itself is devoid of value can have sufficient psychological force to support fairly demanding moral commitments. Charles Taylor has expressed doubt about whether naturalistic morality has sources of motivation sufficient to maintain standards like universal benevolence and justice that arose in contexts where they were supported by religious motivations.[16] On the other hand, it might be asked in return how well religious views have supported the maintenance of these high standards.

Transformative Ideals

Human motivation as we generally find it is sufficient neither for the way of life prescribed by theistic stories nor for the way of life endorsed by naturalistic stories that recognize extensive obligations to others. To live the kind of life either story calls for means transforming common patterns of thinking and desiring. The need for transformation is generally recognized in theistic traditions, where a variety of practices are regarded as vehicles for changing how we think and what we desire. However, there can also be a gap between the way we are and the way we need to be to live out a naturalistic story with demands that are in tension with human inclinations. Without some set of practices that enable us to internalize the ideals the story portrays and discipline our desires, we may find ourselves unable or unwilling to shape our lives in accordance with what is required.

In theistic traditions practices such as prayer play a vital role in helping one to move away from common assumptions about what is valuable and what will make us happy to understandings more in line with the theistic story. Consider, for example the instructions of Teresa of Avila:

> Oh my sisters … how little one should care about honours, and how far one ought to be from wishing to be esteemed in the very least if the Lord makes His special abode in the soul. For if the soul is much with Him, as it is right it should be, it will very seldom think of itself; its whole thought will be concentrated upon finding ways to please Him and upon showing Him how it loves Him. This, my daughters, is the aim of prayer …."[17]

One of the things to be learned in spiritual exercises, such as prayer, is the relative unimportance of things that are widely pursued and the centrality of things connected with God's purposes. Prayer is conceived here not primarily as asking for things, but as a practice that enables one to identify with divine purposes and learn to evaluate our aims from a perspective in which some desires can be seen as trivial in relation to higher priorities.

The teachings of ancient philosophical schools resemble those of religious traditions in treating some kind of transformative task as vital. Julia Annas points out that while all the ancient Greek philosophical schools accepted the idea that happiness (*eudaimonia*) is the proper human end, they dissociate themselves from common understandings of what happiness is. Conventionally it is thought to consist of goods like health, wealth, and power, the things that are commonly pursued. But ancient philosophers give strikingly different accounts. Consider, for example, Socrates' claim that the only relevant consideration when confronted with the possibility of behaving unjustly is that it is unjust. The fact that a particular way of acting is likely to get you killed, he dismisses as simply irrelevant. Annas suggests that while Socrates agrees with the Greek truism that happiness is the human good, what he offers is "a radical redefinition of good such that virtue is the only thing that is good."[18]

Later Stoics allowed that things such as health and wealth could have a certain kind of value, but they follow Socrates in thinking that virtue is sufficient for happiness and has a value of a different kind. Other things are good only for the person who values virtue above all in a way that is incommensurate with other valuations. What is proposed, suggests Annas, is virtue as a transformative ideal: "Happiness is the continuing goal we have, but it can be transformed by virtue; we go on seeking happiness, but our conception of where to look for it and how we have to be to get it can be utterly reconfigured."[19]

The task of coming to think about and pursue happiness in such a different way from what common sense might suggest is clearly a major undertaking. Pierre Hadot connects the needed shift with spiritual exercises:

> The practice of spiritual exercises implied a complete reversal of received ideas: one is to renounce the false values of wealth, honors, and pleasures, and turn toward the true value of virtue, contemplation, a simple life-style, and the simple happiness of existing.[20]

One must unlearn old habits of thinking and desiring and learn new ones by disciplined practice in order to enter into the kind of life that is held up as ideal.

Contemporary advocates of naturalistic stories of the humanist variety have typically not addressed the process by which an individual is expected to acquire far-reaching concerns for improving human welfare that have the power to override concerns with individual comfort. Sometimes this has been the result of excessive optimism about human nature. John Hare describes a utilitarian optimist as thinking, "... if we saw clearly the damage we do to other people, we would not do it."[21] That line of thought suggests an unrealistic intellectualistic bias. Having proper moral motivations is not just a matter of thinking clearly, and treating it as a problem that might be resolved by getting the facts straight seriously underestimates the human tendency toward discounting the interests of others when they conflict with our own.

Ancient moralists realized that they were calling for patterns of living that were at odds with typical behavior and proposed a transformative process to deal with the problem. But contemporary naturalists tend to focus on the issue of whether someone who does not believe in God can have reasons to be moral,[22] while ignoring the question of how these reasons can function as strong motivations for something more demanding than a moral minimum. André Comte-Sponville says, "Where morals are concerned, the loss of faith changes nothing or next to nothing. That you have lost your faith does not mean that you will suddenly decide to betray your friends or indulge in robbery, rape, assassination and torture."[23] No doubt Comte-Sponville is correct that the loss of faith need not precipitate a descent into lawlessness, but he does not set a particularly high standard.

What he says also suggests a failure to recognize the importance of life-orienting stories in supporting a transformative process sufficient to sustain commitment to a morality calling for significant personal sacrifice. Surely he is overconfident to claim that in the movement from a story in which God is a central feature to a story without God nothing of consequence changes. For one who takes a religious story seriously the moral life will differ both in content and in the kinds of motivation available. The naturalist may be quite certain that nothing important is lost, but that judgment would surely differ from the assessment of someone whose moral life is permeated with ideas like divine calls, submission to the will of God, sacred duties, and gratitude to God.

An Objection to Religious Motivation

One of the objections Thomas Nagel raises against religious motivation is that it is the wrong kind of motivation. Refraining from harming other people and treating them well needs to be motivated by a concern for the other person. If we are doing it to gain a reward from God or avoid punishment or even to please God, we are failing to grasp the central point that the relevant reason to consider the interests of others has to do with the importance of those interests. One who doesn't grasp that breaking a promise to someone or cheating someone is wrong because it is bad for the victim surely misses something fundamental. Nagel is surely correct in thinking that some reasons for moral behavior tend to obscure its point. What is more questionable, however, is to suppose that a motivation like concern for the wellbeing of others is completely disconnected with other motivations that might strengthen that concern.

Consider, for example, the person who says, "I am honest in business because if I wasn't, I couldn't sleep at night." On the surface this account sounds like a purely self-interested reason for behavior that coincides with what a moral person would do. However, there are other ways to understood it. The expected difficulty in sleeping at night is presumably a product of a guilty conscience, and having a guilty conscience from immoral behavior is precisely what we would expect of a virtuous individual. At one level avoiding a guilty conscience is like avoiding pain but, seen in a larger context, it is an action of an individual whose conscience is functioning properly to support moral motivation. If we imagine that avoiding pain is the only motivation, then we aren't talking about moral behavior, but in standard cases avoiding a guilty conscience and having concern for the good of others go together.

Similarly, if someone with a theistic life-orienting story says of some moral action, "I did it to please God" or "I did it to become the kind of person God wants me to be," such motivations do not need to be understood as replacing a concern for others. In fact in a theistic context, it ought to be clear that what pleases God will be inseparable from developing concerns for others. One who is thinking clearly about pleasing God won't be thinking that you can achieve that result without developing the right kinds of concerns, but rather has a range of motivations that can help strengthen those concerns.

In a theistic moral system these additional layers of motivation provide mutual support. Sometimes these layers are revealed in the way an action is described. Someone might think of what she is doing as "stopping to help an accident victim" or "being a good Samaritan" or "obeying divine guidance" or "imitating the example of Christ" or "expressing compassion for one of God's creatures." These different ways of thinking evoke a constellation of motivations that can help to sustain the moral life.

Someone who accepts a naturalistic account of morality will likely have a range of motivations as well. But many of the motivators that function to reinforce the moral commitment of a religious individual will not be available. Does this make a difference? Perhaps the place to look for a potential difference is with regard to moral living that far surpasses the moral minimum. One extensive study of individuals identified by others as moral exemplars reported that the kind of extraordinary moral commitment these exemplars exhibited depended on a unifying belief that affected them at the level of habit, judgment, and reflective self-understanding. The psychologists reported:

> Many of our exemplars drew upon religious faith for such a unifying belief. In fact … this was the case for a far larger proportion of our exemplars than we generally expected. But even those who had no formal religion often looked to a transcendent ideal of a personal sort: a faith in the forces of good, a sustaining hope in a power greater than oneself, a larger meaning for one's life than personal achievement or gain.[24]

The researchers also noted that all their exemplars had a faith in human potential: "Although the substance of the faith … was too varied and too elusive to be captured in a final generalization, it can best be described as an intimation of transcendence: a faith in something above and beyond the self."[25]

While we cannot rule out the possibility that a secular life-orienting story can provide this kind of unifying belief, along with a faith in human potential, these ways of thinking surely fit more easily within a theistic story. We can have a morality without such a belief and without such a faith, and if we can find no plausible life-orienting story to support this kind of stance, we will have to make do without it. But we should be reluctant to claim that doing without a story providing these supports for moral living makes no difference for the kind of moral life we will have. Nor should we assume that in removing God from moral thinking nothing of consequence will be lost.

Notes

1   Leo Tolstoy, *The Novels and Other Works of Lyof N. Tolstoi: Essays, Letters, and Miscellanies*, vol. II (New York: Charles Scribner's Sons, 1907), 98.

2   Julian Baggini, *Atheism: A Very Short Introduction* (Oxford: Oxford University Press, 2003), 37. The use of this quotation as an epigraph is by permission of Oxford University Press.

3   A recent example is Erik Wielenberg's *Value and Virtue in a Godless Universe* (Cambridge: Cambridge University Press, 2005). His defense of morality without God is in chapters two and three (pp. 38–97). However, virtually all defenses of atheism argue explicitly for the possibility of a morality without God.

4   Robert Adams proposes that we think of divine commands as commands of a loving God. While he calls his account a divine command theory, the nature of the commander places limits on what commands could produce moral obligation. See his "A Modified Divine Command Theory of Ethical Wrongness," in Gene Outka and John Reeder Jr., *Religion and Morality* (Garden City, NY: Anchor Books, 1973), 318–47.

5   Nonreligious critics often approach sacred texts in a way that is remarkably similar to fundamentalist approaches.

6   Freud viewed it as a despicable teaching, appealing to common sense to show its perversity. Sigmund Freud, *Civilization and its Discontents* (New York: Norton and Company, 1961), 64–74.

7   Peter Byrne follows Aquinas in using the analogy of legislation as a way of discussing divine authority in *The Philosophical and Theological Foundations of Ethics: An Introduction to Moral Theory and its Relation to Religious Belief*, 2nd edn. (New York: St Martin's Press, 1998), 148ff.

8   Plato, *Crito, in The Trial and Death of Socrates: Four Dialogues*, ed. Shane Weller, trans. Benjamin Jowett, (New York: Dover Publications, 1992), 54.

9   E.g., Christopher Hitchens, *God Is Not Great: How Religion Poisons Everything* (New York: Warner, 2007).

10   Thomas Nagel, *What Does It All Mean? A Very Short Introduction to Philosophy* (New York: Oxford University Press, 1987), 62.

11   Immanuel Kant, *The Critique of Practical Reason, in The Cambridge Edition of the Works of Immanuel Kant: Practical Philosophy*, trans. and ed. Mary Gregor (Cambridge: Cambridge University Press, 1996), 235 (5:119).

12   Henry Sidgwick, *The Methods of Ethics*, 7th edn. (Chicago: The University of Chicago Press, 1962), 508.

13   William James, "The Sentiment of Rationality," in *The Writings of William James: A Comprehensive Edition*, ed. John McDermott (Chicago: The University of Chicago Press, 1977), 341–2.

14   James, 342.

15   Michael Martin cites empirical studies on the connection between belief in God or lack of such belief and ethical behavior. *See Atheism, Morality, and Meaning* (Amherst, NY: Prometheus Books, 2002), 27–31. However, much of this evidence does not distinguish between different levels of religious belief, and measures of what constitutes moral behavior concentrate on easily measurable moral minimums. These kinds of studies do not test the kind of claim that James makes.

16   Charles Taylor, Sources of the Self; *The Making of Modern Identity* (Cambridge, MA: Harvard University Press, 1989) 513–21.

17 Teresa of Avila, *Interior Castle*, trans. E. Allison Peers (Garden City, NY: Doubleday, 1961), 228.

18 Julia Annas, "Virtue and Eudaimonism," in *Happiness: Classical and Contemporary Readings,* ed. Steven Cahn and Christine Vitrano (Oxford: Oxford University Press, 2008), 252.

19 Annas, 256.

20 Pierre Hadot, *Philosophy As A Way of Life,* ed. Arnold Davidson, trans. Michael Chase (Malden, MA: Blackwell Publishing, 1995), 104.

21 John Hare, *The Moral Gap: Kantian Ethics, Human Limits, and God's Assistance* (Oxford: Clarendon Press, 1966), 115.

22 Richard Carrier, *Sense and Goodness Without God: A Defense of Metaphysical Naturalism* (Bloomington, IN: AuthorHouse, 2005), 273–302.

23 André Comte-Sponville, *The Little Book of Atheist Spirituality*, trans. Nancy Huston (New York: Viking, 2007), 41.

24 Anne Colby and William Damon, *Some Do Care: Contemporary Lives of Moral Commitment* (New York: The Free Press, 1992), 311.

25 Colby and Damon, 311.

9

Meaning and the Limits of Meaning

"Those who are able to trust in divine providence ... will be as aware as their atheist counterparts are of the terrible suffering in the world; but they believe they have a way of making sense of that suffering, of finding an underlying meaning and value in creation, notwithstanding the dreadful ills that arise within it." (John Cottingham[1])

"We are so structured as to expect a world that comes to meet us halfway, for we cannot make meaning alone." (Susan Neiman[2])

Sometimes events occur that strongly suggest a theological meaning. Psychologist Justin Barrett describes an experience of one of his wife's coworkers, who was doing maintenance work on a farm:

> Doug was working in a grain silo when leaked propane exploded. The first explosion rushed all around him and out the second-level windows high above him. Stunned by not being harmed by the blast, he tried to get out the door, only to discover that the explosion had jammed the doors. Knowing that a second larger explosion was coming, and he had no way out, Doug muttered hopelessly, "Take me home, Lord." He distinctly heard a voice say, "Not yet," and then he felt some invisible hands lift him a dozen feet in the air and out a second-story window, then safely to the ground below. Once he landed outside the silo, a safe distance away, the silo and attached barn exploded into rubble.[3]

Coworkers took Doug to the hospital, and the doctor who examined him said that the amount of propane in his lungs should have been fatal, yet here stood Doug, talking about how God had rescued him.

A married couple of my own acquaintance told me of an incident that left both of them awestruck. Martha and Roy virtually never missed a

Wednesday evening service at their church. But for some reason neither could explain, they lingered at the dining room table one Wednesday evening until it was too late to go. A knock at the door from a frantic neighbor roused them from their lethargy. The woman from next door was shouting frantically that her husband was choking and couldn't breathe. Martha and Roy rushed over, and Roy, who the previous month had completed a class in first aid, performed the Heimlich maneuver he had practiced in class and saved the life of his neighbor. Both Martha and Roy were convinced that their staying home that evening and Roy's knowledge and ability to help had been providentially arranged.

In both of these cases the people involved already believed in God before having the experience. Interpreting the events in the light of their own theistic life-orienting story, they found it natural and obvious to view what had happened as involving the actions of a benevolent deity who is concerned about human wellbeing. In the second story the agents of rescue were human beings who saw themselves as having been put in the right place at the right time. When Doug told his story, he described his belief that angelic messengers had been sent to save him. Others who heard one of these stories agreed in attributing what had happened to supernatural agency. The story they heard fit easily into their own life-orienting narratives, which represent divine action in the world as a real possibility. These events might be unusual, but they conformed to a recognizable pattern of what divine activity might look like.

While an atheist hearing accounts of this kind is unlikely to embrace a theological interpretation of the events, we can imagine an atheist finding such stories noteworthy or even challenging. Naturalistic accounts of the events can no doubt be offered, but the appearance of purposiveness is striking enough to arouse the human tendency to think in terms of an agent who might have arranged things. In fact Barrett uses his story to illustrate the role of a cognitive tool he calls our "Hyperactive Agency Detection Device" in interpreting the meaning of events. Events that are suggestive of a purposive order dispose us to look for an agent or agents capable of causing the events. Since the rescues involved factors beyond the power of human agents to arrange, the incidents can strongly suggest the operation of a higher-level agency.

If events like those described above were typical of the way things usually happen, it might be difficult to refrain from belief in some kind of supernatural agency. But for all the rescue stories we might tell, there are plenty of people who don't get rescued. People die or are seriously maimed in farming accidents. People choke to death for lack of a knowledgeable and skilled rescuer. So even if there are events that strongly suggest divine activity, there are also events in which people are apparently left to their own devices without divine help. Not only that, there are events where the urge to find some kind of purposive meaning is thwarted by what gives every appearance of being random and pointless.

A young newlywed couple plans a romantic balloon trip over the Grand Canyon near sunset. A mishap in the balloon's heating apparatus catches the gondola car on fire, and the balloon crashes to the ground. The woman is killed in the crash, and her husband goes to the hospital with painful and disfiguring burns over most of his body. A newly graduated biochemist, who has impressed everyone with her brilliance and dedicated her life to a promising line of cancer research, is struck with a debilitating disease that leaves her unable to pursue the work. A bus driver on a rainy night misjudges the location of the highway exit ramp, and the bus is plunged onto the highway below, sending most of the passengers to their deaths. A popular and enthusiastic elementary school teacher is forced into a car and taken to an isolated location where a rapist brutalizes her and leaves her lifeless body in a dumpster.

If one kind of story suggests the activity of a benevolent agent, these stories can strike us with the absence of such activity. Far from exhibiting indications of purposeful benevolence, the events reveal an environment where senseless and repugnant things happen. Events of this kind sometimes evoke outrage, even in people who don't believe in supernatural protection. We find ourselves thinking that such things should not happen. The world should somehow operate differently. For someone with a naturalistic understanding of the universe, it is unclear what this reaction means. If nature is the ultimate reality, we can expect that natural laws will sometimes operate in ways that benefit humans and sometimes in ways that bring destruction. Given human nature and society, people will sometimes make bad choices and sometimes make better ones. A naturalist can, of course, blame and be angry at the rapist, but it makes little sense for someone with a naturalistic view to blame or be upset at the natural order.

On the other hand, a theist with a sense that the world should not operate in this way has someone to blame. If God can sometimes rescue people from disaster, why are such rescues not more frequent? Better yet, why isn't there an order that makes dramatic rescues unnecessary? If God should be praised for bringing about circumstances and events conducive to happy endings, then shouldn't God be blamed when things turn out badly?

Complaining About God

It might come as a surprise to people unfamiliar with theistic traditions how often and how passionately believers express their dissatisfaction with the way God runs things. How after all can anyone complain about the actions or omissions of a being presumed to be of unlimited wisdom, goodness, and power? Yet the Psalms are full of laments in which God is taken to task for being too easy on enemies or evildoers. "How long do we have to wait for justice?" asks the struggling victim whose patience has run thin. "When will the wicked get the punishment they deserve?" "When will the righteous be properly vindicated?" Such laments might seem totally out of place when directed toward one deemed worthy of worship, yet their uninhibited presumptuousness suggests a kind of confidence in the deity to whom the complaint is offered. What is the point of complaining unless you believe that God is on the side of righteousness and cares about putting things right? It may be puzzling as to why it takes so long, but the lament gives expression to a hope that God will fix what is currently out of balance.

> The book of Habukkuk begins with the following lament:
>
> How long, O Lord, must I call for help, but you do not listen?
> Or cry out to you, "Violence!" but you do not save?
> Why do you make me look at injustice? Why do you tolerate wrong?
> Destruction and violence are before me; there is strife, and conflict abounds.
> Therefore the law is paralyzed, and justice never prevails.
> The wicked hem in the righteous, so that justice is perverted.[4]

No answers to these questions or explanations for the delay in establishing justice emerge in the book, but despite a vivid awareness of an unprecedented agricultural disaster, the author still affirms at the end, "I will rejoice in the Lord, I will be joyful in God my Savior. The Sovereign Lord is my strength ...."[5]

Contemporary believers are at least as puzzled as ancient ones about things that don't seem to fit into their picture of what God wants for the world. When faced with suffering that seems senseless, they ask, "Why?" Sometimes the puzzle is "Why me?" Sometimes it is why this kind of thing happens to anyone. Often it is why God didn't do something. In a world where tsunamis can quickly destroy huge numbers of people or malicious acts of individuals can suddenly turn happiness to misery, suffering can evoke outrage at the way the world fails to fit our longing for moral order. It seems to us that doing right ought to result in prosperity, and doing wrong ought to result in misery. But instead we find there are no guarantees that doing right won't get you or those you love tortured or killed, and people sometimes get away with despicable evils without showing any signs of receiving the misery they deserve.

A believer, who becomes vividly aware of human suffering, either through personal experience or through learning of what happens to others, may have many kinds of questions. However, a central one is the question of how such suffering can fit into divine purposes. What meaning does it have within some larger scheme of what God intends for the world? A very simple answer to that question, which has frequently been offered, is that suffering should be understood as punishment. Underlying this answer is the assumption that we always get what we deserve, even if it doesn't appear that way. In the book of Job a Hebrew poet portrays Job's "comforters" as offering this answer: "If you are suffering, it must be that you have done something displeasing to God. You need to acknowledge your wrongs and seek forgiveness." What these "comforters" cannot allow is the possibility that justice is not actually done. A moral order that matches deed and desert must be operative, and if it doesn't seem that way, it can only be that we just don't see clearly enough how our own sins bring various miseries upon us.

When viewed as a comprehensive explanation of the meaning of suffering, such an account fails. The book of Job is itself a repudiation of such excessive confidence in the notion that good behavior always pays off and bad behavior always brings punishment. Job is relentless in asserting that he has done no wrong sufficient to deserve the kind of suffering that he experiences, and the narrator of the story assures us that Job is correct and those who offer their supposed wisdom are speaking falsely.

The urge to find some connection between what we get and what we deserve is strong. In religions that posit the idea of karma, previous lives are thought to provide the key to answering the question of why the distribution of good and evil seems so skewed. We may have done nothing in our current life to bring on the suffering we endure, but in the larger picture there are many lives to be considered, and moral consequences may not occur immediately, but in a subsequent life. Whether or not this idea is coherent,[6] when the assumption of previous lives is dropped, the claim of suffering proportional to what we deserve becomes wildly implausible, if not obscene, as a response to what experience reveals. We have to close our eyes to too much that seems obvious to accept such an idea, and furthermore, it seems to undermine our motivation to right the wrongs we observe, since that would risk interfering with a hidden justice.

While Job repudiates the simplistic answer, it is not quite clear what answer is put in its place. Most interpreters of the book conclude that in the messages that Job receives when he encounters a divine appearance in a whirlwind near the end of the book, what replaces an explanation is a raw assertion of God's power and knowledge and a rebuke of Job for the impudence of thinking he can understand such things. There is, however, another way of understanding the book. Throughout God's speeches are images of a wider reality that includes the wild and chaotic forces in nature. The climactic point comes when God refers to Leviathan, the mythical beast that in Hebrew thought represented the forces of chaos. In Hebrew poetic literature about creation God is represented as having destroyed the primordial monsters that opposed divine order, but they are represented in these speeches as still active, and their activity is portrayed by God as displaying magnificent aspects of the created order. For reasons that are not explained to Job, these forces are allowed to operate, hence, what happens in the world does not conform to the pattern of divine justice. Job is right in affirming that there is unjust suffering. Nevertheless, God can be trusted to bring about the good of created things from all the chaos.[7]

To a philosophic mind, such an answer is bound to seem unsatisfactory. Why, we want to know, are chaotic or demonic forces allowed to operate at all? If God is the ultimate power, how can there be anything that opposes God? If there are forces with powers to resist God's work in the world, isn't God responsible for failing to rein in such forces?

God as Micro-Manager

A picture of the relation of God to the universe that is tempting both to believers and unbelievers is of a deity who exercises control over every detail of what happens. This picture is sometimes thought to be a corollary of the attribute of all-powerfulness. If God is all-powerful, then God must be able to make each event happen precisely as it should. Our imagination plays a role here. When we try to conceive of an agent who can produce and maintain a material order, we imagine an agent with the power to manage each state of affairs and think that the failure to put each thing right is a sign either of divine incompetence or lack of concern.

There are alternative ways of thinking about how God might be related to the universe. We might think, for example, that creation involves a relinquishing of control. There are cases in human experience where success in a project can be achieved only through refraining from controlling everything, and instead allowing others to do their part independently without looking over their shoulders to correct any mistakes. Allowing such independence is a strain for some managers who feel strong urges to make sure each thing is done as they would do it. But good managers, like good parents, are able to let go enough to allow others to assume some responsibility for what happens.

Of course, in such cases we can imagine the manager coming in to take over when things are not going well. But what if there were a project in which that was not an option? What if allowing a relative independence for creatures within a material order could happen only by withdrawing to give them room? Louis Dupré suggests,

> For infinite, perfect Being to give rise to being other than itself means … causing emptiness within its own fullness wherein "otherness" can subsist…. Though finite being must remain *within* the infinite, perfect Being from which it draws its entire sustenance, as *other* it assumes a certain independence. By allowing it to be in its own right, infinite Being ceases to wield unlimited power over it and comes to stand in a relation that is no longer exclusively active.[8]

Similarly John Cottingham speaks of creation as "a *withdrawal* by God, a kind of shrinking whereby God, instead of filling all the available space with his supreme and perfect existence, gives way, in order to allow for something *other*, something imperfect, to unfold."[9]

The picture of a divine limitation that arises from the nature of creation may not be the first one that comes to mind when we try to imagine a relationship between God and the world, but when theistic traditions characterize the nature of the relation between God and created things in terms of love, that characterization is hard to square with the image of a divine micro-manager. The kind of love we value most in human relations allows another person to have a significant degree of independence, rather than being an object of manipulative control. However, for a creator to offer that kind of love means a letting go that produces a space sufficient for independent development.

When we try to imagine what it would be like to produce a material order in which self-aware creatures might come to exist, we may imagine the immediate production, as if by magic, of such creatures. But if we take our cue from scientific accounts of the universe, we might instead view the creative act as resulting in a material order, possessing its own nature and capacities for development. Such an order evidently has the potential for producing life from non-loving matter and producing self-aware beings from living things. By giving the material order a kind of independence to develop in accordance with its nature, the creator could be thought of as making something that is not merely an extension of the divine.

Much of our suffering arises from the fact that we are material beings inhabiting a material universe. Such a material order functions by natural regularities that give rise to the conditions of life, but also involve decay and randomness that make our kind of world possible. The fact that we die, that we are vulnerable to diseases or injuries, that we can suffer mental and emotional distress are all products of our nature and the nature of the world we live in. Our tendency toward aggressive and destructive acts is connected with pre-human beginnings that provide raw materials for a nature capable of moral awareness, but also in tension with it. Human nature and the material order it inhabits furnishes conditions for human flourishing, but also potentialities for causing human misery. If nature is created, it is created with capacities to operate against us as well as for us.

But doesn't this picture amount to deism? If God is not able to create an order with relative independence without relinquishing significant control over what happens, doesn't that make God absent from the world in the way the divine "clockmaker" of eighteenth-century thought, whose creative work consisted of setting material particles in motion, was thought to be absent? John Cottingham urges that such a conclusion arises from a false dilemma. If we reject the model of a micro-manager, a deity who is totally uninvolved is not the only alternative. We can envision the possibility of a deity who is involved in a different way. Taking his cue from the Christian tradition, Cottingham offers as an alternative a god who attempts "to redeem and rescue his creation by entering it, not as a superior being, or a fussy micro-manager, but on its own terms, utterly unprotected and vulnerable."[10]

Other writers have theorized that God's action in the world might be thought of as more like persuasive than coercive power. Rather than controlling what happens, this view would suggest that God exerts influences that might be resisted. Theoretical physicist turned theologian, John Polkinghorne, develops a model of "top-down information input" through which God influences what happens in a way that respects, but doesn't overpower, "the integrity" of natural processes. Invoking the theological idea of *kenosis* (self-emptying), he says,

> God interacts with the world but is not in total control of all its processes. The act of creation involves divine acceptance of the risk of the existence of the other, and there is a consequent kenosis of God's omnipotence. The curtailment of divine power … arises from the logic of love, which requires the freedom of the beloved.[11]

An account of this kind is obviously speculative, but it is no more speculative than attempts to say something about divine power by using intuitions about what a perfect being would be able to do. Part of the problem with intuitions about the power of a perfect being is that they are affected by our choice of paradigmatic situations in which power might be displayed. The power of brute force is clearly different from the power to persuade. The power to evoke a response of freely given love is very different from the power to capture and hold as a slave. How God's power is described in relation to creation depends on what we imagine God to be doing in creation, and how we imagine it might be done.[12]

The suggestion that creation involves limitation has been introduced here as a response to the claim that positing powers that might resist God (according to one interpretation of Job) involves an understanding that is deficient from a philosophical point of view. What has been suggested is that these powers might be conceived of as arising from the very existence of a created material order that is relatively independent of God. Such an order would have its own integrity and, in operating within it, God may have to observe parameters that allow it to develop in accordance with its own nature. The divine withdrawal from a certain kind of control may be necessary for having the kind of world in which creatures like us can exist.

Philosophical Questions and Religious Questions

The kind of ultimate explanation sought by philosophers is not generally what a religious believer is looking for when confronted by suffering. Rather than an answer to the question of why there is suffering at all, the believer is typically asking how to think about and deal with suffering in a world where it is undeniably a feature of the way things are. As Clifford Geertz puts it, the religious problem is "how to suffer, how to make of physical pain, personal loss, worldly defeat or the helpless contemplation of others' agony something bearable. ..."[13] The solution offered in theistic traditions involves discerning a meaning in suffering by getting some understanding of how facing various difficulties might contribute to the achievement of God's purposes in the world. This kind of understanding is possible even in the absence of an explanation of why God allows suffering in general or particular instances of suffering.

To the question of why a particular instance of suffering occurred, it is usually unwise for a theist to be confident about having a purposive explanation. Whatever a believer might think with regard to her own suffering, it seems more than a little presumptuous to claim to know that someone else is suffering because God wanted to teach that person a lesson of some kind. One might believe that people can use various difficulties as opportunities for spiritual growth, but explaining each instance of suffering as sent by God to produce some opportunity is likely to result in a fairly monstrous picture of God. "He took my child's life so that I would repent" or "He struck me with paralysis, so I could learn compassion for others." The fact that something may have good results is not by itself a reason for thinking that it was sent for the purpose of producing those results.

Furthermore, belief in a purposive order does not require the belief that everything is purposively ordained. There are views of providential action that don't allow for any randomness, but it is possible to affirm both that God has purposes in the world and that not everything is arranged by God. When it comes to particular cases of suffering, the best explanation for a believer is often the same as the best explanation for a nonbeliever: "He was in the wrong place at the wrong time." Or it was "bad luck."[14] Why was your child born with a genetic abnormality? Why did a hurricane destroy a particular town? Because the world operates in accordance with a combination of natural regularities and randomness that sometimes has these kinds of results. In other words there is no purposive explanation for the particular event, even if there may be such an explanation for the existence of an order that can produce such events.[15]

To admit that there is no purposive explanation for some events is not to deny that they might serve a purpose once they have occurred. Someone who gets unjustly fired from a job might respond to the event as a wake up call to find a different and more fulfilling line of work. Someone whose child is killed by a drunk driver may start an organization to raise awareness of the problem and promote legislative reform. Someone who is struck by paralysis of the lower limbs might respond with admirable attitudes and a determination to make the best of a bad situation. For a believer the most productive question is typically not why a difficulty occurred, but how to respond in a way that can produce something good.

A believer's trust in God need not involve an assurance of protection from the kinds of ills that are a part of human life, but might instead be a confidence that whatever happens won't defeat God's purposes for her. Such a trust can still be difficult at times to maintain, but the difficulty has little to do with the presence or absence of a global explanation of why God allows evils of various kinds, and finding what seems to be a satisfactory answer to that question may not help much in dealing with the experience of suffering. Thinking, for example, that free will is a great good is not particularly comforting for someone who has been victimized by malicious acts. For such a person the more urgent question is how to face up to the difficulties life has brought, and for a believer that will mean responding in a way that is conducive to the achievement of divine purposes in the situation.

Victor Frankl's attempts to aid his fellow prisoners in Nazi concentration camps during World War II hinged on getting them to move from a passive response to their situation to an active one in which they saw their suffering as a task that had been thrust upon them that called for a response. He writes:

> Once the meaning of suffering had been revealed to us, we refused to minimize or alleviate the camp's tortures by ignoring them or harboring false illusions and entertaining optimism. Suffering had become a task on which we did not want to turn our backs. We had realized its hidden opportunities for achievement.[16]

Making use of those opportunities required recognizing that even though they could not control their situation, they could still adopt attitudes that preserve values vital to human dignity and refuse to give in to the pressures to give up that dignity.

It is possible to take this point of view without thinking that the task has been assigned by anyone, but the natural home for the kind of response Frankl urges is a religious view in which facing up to difficulties is a task assigned by God. To invoke this kind of meaning is to see one's response to the situation in terms of a larger story that connects it with worthy ends. When theistic stories tell us to take certain values with ultimate seriousness, they portray those values as playing a vital part in a fulfillment that God intends for human life. You are building your character, not just for the time you spend in earthly life, but for a future one in which your capacity to experience and enjoy the new environment depends on what you become. Human existence here is important not only in its own right, but also as a preparation. In relation to the future destiny earthly life is like a school in which we are either learning or failing to learn the lessons we will need for a fulfillment that goes beyond this world.

John Hick uses the project of "soul-making" as an explanation of why suffering exists. I am invoking it here in a different way, showing how an understanding of suffering as offering opportunities for spiritual development can play a role in shaping believers' responses to suffering. Thinking that even senseless evils can be treated as raw material within a larger project of human fulfillment gives suffering a kind of meaning that provides direction about how to deal with difficult situations. Responding to suffering in the light of this meaning is part of living out a life-orienting story through which life as a whole finds meaning.

Finding Meaning in Life

Our concerns about making life meaningful are rooted in the fact that we are both engaged participants in life as well as reflective thinkers who are capable of considering what we do from an external point of view.[17] As participants we care passionately about some things. We become invested in particular values and goals, developing concerns that become vital parts of our identity. However, we are also reflective enough to be able to stand back and consider our actions and concerns as if we were observers of our lives. When we do so, we sometimes judge what we are doing to be important, and we sometimes judge it to be relatively unimportant. Such judgments are a matter of degree. Some items are very high on the scale of doing something worthwhile, while some at the other end are trivial, with various degrees of importance in between.

The formula for living a life that is *subjectively meaningful* is fairly simple. We are living lives of this kind when our lives include significant involvement in what we reflectively judge to be important. In practical terms it is unrealistic to expect that we can achieve such a life unless we internalize the kinds of concerns that make the activities we judge important a priority for us and allow us to be fully engaged by them. For example, someone who is engaged by scientific investigation cares about scientific truth enough to devote significant amounts of time and effort to seeking it and finds scientific research an absorbing interest. When we are engaged in doing what we reflectively judge to be important, we experience the activity as meaningful, and when such activities play a significant role in our lives, we experience our lives as meaningful.[18]

What we care about need not coincide with what we judge to be important. We can spend our lives doing what is trivial from our own perspective. Someone might think that watching television for three or four hours a night is much less important than writing the novel he has imagined doing, yet lapse into a life in which the relatively unimportant squeezes out other concerns. Hence, people can find themselves neglecting the kinds of things that might contribute to living a more meaningful life.

Judgments of importance are fallible. We can think something important when it is not, and we can think something relatively unimportant when it is vital. So it is possible to live a life that is *subjectively meaningful* that is not *objectively meaningful*. However, while objective meaningfulness might be a goal, in practice we try to approach it by refining our judgments of importance as best we can, even if we recognize that we can get it wrong.

Our judgments of importance are closely connected with the life-orienting stories we find plausible. When a story tells us to view our lives in relation to a divine source or a vision of human fulfillment that transcends our earthly lives, it provides a context within which various values can be understood. It's not that such a story replaces judgments such as it's a worthy thing to feed the hungry or to develop your musical talents. It's more a matter of viewing various relative concerns in the light of something deemed ultimate that transforms how we think about their significance. One who thinks of feeding the hungry as a way of doing service to God may do many of the same things as a secular humanitarian, but it would be a mistake to imagine that the layer of theological meaning makes no difference. It can have a major impact on judgments of what should be done and how it should be done, as well as on the motivation for doing it.

People who have come to understand the meaning of their experiences in theological terms have sometimes wondered whether an atheist could live a meaningful life. If we are talking about subjective meaning, the answer seems clear enough. An atheist might be engaged in the kinds of activities that can be recognized as important from the point of view of his or her own life-orienting story. The theist might think that since the atheist's life-orienting story is false, the assessments of what is important and what is meaningful that depend on it are defective. However, some theists have made a different claim. They have said that if God doesn't exist, no one's life would have meaning. Or alternatively, even if an atheist's life-orienting story is correct, it is not the kind of life-orienting story that could enable one to live a meaningful life.

Is God Needed for Meaning?

Tolstoy came to the conclusion that without God life would be meaningless.[19] As he reflected on his dominant concerns in life (writing novels and caring for his family), it seemed to him that both of these dwindled in significance when he began to think about these things from a viewpoint encompassing a wide enough temporal span. While the concerns that engaged him had seemed important, when he considered his life as it might appear to an observer viewing it as part of a vast temporal span, their importance disintegrated. His novels might be read for thousands of years, but eventually they would be forgotten. The care of his family might seem important now, but one day his family would be dead and gone. So how can either of these things matter? When Tolstoy evaluated his life in this way, he became disconnected from the passions that had allowed him to be engaged in life's activities. The more he thought about it, the more it seemed to him that there was nothing that he could do that really mattered, and these thoughts undermined his motivations, other than those that survived out of habit.

One reaction to this kind of reflection is to say that Tolstoy is setting impossibly high standards for doing something of worth. Surely, we might think, things don't have to endure forever in order for us to think we have accomplished something valuable. Fixing the plumbing might be an important thing to do, even if it may break down again in the next ten years. Saying a comforting word to someone in a time of crisis might be important, even if the effects of the comfort are short-lived. But judgments of the importance of these or any other activities depend on the perspective within which we are considering them. What we judge important in one context is often relatively unimportant in a wider context. Packing the clothes might be important in the context of getting ready for a trip, but the trip itself might be of little importance when thought of in the context of your life as a whole.

Sometimes we try to change people's point of view in order to get them to see the relative unimportance of something. "Look at all of the time you are spending on playing video games. When you think about what it will take to get you where you want to be in 20 years, can't you recognize that this activity is interfering with the achievement of your goals?" We imagine someone to be using too narrow a frame and attempt to broaden it so the person can think about matters more clearly. Tolstoy imagines his own life from an external viewpoint from which he can observe the various events, including his own death, as well as any lasting consequences flowing from his life. When we take such a perspective on our own lives, the things that we treat as vital seem to lose their importance.

Richard Taylor has described the lives of a particular species of worm, inhabiting the dark ceiling of a cave until it is transformed into a flying insect that will live only a day or two. During that time it mates, lays eggs, and then is caught up and devoured by the worms from which it came.[20] Taylor suggests that if we think about the activities of our own species from a perspective that resembles the way we might view those of an alien species, our lives can seem just as pointless. The pointlessness in question arises from the lack of something we can recognize as valuable that is accomplished by the activities that members of the species treat as so important.

Viewing our own species from this external point of view, we might notice that individual humans, including ourselves, are filled with passionate attachments and strong motivations to pursue particular goals, but that the things they regard as important matter only to someone looking at things from a viewpoint constituted by human concerns. From a perspective in which human passions drop out, we can't quite see why any of the things that concern them matter. However, there is something puzzling about this judgment. Are we taking the point of view of an observer for whom nothing matters or are we imagining an observer for whom some things matter, only not the things that concern human beings? In the former case it is not surprising that things seem pointless, since everything is pointless from the point of view of that observer. However, in the latter case, we would have to know what kinds of things matter to the observer and why that observer's perspective should be considered more authoritative.

Sometimes when people attempt to look at their lives objectively, they try to think about things as a scientific observer who is attempting to remain neutral about value questions. They think of a universe described in acceptable scientific terms and of humans as a particular species, existing a relatively short time, compared to the age of the universe, and occupying a miniscule portion of a vast and rapidly expanding space. It's easy to generate feelings of insignificance from this line of thought. But it is not clear what those feelings tell us. When we think from a perspective that excludes values, we cannot judge our value to be either high or low. An alternative is to think that there is some ideal valuing perspective from which human life can be seen as significant or insignificant. But in that case we are thinking about something close to the question of whether our lives could be seen as significant from God's point of view.

In living our lives we recognize the validity of thinking more objectively about ourselves. On the one hand, we care about and become deeply involved in things that matter to us from our individual point of view, but we will also recognize that this point of view is only one among many. Our individual point of view may be corrected to some extent as we move to the more objective point of view of what is good for our community or for members of our species. We can integrate the more subjective with the more objective by assuming a moral point of view that recognizes the legitimacy of what individuals care about, but only within limits. However, the moral point of view itself can be seen as something that is a product of human subjectivity, and if we think that the more objective way of thinking is a picture of reality in which our moral concerns and our judgments of importance drop out, it is unclear how we are to integrate this with the moral perspective by which we evaluate our lives. If the most objective perspective we recognize is one that is devoid of value, the result is a kind of tension in the way we think about the meaning of our lives.

We could say that certain things matter to us, even if they don't matter from the point of view of the universe. However, we are creatures who understand ourselves both from the point of view of living a life and from the more objective point of view of seeing ourselves as parts of a larger whole. We recognize the validity of the wider perspective because it is part of our own self-image. When I judge certain of my concerns as excessive, it is often because I recognize that I am only one person and the world does not revolve around me. So when I think about the human species and concerns that members of that species have, shouldn't I remind myself that the world does not revolve around the concerns of my species? Some writers have urged that we should attempt to make our ethics less anthropocentric, and this urge could be viewed as a reflection of our concern to adopt more objective ways of thinking about ourselves. However, the move only makes sense if we can find a coherent value perspective that integrates our anthropocentric concerns with something wider.

Someone who accepts a naturalistic life-orienting story holds that when we tell the ultimate truth about ourselves, we need to recognize that human concerns do not fit into any larger picture that reveals any of them to be important. At some point we reach the limits in our judgments of what is important, and those limits are from within a human point of view that makes claims about value in a universe that apart from us (and other species) is mindless and purposeless. We see some of our concerns as important enough to give our lives meaning, but when we are thinking objectively, those concerns don't look so important. They look like the expression of an anthropocentric point of view, which we have reason regard as having limited authority.

The conclusion is not, as some theists have thought, that there can be no meaningful life without God. It is rather that without an authoritative value perspective that transcends the human perspective, we can't have the kind of meaning that allows us to integrate our subjective sense of importance with our objective sense of reality. We will undoubtedly find things we think important enough to give our lives meaning, whether we believe or don't believe in God. But our sense of their importance will be in tension with thinking that we will unavoidably do when we view our lives in the context of a more objective picture of reality.

Perhaps the issue comes down to a yearning we might have for our lives to be meaningful in a way that can integrate the more objective and the more subjective viewpoints. One who is convinced that God does not exist will likely say that if we have such a yearning, we should recognize it as something that can't be satisfied and get on with our lives. However, someone who is not convinced might regard the yearning as a reason to consider a story telling how such a longing might be fulfilled. Stories that speak of God offer such a prospect. When we believe in God, the most objective perspective on what matters in human life allows for a kind of union between fact and value.[21]

Theistic stories that attempt to link human judgments about importance to the divine perspective are not simply endorsements of our ordinary point of view. They characterize many of our ordinary concerns as limited, confused, or sinful. When we attempt to see our lives in the light of God's purposes or plans for human life, such stories portray the need for transformation. Our self-centered and anthropocentric concerns need to be modified in the light of what is ultimately important.

If we view our lives in terms of a theistic life-orienting story, we are neither all-important nor insignificant. No doubt much of what we do and concern ourselves with can be recognized as trivial in relation to an understanding of what is most important. But such a story will tell us how we can give even ordinary actions a far-reaching significance. Making a pair of shoes may not look like a big thing, even from a human point of view, but in a theistic account using your talents to do a service well can be pleasing to God. Similarly, experiencing and expressing gratitude can be an act of worship. Raising your children can be viewed not just as a human duty, but as fulfilling a sacred trust.

When Tolstoy considered the prospect of a theistic life-orienting story, it was apparent to him that such a story allowed for a way of viewing human life as mattering that linked human concerns to something that could be recognized as valuable from the most authoritative point of view. When he tried to see his activities as meaningful from the perspective of the scientific story of the universe he had been treating as the ultimate truth, he couldn't quite see how any human concerns could matter. He might have explored the possibility of finding values that matter in a more limited way, even if nothing had the kind of ultimate significance he longed for. But his longing for a deeper significance motivated him to search for a life-orienting story that could satisfy it and, through this search, he came to believe that a story satisfying his longing was true.

Notes

1   John Cottingham, *On the Meaning of Life* (New York: Routledge, 2003), 38–9. The use of this quotation as an epigraph is by permission of Taylor and Francis Books.
2   Susan Neiman, *Evil In Modern Thought: An Alternative History of Philosophy* (Princeton: Princeton University Press, 2002), 323. The use of this quotation as an epigraph is by permission of Princeton University Press.
3   Justin Barrett, *Why Would Anyone Believe in God?* (New York: Altamira Press, 2004), 34.
4   Habukkuk 1:2–4, New International Version.
5   Habukkuk 3:18–19, New International Version.

6 Bruce Reichenbach, *The Law of Karma* (Honolulu: University of Hawaii Press, 1990).

7 For contemporary discussions of the book of Job, see Carol Newsome, *The Book of Job: A Contest of Moral Imaginations* (New York: Oxford University Press, 2003) and Norman Whybray, *Job* (Sheffield: Sheffield Academic Press, 1998).

8 Louis Dupré, *Religious Mystery and Rational Reflection* (Grand Rapids, MI: William B. Eerdmans Publishing Company, 1998), 56.

9 John Cottingham, *The Spiritual Dimension: Religion, Philosophy and Human Value* (Cambridge: Cambridge University Press, 2005), 32.

10 Cottingham, *Spiritual*, 34.

11 John Polkinghorne, *The Faith of a Physicist: Reflections of a Bottom-Up Thinker* (Princeton: Princeton University Press, 1994), 81.

12 See the discussion of the power of a perfect being in Chapter 6.

13 Clifford Geertz, *The Interpretation of Religion* (New York: Basic Books, 1973), 104.

14 Peter van Inwagen responds to the problem of evil with a story of God bringing good out of evil that God could not have brought about without allowing the evils. He says of his story: "If the story is true, much of the evil in the world is due to chance. There is generally no explanation of why *this* evil happened to *that* person." "The Argument from Evil," in *Christian Faith and the Problem of Evil* (Grand Rapids, MI: William B. Eerdmans Publishing Company, 2004), 72.

15 William Hasker, "The Necessity of Gratuitous Evil," *Faith and Philosophy* 9 (1992), 23–44.

16 Victor Frankl, *Man's Search For Meaning: An Introduction to Logotherapy*, trans. Ilse Lasch (Boston: Beacon Press, 1959), 78.

17 My discussion is indebted to Thomas Nagel, especially "The Absurd," in *Mortal Questions* (Cambridge: Cambridge University Press, 1979), 11–23 and *The View from Nowhere* (New York: Oxford University Press, 1986), 208–31.

18 David Holley, *Self-Interest and Beyond* (St Paul, MN: Paragon House, 1999), 137–53.

19 See the discussion of Tolstoy in Chapter 5.

20 Richard Taylor, "The Meaning of Life," in *The Meaning of Life*, ed. E. D. Klemke (Oxford: Oxford University Press, 1981), 145.

21 Clifford Geertz says that the "peculiar power" of sacred symbols comes from "their presumed ability to identify fact with value at the most fundamental level …" Geertz, 127.

10

Conviction, Doubt, and Humility

"It is a terrible thing to try to live a life without believing in anything.*"*
(David Wiggins[1])

"None of us stands at the point of view of the universal. Our attachment to our own faith cannot come from a universal survey of all others from which we conclude that this is the right one. It can only come from our sense of its inner spiritual power, chastened by the challenges which we will have had to meet from other faiths." (Charles Taylor[2])

Piscine Patel, the title character of Yann Martel's novel *Life of Pi*, has more than the typical interest in religion. As a young boy in India, he is captivated by Hindu spirituality. The rituals appeal to his senses and offer hints of a mystery that draws him. He says, "I became loyal to these sense impressions before I knew what they meant or what they were for."[3] Later he learns a Hindu account of the universe that makes sense to him. He learns of Brahman that is beyond description, the ultimate source reality, and Brahman as manifest in various Hindu deities. He learns of the identity of the inner self (Atman) with the ultimate reality, how at the deepest level we seek liberation from the illusion of separateness, and how there are many paths to liberation.

At the age of 14 Piscine ventures into a Christian church and begins a relationship with a priest who tells him the strange story of God's son dying for humanity's sins. The story doesn't fit at all with what he has learned of the gods of Hinduism. He has never heard of a Hindu god dying, and he's puzzled about why God would bring death upon himself. The answer of the priest to this puzzle and other questions Piscine raises is always a single word: "Love." At first Piscine is so put off that he says he'll stick with Krishna.

But there's something about the humanity of Jesus that he can't get rid of, and eventually he decides he would like to become a Christian, giving thanks to Krishna for having brought Jesus to him.

At the age of 15, Piscine meets a Sufi Muslim who introduces him to the beauty of Islam. When he watches Muslim prayer, his first impression is that it is like an athletic exercise. When he asks what this religion is about, he is told "It's about the Beloved."[4] He gets to know a man who is seeking union with a very personal and loving God, and he finds in the presence of this man intimations of the sacred. After an initiation into Islamic practice, Piscine has a mystical experience in which he becomes aware of things existing in a harmonious relation. He reports, "I knelt a mortal; I rose an immortal. I felt like the centre of a small circle coinciding with the centre of a much larger one. Atman met Allah."[5]

Piscine happily practices all three of his religions until one day his teachers and his parents discover that he is a practicing Hindu, Christian, and Muslim. They all agree in telling him that he can't be all of these things, each of the religious teachers defending his own faith and disparaging the faith of the others. Piscine will have to choose, they insist. But Piscine doesn't want to choose. Each of his religious practices seems to him to be a way to love God. He quotes Gandhi's claim that "All religions are true." His father, who is completely secular in orientation, is puzzled by all of this. Why, he wonders, can't his son have "the normal interests of a boy his age?" However, in the end Piscine gets what he persistently requests. He is permitted to be baptized as a Christian *and* to get a Muslim prayer rug.

There is something charming about this story. The idea of a boy able to appreciate and practice these diverse religions, viewing each as a way to God, seems possible, even if unlikely. There is something refreshing about the boy's openness, compared to the dogmatism and intolerance that religion often generates. But we have to wonder how anyone could adopt all these religions. It's all very well to appreciate that different traditions may have wisdom from which we can learn, but it's not so easy to see how a single individual can combine such diverse teachings. Is one a Christian in belief and practice on Sundays and Wednesdays, a Muslim on Tuesdays, Thursdays, and Fridays, and a Hindu on Mondays and Saturdays? Or do the practices and the stories mix in some more complex way? Perhaps Piscine has a master story that provides a place for each religion's accounts. Or perhaps he simply adopts what he likes in each without much thought about reconciling the various teachings.

Conflicting Truth Claims

One reason why we have trouble seeing how a person could adhere to so many religions is that each tradition makes claims about ultimate reality, the human condition, and how the human problem can be fixed that are not interchangeable. In the case of Islam and Christianity, each explicitly affirms some things that the other denies, and a Hindu account of the ultimate and of the human condition does not fit easily with the accounts of the other faiths. Hinduism generally affirms the possibility of multiple paths to liberation, but this openness presupposes a Hindu understanding of the place of alternative revelations that is unlikely to seem acceptable to the others.

If we do not think of these religions as alternative belief systems, it is easier to entertain the legitimacy of refusing to settle on a single one. A person can enjoy many varieties of ethnic foods without worrying about how all the taste combinations fit together. So perhaps a religion is like culinary appreciation.[6] Or perhaps different religions are different methods for achieving some recognizable goal. Piscine defends the possibility of having more than one religion to his mother by pointing out that a person can have passports from more than one nation. His mother replies that passports are valid on the earth where there are multiple nations, but points out that there is only one spiritual reality. Piscine responds that in that case all passports for it should be valid.

Surely Piscine overstates his case. Even if there are multiple paths to God, it can't be assumed that every practice moves you in the right direction. Piscine himself is attracted by teachings that arouse his sense of the sacred. But his attraction suggests that he has at least a rudimentary idea of how to recognize the sacred. He can view his mystic vision of harmony as a revelation of the way things are, but there are possible visions and possible teachings he would have to dismiss. In other words even someone as open to alternative accounts as Piscine must have some way to distinguish between what brings him closer to the divine and what does not, and that seems to involve beliefs about the nature of that ultimate reality. It is difficult to imagine how one could have such beliefs without accepting claims that some religions would dispute.

Hick's Pluralism

One of the most prolific and influential writers on questions of religious diversity is John Hick. Hick defends the validity of alternative religious practices with conflicting beliefs by viewing different religions as alternative ways of achieving a transformation of the individual from self-centeredness to what he calls reality-centeredness.[7] He attempts to keep the account of the nature of this transformation general enough to accommodate very different ideas of the kind of change involved. So, for example, a Christian account of salvation will not match a Buddhist or Hindu view of what it means to achieve liberation. Nevertheless, Hick thinks that the ideal results in each case, even if very different, can be recognized as diverse examples of a general type of change. This focus on the practical function of religion allows Hick to think of different belief systems as instruments for producing the desired change and to postulate that there are diverse traditions that are more or less equally effective in achieving the goal.

Hick postulates that the transformation sought in each tradition involves a kind of opening of the self to a transcendent reality, resulting in what particular traditions call salvation, liberation, or enlightenment. He views different religions as responses to this same reality, even if they characterize the transcendent in diverse and conflicting ways. Such a view, of course, raises the question of the nature of the transcendent reality. Hick wants to answer in a way that allows each of the various religions to be right from a certain point of view, but in order to do this, he postulates a sharp separation between the ultimate as it is in itself and human descriptions of the ultimate. The transcendent, which Hick calls the Real, is in itself beyond human comprehension. Hick compares it to the ultimate reality postulated by Kant. Kant held that we can't know reality as it is in itself (noumena), but only as it fits into human ways of perceiving and thinking. The reality we can describe is phenomenal – reality as it appears to human consciousness. But while Kant spoke of only one phenomenal reality, Hick postulates multiple phenomenal realities in different religious traditions.

The result is a *pluralist* view in which truth claims from various religions are acceptable, even if they are not compatible with each other. Each religion is talking, not about the Real itself, but about the Real as experienced within a particular limited human mode of understanding. When one religious tradition talks about a personal being who acts in purposeful fashion and another speaks of an impersonal absolute, they are not contradicting each other because each is referring to the phenomenal reality experienced in that religious tradition. Hick thinks of each tradition as having developed the conceptual resources of a particular location and era to describe its experience of the transcendent. The use of particular cultural and historical ways of thinking results in alternative ways of conceiving a reality that defies human representation. None of these ways gives us the absolute truth, but each can be regarded as playing a role in a legitimate way of responding to the divine. The test of legitimacy for a mode of thought is its effectiveness in producing the kind of transformation Hick views as the point of religion.

Hick's openness to a diversity of understandings is purchased at the price of denying our ability to characterize the ultimate reality that religions are said to respond to. In fact Hick emphasizes that the Real itself is beyond understanding. It

> … cannot be said to be one or many, person or thing, conscious or unconscious, purposive or non-purposive, substance or process, good or evil, loving or hating. None of the descriptive terms that apply within the realm of human experience can apply literally to the unexperienceable reality that underlies that realm.[8]

While something similar to this acknowledgment of the limitations of human conceptions is made within the reflective thought of theistic religious traditions, in those traditions the claim that God is beyond human understanding should not be identified with the idea of something completely unknowable. There is an admission that when we try to use human perfections to think about God, our comprehension fails. The infinite being of God is greater than what we can imagine. Even so, it is better represented by some terms than others. The idea that God is worthy of worship conveys some content by directing us to think of a supreme perfection of which our experience gives us some intimations, and at the heart of any theistic tradition is the belief that this supreme perfection has been encountered experientially.

By contrast, the skepticism displayed in Hick's denial of human ability to say anything about the Real makes it problematic to think of it as an object with religious significance or to judge what might be a valid response to it. If we don't know anything about the Real, how can we distinguish between appropriate responses and inadequate ones? How can we say that a religion that urges child sacrifice or the systematic practice of genocide is unacceptable, but one that promotes universal love is appropriate? If the answer is that we can rule out certain things on moral grounds, how can we say that moral behavior is an appropriate response to a Real that can't be called good or evil, but immoral behavior is not? Hick wants to use a transformative test to decide whether a religion is a genuine response to the Real, but unless we can say something about the Real, how could we have any idea of what kind of transformation to look for?

Keith Ward points out that despite Hick's official position that nothing can be said about the Real, he actually says various things about it: "that it is supremely valuable; that it is one cause of everything other than itself; that it manifests to human experience in a number of ways. ...."[9] Ward suspects that it might be better to discount the most skeptical claims and to characterize Hick as a theist who is trying to show how God could be manifest in many traditions. Whether or not Ward is right about that, it seems apparent that Hick needs at least a minimal account of the Real to be able to give content to the claim that religions are genuine responses to it. However, giving such an account threatens to break down the claim that religious descriptions are only phenomenal.

With or without a minimal account, Hick is in the position of contradicting the self-understanding of practitioners of particular traditions. If they think they are giving the truth about the Real, they are mistaken. From a higher point of view we can say that the Real is unknowable. Furthermore, Hick's view requires significant reinterpretations of the meaning of a variety of specific claims within religious traditions. So, for example, Hick suggests that the Christian doctrine of Jesus as a unique incarnation of God should be treated as a myth. By "myth" he means an account that is not literally true, but that can produce dispositional attitudes conducive to responding to the Real. What is apparent from this example is that Hick is committed to a procedure that in some cases will tell adherents of particular religious traditions how their doctrines should be understood. In some cases he is asking reflective adherents to give up understandings that they have for ones that fit better within a pluralist theory. His openness to various religions traditions in the end is conditioned by a willingness to accept those traditions only on terms that cohere with the project of putting the claims of major world religions on a more or less equal footing.

Responses to Religious Diversity

The pluralist impulse to refrain from viewing the truth claims of a particular religion as superior to those in other religions arises from considerations that challenge the human tendency to think with regard to religious matters, "I am right, and others who see things differently are wrong." A well-informed and reflective believer will be aware that his or her own life-orienting story is not the only possible one. The awareness of diversity by itself, however, does not pose a problem. If I can view those who think differently as uninformed or unintelligent or suffering from some other defect, I can dismiss their views as mistaken or misguided. However, in the modern world well-informed believers are likely to have firsthand or secondhand awareness of people with very different life-orienting stories who seem as intelligent and well informed as they are. Such awareness raises the question, "Do I have any reason to think that my beliefs are superior to the beliefs of those who disagree with me?"

If I am a reflective believer, I should be aware of the kinds of processes that have led to the formation of my religious beliefs. These processes may include such practices as listening to religious teaching, studying sacred scripture, engaging in prayer, and participating in public worship. From these practices people develop confidence in a particular set of beliefs. So, for example, one might discover an awareness of God's presence and an inner sense of the need for repentance and forgiveness during prayer or scripture reading. Whatever the particulars of the process, a reflective believer should be able to recognize that there are similar processes that have produced belief in religions with very different teachings. In fact such a believer might think something like, "While I strongly believe in Christianity, if I had been exposed to Islam or to Buddhism in the way I have been exposed to Christianity, I might have come to believe one of those religions instead."

Such thoughts can make one's head swim. It's not that they show a particular set of beliefs to be wrong or show that one should give up these beliefs. It's that this line of reflection gives rise to a kind of doubt that makes it difficult to confidently assert, "I am right, and those with alternative life-orienting stories are wrong." Unless there is a special reason, which doesn't just assume the truth of your own view, for thinking that the process that brought you to belief is reliable and that the processes that produced belief in those who disagree are unreliable, it's hard to avoid the realization, "I might be wrong, and those who defend an alternative view might be right." Of course, such a possibility will seem viable only in relation to an alternative that has at least some plausibility in your eyes, but in cases where you are able to find intelligent and well-informed believers on the other side, some willingness to enter imaginatively into the alternative religion may reveal something of what attracts others to that view. No doubt some alternatives can be dismissed as clearly inadequate, but some alternatives that could be viewed as serious competitors are likely to remain.

So what is the appropriate response in such a situation? Hick's response could be described as an *outside-in approach*. Look at your own tradition as if it were one of many equally legitimate responses to something real. Recognize it as limited and partial, with none of these traditions giving *the* truth, but each from a particular perspective exemplifying a response that can be recognized as equally valuable for the practical purposes of having our lives transformed.

Seeing my own religion in that way ought to be conducive to developing a tolerant and open attitude. My truth doesn't have any priority over the truth of someone with another faith. However, there is a question of whether thinking in this way is conducive to achieving the kind of transformation Hick views as central. If I can think of my religion as telling me the truth about things, I may be able to embrace the way of life it advocates whole-heartedly. But if I view the teachings of my religion as ways of thinking that are useful, but not actually true, there is a psychological obstacle to the same kind of commitment. It's as if each of the elements of the story that guides my life is affirmed by me in quotation marks. I am to operate as one who is fully engaged by the life-orienting story of my tradition, but also aware of a superior disengaged perspective that treats the truths of that tradition as merely useful for certain purposes. But regarding this disengaged perspective as superior threatens to undermine my capacity to be fully engaged by a particular story. If I think that my detached judgment is superior, won't I be inclined to rein in the excesses of a self that acts as if it really believes a particular story?

Contrast the outside-in response to awareness of religious diversity with another kind of response, an *inside-out approach*. Suppose I begin with the particular life-orienting story I have embraced, one that I regard as true. But as I reflect on the facts of religious diversity described earlier, I realize that there are other traditions and other stories accepted by equally intelligent and well-informed people. Unless I have a non-question-begging way of certifying my claims to truth and of understanding how these others went wrong, I have reason to think of my beliefs as fallible. That is, I have reason to think that while I regard my story as true, I approach the matter as a human being with a particular, limited perspective who could be wrong. However, thinking from the inside out, I do not assume that all views are equally correct, but instead think that there is a truth to be found, and my own experience and reflection leads me to affirm my own life-orienting story as closest to the truth and reject alternatives that conflict with it. Even if I might be wrong, I may still find reasons for thinking my understanding superior to alternatives I am aware of, as well as considerations I can't fully articulate that convince me of the truth of my story.

Accepting the possibility that I could be wrong is not at all the same as thinking that I am wrong or that my truth claims should be put in quotation marks. While this awareness introduces a kind of doubt, it need not be the kind that cripples belief. One way to see this is to compare religious beliefs to beliefs in other areas where intelligent and well-informed people disagree.[10] People can be very sure about their *political beliefs*. They can be confident that electing a particular individual would be good for the country and that electing someone from the other party would be bad. At the same time, they may be aware that there are intelligent and well-informed people on the other side who make the opposite assessment. They may also realize their inability to make a case that those who disagree would find convincing. People don't always admit their fallibility in such circumstances, but for those who do, the admission "I could be wrong" need not generate the kind of doubt that undermines their own passionate conviction, though awareness of fallibility might be conducive to greater humility and a reluctance to demonize those who disagree.

Similarly there are *philosophical beliefs* about issues such as freedom or the nature of morality or the relationship between mind and body or human motivation that generate interminable discussion. In the process of considering these beliefs, some views are revealed as inadequate, but there continue to be a range of conflicting views adopted by competent thinkers who become convinced of the truth of their positions. The awareness that someone whom I recognize to be my equal in intelligence and philosophical ability holds a different view is something that can fit with my own conviction that I am right on the matter, but with the judgment that I am right ought to go a realization that these are difficult matters about which error is possible and that even though I don't think I'm wrong, I could be.

How then should someone who approaches the awareness of alternative life-orienting stories from the perspective of belief in and commitment to her own life-orienting story think about truth claims that conflict with that commitment? In the political case and the philosophical case we ordinarily assume that there is a truth to be found and that some people come closer to it than others. We may be frustrated by our inability to convince those who think differently, but we are not generally tempted to think that all views are equally right (or that none of them are true or false). If, after reflecting as fully as we can, we find ourselves convinced of the truth of some view, then as a matter of logic we will think that conflicting accounts are incorrect. So unless there is a convincing reason for thinking that religious truth claims do not really conflict, being convinced of one means rejecting what is inconsistent with it.

It is important to remember, however, that not all apparent conflicts are genuine conflicts. Often views that sound alien to your own can be reconciled by means of further clarification and discussion. Religious traditions have different vocabularies and different approaches, but an investigator who is intent on looking for convergence rather than divergence can often find a significant amount of agreement or the potential for agreement at deep levels. For example, consider a thinker in one tradition who affirms the experience of God as a personal reality and one in another tradition who describes the ultimate as "the limitless ocean of being." Whether or not these claims conflict depends on whether the limitless ocean of being can relate to humans as a person. As Keith Ward puts it,

> If I am prepared to concede that God is much more than a person, as I understand the term, and you are ready to say that unlimited being can take a limited form for the sake of creatures, then a straight contradiction has disappeared.[11]

Hence, it is sometimes possible to recognize even in a life-orienting story very different from your own resemblances in the nature of the quest that seem more important than differences in doctrine. Perhaps we can see Piscine Patel's attraction to various religious traditions in these terms. Hinduism, Christianity, and Islam all seem to him to be ways to love God. Even if this kind of appreciation is possible, however, in practice it calls for some kind of understanding of how the various approaches fit together, and that is likely to be supplied either by enlarging one tradition in such a way as to make room for the claims of the others or by using a philosophical theory to develop an integrated account of what is important in various traditions.

Openness to Other Traditions

While what I have called the inside-out approach is potentially compatible with openness to appreciating and learning from other traditions, there are ways of starting from one's own story that could preclude that possibility. If it is an essential part of my story that there is only one true revelation and that people can gain right standing with God only by responding in terms of the formulas of faith it authorizes, then there is not much room for seeing value in other religions (or even in some cases different versions of my own religion). However, within monotheistic traditions that proclaim God's concern for all people, there is a tension in thinking that saving truth is revealed only to a few and that everyone else is out of luck. The tension is particularly acute if what is at stake is an eternal destiny which might include eternal punishment for failing to find the right religion.

It is instructive to see here how a reflective defender of the truth of his own tradition might handle such issues. C. S. Lewis, an eloquent apologist for the truth of Christianity, offers an interpretation of the doctrine of hell as the natural consequence of what each of us freely chooses. In a striking metaphor he claims, "… the doors of hell are locked on the *inside*."[12] On his account God gives each of us what we finally and decisively choose, and given that God's nature is love and that God is the ultimate reality, the final choice is between accepting the way of love or withdrawing from reality. In his story *The Great Divorce* characters after their earthly life choose either to become more solid (closer to reality) or to become more ghostlike, potentially over time to the point of ceasing to exist as persons.[13] The hellish possibility of choosing to reject God is in part a continuation of choices made during one's earthly life, but whatever chances might enable one to choose the way of love are provided, even extending into the afterlife. Lewis also suggests that the test for each individual is not a narrow doctrinal one. In his Narnia series a character who has been an ardent follower of a false god receives a final judgment in which it is declared that in his devotion to that god, he was actually following the true God without knowing it.[14]

What we have here in part is a reflection on how narrowly to construe one's own claims about how to be right with God. While Lewis sees his own faith as the truth (or the closest to the truth), his reflections on the universality of God's love leads him to think that there are ways of responding to God that don't involve an explicit understanding or appreciation of that revelation. While he assumes having an accurate understanding of one's situation in relation to God is better than having a confused or mistaken understanding, what is vitally important is responding to the light one has. Obviously, not every Christian would be willing to grant this much, but the point to notice is that it is reflection on the facts of religious diversity in the light of his own understanding of central Christian claims that leads to a broadened understanding of what it means to respond to God.

What I am suggesting is that within theistic traditions there are ways of correcting understandings that are judged too narrow or too exclusive to fit with the tradition's own claims about the universal benevolence of God. However, unlike the outside-in approach, correcting these understandings does not depend on assuming that all religions are equal with regard to truth claims or saving power. A reflective Muslim might think that the Koran is the fullest and best revelation of the truth, but that after all God is the merciful and the just one who will respond with compassion to all and has supplied other more limited revelations as well. The inside-out approach attempts to interpret the truth claims that come from within a tradition in such a way as to accommodate both theological concerns from within the tradition and the facts of religious diversity that reflective people in a pluralistic environment need to consider. Obviously, this kind of project can be carried out in a variety of ways, and there will be conflicting judgments about what is essential to a religious tradition, but the project is not unlike an attempt to see how something like new scientific or historical understanding can be integrated into a religious tradition that has not fully come to grips with these matters.

Attitudes Toward Those Who Disagree

I have characterized the inside-out approach as starting with a commitment to the truth you find convincing. But being convinced you are correct is consistent with more than one attitude toward those who disagree. You might regard those with alternative life-orienting stories as blameworthy for some epistemic or moral failing and respond to them accordingly. Depending on the nature and extent of the blame, you might think that means stronger than rational persuasion should be used to respond to their mistaken views. You might regard them as unworthy of such an effort. You might adopt a condescending attitude toward them. What I want to suggest, however, is that an awareness of human fallibility and of the role of contingent features affecting responsiveness to a particular life-orienting story should in most cases lead to a reluctance to blame and a humility about claims to have the truth.

While believing something commits you to think that those who believe what contradicts your belief are incorrect, an awareness of how difficult it is to get things completely right with regard to life-orienting stories suggests that in relation to those accepting a different story one should refrain from overconfidence about who has the truth. I can firmly believe something to be true, but at the same time admit, "I might be wrong, and you might be right." If I am a reflective and well-informed believer, I will be aware that the version of the story I have adopted from my own tradition is a product of a long historical development in which a great many understandings have been revised over time. I will also be aware that there are those within my tradition now who understand its essential teachings differently from the way I understand them, which suggests that even if I have managed to find the religious tradition closest to the truth, my understanding of that tradition may be defective in a variety of ways.

So while I am doing my best to live by the truth as I see it, my realization that what I see is partial and prone to error should lead me to view those with different understandings as working within the same limitations. I may still find some views to be irrational or immoral, but I can often charitably assume that many of those who disagree are striving to live by the truth as they see it. I can fully believe something while at the same time maintaining humility about my own truth claims and respectful attitudes toward those who don't share my beliefs.

I have been speaking of reflections on human fallibility in relation to someone who accepts a religious life-orienting story. However, the awareness "I could be wrong" is appropriate for any life-orienting story, not just religious ones. Those who accept a naturalistic story are often as reluctant as those who are attached to a religious story to reflect seriously on the possibility of error, but as I have pointed out throughout this book, a naturalistic view involves commitments to particular ways of understanding the human context that are not empirically verifiable. Just as a religious individual may be very confident of her own story, a naturalist may be very confident that her story is correct. But in either case that confidence needs to be tempered with an admission that humans are not in a position to put claims of this kind beyond all doubt.

Certainty and Doubt

Questions about certainty arise at different levels. Someone who is using a life-orienting story may find it easy enough to think and act in terms of the fundamental assumptions of the story. So, for example one may be able to experience a world that is devoid of theistic meaning, thinking and acting in ways appropriate to viewing the ultimate frame as the natural world. Or one might experience a world in which the presence and activity of God seems evident, thinking and acting in ways appropriate to a theistic understanding of the human context. At one level the question of certainty is just the question of how well a person is able to live out a particular life-orienting story, and people who are actually living out naturalistic or theistic stories often find convincing reasons to be confident of the stories that shape their understanding.

Sometimes, however, people lose confidence in the story they are using. The kind of doubt that creeps in keeps them from fully entering into the patterns of thinking and behaving that the story calls for. Occasional doubt may be manageable, but doubt can reach a level that seriously interferes with living a particular way of life. One may "go through the motions" for a considerable time before recognizing that the experiential and motivational connections which made a particular way of life possible have been weakened, sometimes beyond repair. Often people remain committed to the way of life structured by a life-orienting story in the absence of experiential confirmations, but sometimes the inability to be fully engaged motivationally and experientially can make an individual receptive to an alternative life-orienting story.

The kind of *practical certainty* that enables one to live out a story should be distinguished from what might be called *theoretical certainty*. Practical certainty is fueled by confidence derived from thinking and living in accordance with a particular life-orienting story. But gaining this kind of confidence depends on entering into the patterns of thought and feeling that the story structures. For example, living in accordance with the assumption that there is no transcendent realm and finding this way of living effective and satisfying can make one confident that the assumption of naturalism is correct. Living in accordance with the idea that each person is responsible before God and finding the sense of such responsibility central in one's everyday experience can increase confidence in God's existence. But in each case the reasons for confidence depend to some extent on being drawn into patterns of thought that some alternative stories reject.

The desire for theoretical certainty is a desire for the kind of reasons that would be convincing to anyone who is sufficiently rational. Sometimes people think they have this kind of evidence for the fundamental assumptions of disputed life-orienting stories. There are naturalists who think that something about scientific knowledge proves that God does not exist or shows that belief in God is irrational. There are theists who think they can provide arguments for God's existence that one would have to be irrational to reject. Partisans on either side tend to underestimate the extent to which the evidence they cite seems convincing because they view it in the light of ways of thinking that are closely connected with the story they are defending, but not accepted by the other side. They also underestimate the capacity of alternative stories to be developed in ways that accommodate what might seem puzzling.

The main problem with trying to satisfy the desire for theoretical certainty is that when we pull back to a level where we might expect any rational person to agree, we are left with too little in the way of evidence to compel us to move toward a full-blooded life-orienting story. When we refrain from accepting whatever is open to dispute, the meaning of the evidence becomes indeterminate. It is indeterminate, however, because we have filtered out many of the features of our experience that render the assumptions involved in particular orienting stories plausible. In actual practice we will be drawn toward thinking in ways that make particular religious or nonreligious stories convincing, and once we begin to operate within the patterns of a story, we find confirmations of the appeal that drew us in.

John Bishop characterizes what is going on when we are drawn into accepting fundamental assumptions that might underlie a life-orienting story as a "doxastic venture." On his account such a venture is a matter of taking something to be true in practical reasoning, while recognizing that its truth is not adequately supported by the total evidence.[15] However, that way of describing things gives priority to the evidential situation of one who puts on hold a range of dispositions and inclinations that produce judgments of plausibility that not everyone shares. If we consider evidence from the viewpoint of what we actually find plausible, we might alternatively describe ourselves as trusting particular dispositions and inclinations to reveal what is evidentially relevant. We could ask whether we have sufficient reason to trust these dispositions, but we are misguided to think that we might have evidential guarantees for such trust. The evidence that we gather comes from using ways of thought that seem reliable and becoming convinced that they are. When life-orienting stories are elaborated enough to serve as guides for life, there are certainly elements that could be judged to go beyond available evidence, but becoming convinced of the basic truth of a story typically seems like getting into a position where it is possible to read the available evidence correctly.

In earlier chapters I have emphasized the role of receptiveness with regard to considering life-orienting stories. Responding positively to a theistic story, for example, presupposes human tendencies to posit agency when confronted by apparently purposive phenomena. Such tendencies are at the roots of our awareness of other people and our interpersonal responses. One may decide that these tendencies are unreliable and distrust them when they lead to thinking of the world or particular events in theological terms. But for someone who allows these tendencies to operate, subject to correction by critical reflection, a theistic narrative may seem more plausible than available alternatives.

Since life-orienting narratives purport to tell us about how to understand ourselves, other kinds of receptiveness are relevant as well. For example, our willingness to seriously consider a story may be hampered by resistance to the self-image it portrays or the mode of life it would require. In responding, for example, to a picture of ourselves as responsible to God, we are not just dealing with facts that could be kept at arm's length, but with matters that are close to the core of what we care about and how we conceive ourselves. We may be drawn to or repulsed by the self-understanding implied in some life-orienting story. Our position resembles having to consider some alleged insight that might emerge in a therapeutic encounter. Our ability to discern what the relevant evidence means depends not just on our inferential skills, but on attentiveness to patterns of potential significance that could be dismissed. It also depends on whether a love for the kind of good a story portrays can be awakened.

We don't stand outside all stories and look at them in an objective "view from nowhere." We are instead in the position of relying on some story to shape our understanding, even if the story that guides us is not something we could explicitly articulate. We approach potential life-orienting stories as agents who are actually living our lives, though aware of alternative understandings that could structure our lives in different ways and having varying degrees of willingness to seriously considering an alternative.

Is God a Hypothesis?

At the beginning of this book I questioned the assumption that belief in God should be thought of as a hypothesis. My point is not just that people don't come to belief in this way. It is that considering belief in God in these terms involves us in a project that has little relevance to the question of whether to believe. Instead of considering whether a life-orienting story evokes a strong inclination to believe and reflecting on whether the inclination should be trusted, we put the issue in terms of evidence that we might test from a position of detached neutrality. It is understandable that the influence of natural science has inclined us to think that we could investigate any knowledge claims in terms of verification of hypotheses. But it is a leap to think that a method we find effective for acquiring knowledge of the physical world is equally effective for discerning whether or not the ultimate frame for understanding our lives should be depicted in purely physical terms. Many of the beliefs we depend upon to make sense of our lives do not fit the hypothesis-verification model, and such a model seems particularly ill-suited to determining how to judge inclinations to understand our lives in relation to a dimension beyond the physical.

When we consider the question of God in terms of whether a particular kind of explanation is needed for some set of agreed-upon facts, we enter into a theoretical mode where the appropriate attitude is one of disengaged rationality. We are thinkers, attempting to arrive at an adequate theoretical account. However, when believers talk about revelatory events or signs that point toward the divine, they are not operating primarily as thinkers, concerned with finding the answer to a theoretical issue. They are operating as agents who have a range of concerns with which a story of the divine might connect. When we filter out all the practical concerns to do a theoretical inquiry, the response of belief in God becomes virtually unintelligible.

Filtering out considerations that arise from the point of view of agency also misrepresents the nature of belief in a story that denies any transcendent realities. The appeal of naturalistic stories is tied to a conception of human life in which a particular epistemic ideal takes on moral significance. We view ourselves as agents who are capable of a kind of rationality that fulfils us and puts us in touch with the way things are. Only as we exert the proper discipline to refrain from asserting what we cannot verify through means other than empirical investigation can we hope to rid ourselves of superstition and achieve our good. The conviction that reality must be without gods is bound up with the appeal of a picture about how we achieve our dignity as rational agents, and being drawn to that picture is not a product of the kind of detached inquiry that naturalistic stories privilege.

When we think about questions of the nature of ultimate reality as arising in a practical context, our understanding of what considerations are relevant to judging between alternatives differs from what we might assume relevant in a more theoretical context. We are offered various ways of construing the human condition that tell us what is important, how to deal with suffering and death, how to achieve our full potential as human beings. In evaluating these accounts, we need to make sure that they square with what we consider the relevant facts to be, but it is equally important that they present us with a way of life which resonates with our deepest understanding of value. We must find the moral order a story reveals to be something that engages us.

Our concern that life-orienting stories lack theoretical certainty arises when we think of their fundamental assumptions as matters to be decided by the exercise of detached rationality. But we don't confront stories that affirm God or stories that deny God in that way. We encounter them as potential ways of dealing with the practical need for finding orientation in life. We can raise the question of whether one who finds orientation in a particular story and reflectively judges it superior to alternative stories really knows. But we should not assume that we have some way of evaluating these stories that removes us from the actual human condition. The desire to certify our understandings from some absolute perspective that puts them beyond question is a craving for something beyond our grasp. What we can actually attain is the practical certainty that sometimes results from trying on, living out, and reflecting on those stories that convince us.

The Practice of Belief

Ordinarily we think of belief in God as something a person either possesses or lacks. We identify ourselves as believers or as unbelievers, and while we recognize that one may both believe and have doubts, we imagine that there is some predominant state of mind that can be called belief or unbelief, or perhaps suspension of judgment. In many instances, however, belief in God is less a state of mind or a completed achievement and more of a practice to which one is committed, a practice that may involve elements of struggle.

Why should struggle have anything to do with belief? One kind of struggle arises from the fact that human psychology is complicated. We may believe something at one level, but have difficulty believing it at a different level. Imagine, for example, someone who has difficulty fully accepting what is perfectly obvious to everyone else – that her spouse really loves her. Say that she has had a life in which she was mistreated by those close to her and in response has developed a deep cynicism about the possibility of genuine love, or perhaps a reflexive pessimism about her own lovableness. We could imagine a therapist of a cognitive orientation advising her to focus her attention on facts about how her husband treats her, as well as what he says to her and to others about her. Perhaps we can imagine a process of coming closer to being able to realize that she is loved. In such a case we might say that she is practicing the belief that she is loved. At one level she accepts what she is trying to bring herself to accept at a deeper level.

Often our ability to believe is not just a matter of the evidence that we have available. Especially when a belief has deep personal significance, there is the question of whether we are able to integrate the belief into a complex emotional and attitudinal structure. The realm of religious belief is a paradigmatic place for the kind of adjustment involved in bringing something that one accepts at one level to become real at a deeper level. Consider, for example, one who has heard teaching all his life about being forgiven by God, but has difficulty feeling forgiven. Part of the point of religious practices, such as prayer and meditation, is to focus an individual's attention in a way that is conducive to making such beliefs experientially real. One who is engaged in such practices will not typically think of what is being done as practicing belief, but the practical effect is to integrate what is accepted on a surface level with deeper sources of motivation.

It is by cultivating the right habits of thought, feeling, and behavior that one is able to acquire the sensitivities of a believer. Consider a religious belief from an Eastern tradition. Suppose I have accepted the proclamation of the *Upanishads* that Atman is Brahman. I acknowledge the insight of those advanced practitioners of the meditative arts that the fundamental reality of my deepest inner self is the same as the ultimate reality behind the universe. Furthermore, imagine that I accept the diagnosis that major problems arise from clinging to the illusion of a separate individual existence. If I can genuinely recognize my identity with Brahman, I will cease the futile egoistic cravings that lead to so much unnecessary pain and suffering. There is likely to be a huge gap between my intellectual acceptance of the teachings of my tradition and the kind of realization that enables me to consistently exemplify the way of life that tradition calls for. By continual practice I may be able to reach the point where what initially is a surface assent becomes a pivotal feature of my understanding of daily events and my reactions to them. By engaging in the proper practices, I enable myself to transform what I accept intellectually into a conviction that shapes my basic identity.

Most people who lose their faith do not lose it through coming across decisive counterarguments, but rather by a process in which it becomes disconnected with the deep sources of motivation. Belief in God can die without sufficient support from the cognitive and emotional structures that surround it, and it can come to seem unreal if the experiences that evoke it begin to lose their saliency. Depending on our frame of mind, we can discern the heavens declaring the glory of God or we can discern a natural order devoid of human significance. The starry heavens that struck Kant as awe inspiring may also leave us cold with fear and loneliness. The events that give us comfort and hope can, in the light of later experiences, come to seem like a cruel joke. To hold onto belief in God requires a cultivation of the soil in which that belief grows.

But it is precisely this sort of special nurture that strikes many nonbelievers and some believers as perverse. There is a widespread idea that we should cultivate a critical distance from our beliefs, holding on to them loosely lest contrary evidence arise. This picture of maintaining a detached analytical viewpoint conflicts sharply with the picture of a religious person who is struggling to nurture and protect a belief. From some points of view providing nurture for a treasured belief seems unworthy, if not disgusting. It is noteworthy, however, that attempting to maintain a detached objectivity toward our beliefs itself involves a kind of practice. One who thought that the exercise of this kind of detachment was ethically required should seek to cultivate the attitudes and emotional inclinations needed to support this exercise. Such a person would need to resist the temptation to hold on too tightly to beliefs. Maintaining the ideal of belief formation underlying this picture could require considerable discipline, including the discipline of repeated reminders of the danger of becoming too attached to particular beliefs. Such a practice differs from that of the theistic believer who appears to privilege belief in God, but it doesn't escape privileging an epistemic ideal of its own.

Furthermore, the ideal of maintaining a critical distance in relation to our deepest convictions is unrealistic. Human beings need some identity-shaping convictions, and nothing can play that role if it is subject to being put on or taken off with ease. It is difficult to be fully engaged in something and be fully open to the possibility of rejecting it at the same time. Imagine someone who is engaged in the practice of law, but finds herself frequently questioning the value of justice. There comes a point where the questioning can undermine the ability to be wholeheartedly involved in the activity. A believer can have moments of wondering whether God really exists, but to treat the belief as something to be examined with dispassionate aloofness is close to abandoning the conditions needed to sustain any recognizably religious belief. We can examine our beliefs, even our fundamental convictions, but in the case of beliefs that give shape to our lives, the kind of examination we can expect to do is tempered by the pressing need to become fully engaged in a way of life.

What I have been urging throughout this book is not blind acceptance of a life-orienting story. We can reflect on our stories in many ways, including comparing our way of life to alternatives we find attractive. What we cannot do, however, is to hold back indefinitely from committing ourselves to some story, for the attempt to do so involves the pretense that we can live without fundamental convictions that shape who we are and how we live. We can be skeptical about a great many things, but adopting skepticism that keeps us undecided about the truth of all assumptions about ultimate reality is futile from a practical standpoint.

Additionally, cultivation of this kind of skepticism risks being closed to potential awareness of the truth. Yann Martel imagines alternative reactions to a deathbed experience by an atheist and an agnostic:

> I can well imagine an atheist's last words: "White, white! L-L-Love! My God!" – and the deathbed leap of faith. Whereas the agnostic, if he stays true to his reasonable self, if he stays beholden to dry, yeastless factuality, might try to explain the warm light bathing him by saying, "Possibly a f-f-failing oxygenation of the b-b-brain," and to the very end, lack imagination and miss the better story.[16]

There are truths that we may miss if we are unreceptive to their possibility or if we insist on the wrong kind of verification. While we need to guard against gullibility, it is at least as important not to close our minds and hearts prematurely to what might turn out to be "the better story."

Notes

1   David Wiggins, *Needs, Values, Truth: Essays in the Philosophy of Value*, Aristotelian Society Series, vol. 6 (Oxford: Basil Blackwell, 1987), 89. The use of this quotation as an epigraph has been accepted as fair dealing by Wiley-Blackwell Publishers.
2   Charles Taylor, *A Secular Age* (Cambridge, MA: Harvard University Press, 2007), 680. The use of this quotation as an epigraph is by permission of Harvard University Press.
3   Yann Martel, *Life of Pi* (New York: Harcourt Inc., 2001), 48.
4   Martel, 60.

5   Martel, 62.

6   Kevin Meeker, "Exclusivism, Pluralism, and Anarchy," in *God Matters: Readings in the Philosophy of Religion*, ed. Raymond Martin and Christopher Bernard (New York: Longman, 2003), 524–35.

7   Hick's views are developed in numerous writings. See, for example, *An Interpretation of Religion* (New York: The Macmillan Press, 1989).

8   Hick, *An Interpretation of Religion*, 194.

9   Keith Ward, "Divine Ineffability," in James Kellenberger, *Introduction to Philosophy of Religion Readings* (Upper Saddle River, NJ: Pearson Education, 2007), 569.

10 Peter van Inwagen, "It Is Wrong, Everywhere, Always, and for Anyone, to Believe Anything upon Insufficient Evidence," in Jeff Jordan and Daniel Howard-Snyder, *Faith, Freedom, and Rationality: Philosophy of Religion Today* (Lanham, MD: Rowman & Littlefield Publishers, Inc., 1996), 137–53.

11 Keith Ward, *Revelation and Religion* (Oxford: Oxford University Press, 1994), 331.

12 C. S. Lewis, *The Problem of Pain* (New York: Macmillan Publishing Company, 1962), 127.

13 C. S. Lewis, *The Great Divorce* (New York: Macmillan Publishing Company, 1946).

14 C. S. Lewis, *The Last Battle* (New York: Macmillan Publishing Company, 1956), 164–5.

15 John Bishop, *Believing By Faith: An Essay in the Epistemology and Ethics of Religious Belief* (New York: Oxford University Press, 2007), 20.

16 Martel, 64.

Suggestions for Further Reading

The following list is intended as a help to getting started for the reader who wants to explore further some of the issues dealt with in this book. There are some additional sources mentioned in the endnotes to the chapters.

Atheism

A number of recent best-selling works have argued for atheism and criticized theistic religion. These include books by Richard Dawkins, Christopher Hitchens, and Sam Harris. I don't recommend these books because of their strident tone, which displays contempt for opponents and exhibits virtually no effort toward charitable understanding of what is rejected. Various responses to these works have pointed out weaknesses of what has been called the "new atheism." One recent response is:

Reitan, Eric, *Is God A Delusion? A Reply to Religion's Cultured Despisers* (Malden, MA: Blackwell Publishers Inc., 2009). Reitan distinguishes between the kind of religion he thinks defensible and the kind he thinks deserves the new atheists' scorn.

For a better introduction to atheism, I recommend the following more restrained and better informed discussions:

Antony, Louise (ed.), *Philosophers Without Gods: Meditations on Atheism and the Secular Life* (Oxford: Oxford University Press, 2007). This book contains a collection of essays by philosophers who reject theistic belief. They attempt to explain their reasoning, sometimes with personal stories of how they arrived at their position. The autobiographical approach parallels corresponding collections that have appeared in recent years in which Christian philosophers describe their belief.

Baggini, Julian, *Atheism: A Very Short Introduction* (Oxford: Oxford University Press, 2003). Baggini presents atheism as a form of naturalism and argues that naturalism is the best explanation of things.

Comte-Sponville, André, *The Little Book of Atheist Spirituality*, trans. Nancy Huston (New York: Viking Penguin, 2006). Comte-Sponville argues for an atheist view in a way that shows respect for the religious quest and seeks common ground with those who disagree.

Cognitive Psychology and God

Barrett, Justin, *Why Would Anyone Believe in God?* (New York: Altamira Press, 2004). Barrett explains psychological research findings with regard to belief in supernatural agents, showing why the formation of these beliefs is natural for human beings.

Tremlin, Todd, *Minds and Gods: The Cognitive Foundations of Religion* (Oxford: Oxford University Press, 2006). Tremlin offers a helpful summary account of the relevance of cognitive psychology to religion.

Conceiving God

Soskice, Janet, *Metaphor and Religious Language* (Oxford: Oxford University Press, 1985). Soskice defends the meaningfulness of metaphorical language in speaking about a transcendent deity.

Westphal, Merold, *Transcendence and Self-Transcendence: On God and the Soul* (Bloomington, IN: Indiana University Press, 2004). Westphal provides an account of three ways of conceiving divine transcendence through a discussion of major philosophers and theologians. He links ways of thinking about God with ways of viewing the self.

Divine Hiddenness

Howard-Snyder, Daniel, and Moser, Paul (eds.), *Divine Hiddenness: New Essays* (Cambridge: Cambridge University Press, 2002). This book is a collection of philosophical essays on divine hiddenness, containing various responses to Schellenberg.

Schellenberg, J. L., *Divine Hiddenness and Human Reason* (Ithaca, NY: Cornell University Press, 1993). This book presents Schellenberg's argument against belief in God, which proceeds from an account of the nature of God and the facts of divine hiddenness.

Evil

Adams, Marilyn, *Horrendous Evils and the Goodness of God* (Ithaca, NY: Cornell University Press, 1999). Adams emphasizes the need to think of evil not just as a global issue, but in relation to individuals. She attempts to give a Christian response to the kinds of evils that can lead an individual to doubt that his or her life could be a great good on the whole.

Hasker, William, *The Triumph of God Over Evil: Theodicy for a World of Suffering* (Downers Grove, IL: Inter Varsity Press, 2008). Hasker gives clear accounts of much of the current literature and offers his own response to arguments against God based on evil.

Howard-Snyder, Daniel, *The Evidential Argument from Evil* (Indianapolis: Indiana University Press, 1996). This book contains essays by a number of contemporary philosophers for and against the claim that the amount or types of evil in the world make the existence of God unlikely.

Faith

Bishop, John, *Believing By Faith: An Essay in the Epistemology and Ethics of Religious Belief* (Oxford: Oxford University Press, 2007). Bishop develops and expands on ideas from William James to defend the moral justifiability of taking propositions to be true in practical reasoning in some cases where the truth is not adequately supported by the total available evidence.

Evans, C. Stephen, *Faith Beyond Reason: A Kierkegaardian Account* (Grand Rapids, MI: William B. Eerdmans Publishing Company, 1998). Evans defends a version of fideism inspired by Kierkegaard's thought that regards human reason as limited and recognition of the truth of God's revelation dependent on a passionate response, which might be called faith.

Helm, Paul, *Faith With Reason* (Oxford: Oxford University Press, 2000). Helm provides a closely argued account of the relevance of faith to reasonable religious belief. He discusses a range of positions in philosophy of religion. One noteworthy aspect of his view is the idea that moral considerations can be relevant to our appreciation of evidence.

God, Morality, and Meaning

Byrne, Peter, *The Philosophical and Theological Foundations of Ethics*, 2nd edn. (New York: St. Martin's Press, 1999). Byrne offers a defense of virtue theory and a careful analysis of morality with and without religion.

Klemke, E. D. (ed.), *The Meaning of Life*, 2nd edn. (Oxford: Oxford University Press, 1999). This collection of philosophical essays includes a few articles by philosophers who defend a theistic account, but mostly defenses of nontheistic views of the meaning of life and discussion by philosophers who reject the question of whether life has meaning.

Martin, Michael, *Atheism, Morality, and Meaning* (Amherst, NY: Prometheus Books, 2002). Martin argues for a nonreligious account of morality and against claims of the need for a theistic foundation. He also defends the claim that life can have meaning without God and argues against a Christian conception of the meaning of life.

Wainwright, William, *Religion and Morality* (Aldershot, UK: Ashgate Publishing Limited, 2005). Wainwright discusses whether morality can be used as an argument for God. He also examines divine command theory and other issues relevant to a religious approach to ethics.

Wielenberg, Erik, *Value and Virtue in a Godless Universe* (Cambridge: Cambridge University Press, 2005). Wielenberg argues that God is not needed for life to have meaning or as a foundation for morality.

Wolterstorff, Nicholas, *Justice: Rights and Wrongs* (Princeton: Princeton University Press, 2008). Wolterstorff offers an account of justice and defends the claim that our notion of rights makes more sense in a theistic than a secular context.

Historical Development of Atheism

Buckley, Michael, *At the Origins of Modern Atheism* (New Haven: Yale University Press, 1987). Buckley gives a historical account of how the attempt to defend belief in God through philosophical arguments in the Western world had the effect of undermining belief in God.

Taylor, Charles, *A Secular Age* (Cambridge, MA: Harvard University Press, 2007). Taylor presents a massive historical analysis of shifts in the modern West (since the 16th century) that made it possible to move from a world in which it was difficult not to believe in God to the current situation in which unbelief is an option, or for some people virtually inescapable.

Narrative

MacIntyre, Alasdair, *After Virtue*, 3rd edn. (Notre Dame, IN: University of Notre Dame Press, 1981). MacIntyre develops an account of virtue ethics as it functions within a narrative context for understanding one's life.

Smith, Christian, *Moral Believing Animals: Human Personhood and Culture* (Oxford: Oxford University Press, 2003). Smith offers a sociological account of human life that emphasizes the importance of moral orders and the role of narratives that shape our sense of what is significant. My account of life-orienting stories is indebted to his discussion.

Naturalism

Goetz, Stewart, and Taliaferro, Charles, *Naturalism* (Grand Rapids, MI: William B. Eerdmans Publishing Company, 2008). The authors give a clear account of various types of naturalism and offer their own critique.

Haught, John, *Is Nature Enough? Meaning and Truth in the Age of Science* (Cambridge: Cambridge University Press, 2006). Haught argues for a theistic alternative to the view that nature is all there is, which he defends as scientifically informed and adequate to deal with a range of reflective concerns.

Passionate Reasoning

Wainwright, William, *Reason and the Heart: A Prolegomenon to a Critique of Passional Reason* (Ithaca, NY: Cornell University Press, 1995). Wainwright challenges the sufficiency of objective reasoning with regard to religious matters and argues for the relevance of aspects of our nature other than reason in responding to religious truth claims. This book is an important influence on my own position.

Wynn, Mark, *Emotional Experience and Religious Understanding: Integrating Perception, Conception and Feeling* (Cambridge: Cambridge University Press, 2005). Wynn argues that affective responses play an important role in the formation of moral and religious knowledge. He argues persuasively for the cognitive significance of emotions in religion.

Philosophical Classics

Hume, David, *Dialogues Concerning Natural Religion*, ed. Norman Kemp Smith (Indianapolis: The Bobbs-Merrill Company, 1947). Hume's character Cleanthes argues for the existence of God as a conclusion that may be drawn from the same kind of reasoning used in science and common life. He argues that just as we explain the purposive order in machines as products of human minds, we can reason to a divine mind as the explanation of the order of the universe. Hume's Philo criticizes the argument to God based on an analogy between human artifacts and things in the natural world. An underlying assumption of the whole discussion is one that I reject in this book: that a disengaged form of reflection of the kind that might be used for scientific claims is the appropriate way to decide about God.

James, William, *The Will to Believe and Other Essays in Popular Philosophy* (New York: Dover Publications, 1956). James's discussion in "The Will to Believe" furnishes the basis for my account of the practical necessity of adopting a life-orienting story.

Kierkegaard, Søren, *Concluding Unscientific Postscript to Philosophical Fragments*, vols. 1-2, ed. and trans. Howard V. Hong and Edna H. Hong (Princeton: Princeton University Press, 1992). Kierkegaard's pseudonym Johannes Climacus argues for subjectivity with regard to ethical and religious claims. He is sometimes understood to be an irrationalist. I understand his rejection of objectivity in these matters to parallel my rejection of disengaged reasoning. Passionate concerns connected with our awareness as agents play a vital role in convincing us about truths that will shape how we live. We are not in a position to achieve theoretical certainty about these kinds of truths, but can have what in Chapter 10 I call practical certainty or what Kierkegaard might call subjective truth.

Pascal, Blaise, *Pensées*, ed. and trans. Roger Ariew (Indianapolis: Hackett Publishing Company, 2005). Pascal's distinction between the god of the philosophers and the God of Abraham, Isaac, and Jacob is important in my discussion in Chapter 2. His thoughts on divine hiddenness and human receptivity are discussed in Chapter 4.

Peirce, Charles, *Philosophical Writings of Peirce*, ed. Justus Buchler (New York: Dover Publications, 1955). Peirce defends fallibilism with regard to knowledge claims, a view that is important to the position developed in this book. See, for example, his essay on "The Scientific Attitude and Fallibilism."

Practical Understanding

Cottingham, John, *The Spiritual Dimension: Religion, Philosophy and Human Value* (Cambridge: Cambridge University Press, 2005). Cottingham argues for the inadequacy of trying to evaluate religion in purely intellectual terms and for recognizing how religious understanding arises from a kind of practical involvement directed toward transformation.

Taylor, Charles, *Sources of the Self: The Making of Modern Identity* (Cambridge, MA: Harvard University Press, 1989). Taylor argues that our understanding of what is ultimately real needs to take into account our thinking as agents, not just our thinking as theorists. Much of this book traces the historical development of modern ideas of the self. His thoughts about disengaged reasoning are an important influence on my position.

Religious Diversity

Hick, John, *An Interpretation of Religion* (New York: The Macmillan Press, 1989). Hick defends a form of pluralism about religious truth claims.

Quinn, Philip, and Meeker, Kevin (eds.), *The Philosophical Challenge of Religious Diversity* (Oxford: Oxford University Press, 2000). This book contains a collection of philosophical responses to the issue of truth claims and religious diversity.

Religious Experience

Alston, William, *Perceiving God: The Epistemology of Religious Experience* (Ithaca, NY: Cornell University Press, 1991). Alston defends the legitimacy of forming experiential religious beliefs in accordance with a general practice that he calls Christian mystical practice.

Davis, Carolyn Franks, *The Evidential Force of Religious Experience* (Oxford: Oxford University Press, 1989). Davis develops a classification of types of religious experience and an assessment of the evidential value of these experiences.

Dupré, Louis, *Religious Mystery and Rational Reflection* (Grand Rapids, MI: William B. Eerdmans Publishing Company, 1998). In a series of essays Dupré explores the question of how philosophy can consider religious experience in a way that does justice to its nature.

James, William, *The Varieties of Religious Experience* (New York: The Macmillan Company, 1961). James's classic study, published originally in 1902, gives a respectful discussion of religious experience and a measured analysis of the significance of mystical experience for belief.

Revelation

Abraham, William, *Crossing the Threshold of Divine Revelation* (Grand Rapids, MI: William B. Eerdmans Publishing Company, 2006). Writing from a Christian perspective, Abraham attempts to establish the importance of revelation as an epistemological category.

Menssen, Sandra, and Sullivan, Thomas, *The Agnostic Inquirer: Revelation from a Philosophical Standpoint* (Grand Rapids, MI: William B. Eerdmans Publishing Company, 2007). Menssen and Sullivan argue for the relevance of accounts of what God has revealed to deciding about God's existence. Their work is addressed to people who are agnostic about God.

Index

and reward and punishment 24,
130, 151, 152, 162–4
as subject 125–7
and submission to divine
authority 159–61, 168
and suffering 173–8
and theistic stories 59–61
goodness:
divine 75, 87–8, 118, 176
love for 72–3

Hadot, Pierre 82, 167
happiness:
in ancient philosophy 167
and morality 164–6
Hare, John 168
Haught, John 11, 136–7
Heidegger, Martin 38
Helm, Paul 69
heroism, moral 165
Heschel, Abraham 125–6
Hick, John 75
and religious pluralism 194–7, 198–9
and suffering 184
Hinduism:
Advaita Vedanta 123–4, 210
bhakti tradition 87
and religious diversity 192, 194
Hugo, Victor, *Les Miserables* 69–71,
88
humanism, naturalistic 137, 167–8
Hume, David 16, 120–1

identity:
and belief 40–1, 211
and life-orienting stories 15,
16–17, 25, 58, 184
and moral values 144
illusion:
experience as 20
and morality 131, 145
reality as 123

incarnation 76, 180, 197
intelligibility, and experience
of God 37, 43, 55
Islam, and religious diversity 193, 194

James, William 21–2, 29 n.7, 90,
107 n.3, 165
Joan of Arcadia (TV series) 109, 111
Job (biblical book) 177–8, 181
judgments, and background
stories 3–5

Kant, Immanuel 60–1, 122, 144, 164,
195, 211
karma 177–8
kenosis 181
Kierkegaard, Søren 10 n.6, 75–6
knowledge:
divine 118, 119, 178
experiential 39–40
of God 125–6
moral 154–5
revelatory 46, 53–4, 79–80
and science 133–4, 148–9
self-knowledge 70–1, 72, 79
theoretical 38–9

language, religious 109–11, 120–4,
126–7
and analogy 122, 123
and children 113–15
and metaphor 111, 116, 126
Lewis, C. S. 202
life, meaning of *see* meaning
life-orienting stories *see* stories,
life-orienting
love:
divine 75, 76–7, 80, 179–80, 202
for God 75–6, 87–8

McGhee, Michael 51
MacIntyre, Alasdair 90

BT
103
.H66
2010